Class Meetings That Matter

A Year's Worth of Resources for Grades K–5

Vicki Crocker Flerx, Ph.D.

Susan P. Limber, Ph.D.

Nancy Mullin, M.Ed.

Jane Riese, L.S.W.

Marlene Snyder, Ph.D.

Dan Olweus, Ph.D.

HAZELDEN®

Hazelden
Center City, Minnesota 55012
hazelden.org

ISBN: 978-1-59285-722-7

13 12 11 10 09   1 2 3 4 5 6

Cover design by David Spohn
Interior design and typesetting by Ryan Scheife, Mayfly Design

What Is the Purpose of This Manual?

The purpose of this manual is to provide teachers and other school staff members with developmentally appropriate activities to use as part of their *OBPP* class meetings in kindergarten through grade 5. These class meetings are grouped according to grade levels (kindergarten–grade 2 and grades 3–5). Within grade levels, the meetings are further grouped according to one of eight subject areas. When planning class meetings with your students, we encourage you to keep in mind several principles:

1. Even within these fairly narrow grade groupings, not all class meetings will be appropriate for each grade level or even each class within a grade. Choose class meetings as appropriate—make sure "prerequisite" class meetings are completed first so concepts build upon each other.

2. Although it is appropriate to revisit concepts regularly, class meetings should be varied in terms of how ideas are presented, and the focus of discussion. We hope that you will adapt and expand on ideas in this manual as appropriate for your students.

3. It is not expected that you complete all the class meetings each year at each grade level. Rather, we recommend that as a school you determine what sessions might be most appropriate at each grade level. There are a broad range of curriculum connections associated with each class meeting. It is not our expectation that you will cover all of these curriculum connections within any one class meeting.

4. Some class meetings may require more than one class period to complete. In such cases, be sure to leave some time at the end of each session to process the portion of the activity to that point and let students know what to expect during the next session.

5. Be creative! Utilize your own ideas and student feedback to put your own "stamp" on these class meetings. We also recommend that you link these class meetings and the underlying concepts to your academic content whenever possible.

This manual is not meant to be used as a stand-alone program. It should be used as part of a comprehensive, schoolwide implementation of the *Olweus Bullying Prevention Program*. The class meetings in this book build upon those provided in the *OBPP* Teacher Guide.

Contents

Part 2: Class Meetings for Grades 3–5

Acknowledgments

Educators implementing the *Olweus Bullying Prevention Program* in the United States have been asking for more ideas for engaging students in conversations about bullying behaviors and other related topics during class meetings. (Initial class meeting topics and videos with discussion questions are included in the *OBPP* Teacher Guide.) We thank them for their dedication to bullying-prevention efforts and for providing time for students to discuss and consider topics important to improve school climate.

Our *Olweus Bullying Prevention Program* trainers provide training for schools' Bullying Prevention Coordinating Committees (BPCC) and provide basic information for setting ground rules and practice in conducting class meetings in their training agendas. We are proud of our trainers and thank them for their work with BPCC members to implement the program with fidelity, including training to support class meetings.

We would like to thank educators from all over the United States, including Regina Anderson, Katie Armstrong, Shelly Baier, Sherri Baker, Marcia Bassler, Carol Cox, Sally Hash, Deana Mahlandt, Tonya Nickerson, Lindsay Pepler, Barb Schafer, Tamera Weisweaver, and Anne Zernicke, who provided invaluable feedback and suggestions for this collection of class meeting ideas.

In addition, Rebecca Ninke, Debbie Trafton O'Neal, and the editorial team of Pamela Foster and Sue Thomas at Hazelden Publishing helped shepherd the development of this curriculum. Without their support, creativity, and assistance, this project would not have been produced.

As a group of authors, we thank all our family members who continue to inspire and support our work.

Introduction

What Is the Olweus Bullying Prevention Program?

The *Olweus Bullying Prevention Program (OBPP)* is the most researched and best-known bullying prevention program available today. With over thirty-five years of research and successful implementation all over the world, *OBPP* is a whole-school program that has been proven to prevent or reduce bullying in schools.

OBPP is used at the school, classroom, and individual levels and includes methods to reach out to parents and the community for involvement and support. School administrators, teachers, and other staff are primarily responsible for introducing and implementing the program. These efforts are designed to improve peer relations and make the school a safer and more positive place for students to learn and develop.

What Is the Purpose of This Manual?

As part of *OBPP*, classroom teachers are asked to hold regular class meetings with students. The *OBPP* Teacher Guide provides outlines and suggested discussion questions for class meetings that are held as an initial part of this program.

This manual provides thirty-five additional class meetings for kindergarten–grade 2 and thirty-five additional class meetings for grades 3–5. The manual gives specific content for class meetings beyond the initial phases of implementation and into subsequent school years. The purpose of class meetings is to broaden bullying topics to include a variety of content related to peer relations.

The thirty-five class meetings in each grade grouping are organized into eight categories. Within each category, class meetings are arranged in a specific order so as to build on one another. These categories include

- Building a Positive Classroom Climate (four class meetings)
- Identifying Feelings (four class meetings)
- Communication (six class meetings)
- Hot Spots (five class meetings)

- Peer Relationships (ten class meetings)
- Respecting Differences and Promoting Acceptance (three class meetings)
- Serving the Community/Reaching Outward (two class meetings)
- Using Current Events (one class meeting)

Because this manual is meant to be used as part of a comprehensive, schoolwide implementation of the *Olweus Bullying Prevention Program*, classroom teachers will want to review and apply the class meeting guidelines outlined in the *OBPP* Teacher Guide (chapter 6) before implementing ideas in this manual. It is recommended that every classroom teacher have a copy of this manual or, at a minimum, there should be one copy for every three teachers. If teachers must share, the Bullying Prevention Coordinating Committee can assist with a plan that facilitates teachers sharing this resource.

The class meeting activities in this manual are organized by grade and by topic. Although it is not necessary to follow topics in order, they are listed in a logical sequence so that concepts build on each other. Make sure students have covered "prerequisite" concepts first.

While topics are repeated within and across each grade grouping, we recommend that class meetings not be repeated verbatim; that is, class meetings for grades 1 and 2 should not repeat exactly what was presented in kindergarten. Students and teachers need variety in materials, activities, and follow-up discussion to keep class meetings fresh and interesting. We encourage teachers to be creative, and particularly to rely on student ideas, needs, and concerns, and to include student writing and age-appropriate literature as springboards for discussion.

A list of recommended resources is provided on pages 351–356 of this manual. We encourage you to use these resources as supplements to class meeting activities to provide variety.

How Are the Class Meetings Structured?

General guidelines for conducting class meetings appear in the *OBPP* Teacher Guide. In this manual, each class meeting is organized in the following structure:

Background Information

This brief paragraph provides insight into the purpose of the class meeting activity and issues teachers should be aware of as they facilitate the meeting. Information regarding prerequisite activities/concepts will also appear in this section.

Learner Outcomes

This text identifies the learning that will occur as a result of implementing the class meeting.

Materials Needed

This list contains the resources needed to conduct the class meeting. These materials have been kept to a minimum to make implementation easier. Any handouts on the materials list will be found in the manual following the class meeting outline.

Preparation Needed

This list will give you step-by-step instructions to prepare for the opening activity and follow-up discussion for the class meeting.

Class Meeting Outline

Each class meeting outline contains the following components: opening activity, discussion questions, and wrap-up. All text in the outline that is **bold** is scripted text. Facilitators may choose to read this text from the manual, use it as a guide, or not use it at all.

Opening Activity
This activity introduces the class meeting theme and gets students motivated and thinking about the topic. Opening activities last about half of the total class meeting time (a time frame is suggested for each). In some cases, the class meeting may require more than one class period and may be carried over from one week to another.

Discussion Questions
Following the opening activity are discussion questions to help students process the activity and apply it to their lives at school and outside of school. Questions are arranged in a general sequential order (from most basic to more in depth) and allow teachers to provide more nuanced discussions with students at different ability and age levels. Teachers should realize that they might not get through all of the discussion questions for each class meeting, and they might want to make adjustments according to student interest. Student discussion and debriefing is a key part of the class meeting, so allow most of the remaining meeting time for this.

Wrap-Up
Each class meeting includes a short wrap-up that should be used to summarize the key concepts discussed and provide an opportunity to extend the activity or student thinking about the topic.

Additional Components

Teacher Tips
These include strategies and resources to help the class meeting run smoothly. They are located in the margins.

Dig Deeper
These include concepts or ideas to further facilitator and/or student understanding. They are located in the margins.

Curriculum Connections
This section, found at the end of each class meeting outline, provides ideas for integrating the class meeting topic into other subject areas.

What Are Class Meetings?

Class meetings are an important component of *OBPP*. The purpose of these meetings is to build class cohesion and community, to teach the four anti-bullying rules, to help students understand the consequences of bullying and their role in bullying situations, and to address issues about bullying as they arise. At first, class meetings should focus on various aspects of bullying, but classroom teachers will also want to use these meetings to address additional related themes and topics.

There is no one right way to lead a class meeting. Some teachers prefer to have a step-by-step plan for what is going to be discussed. The class meeting activities in this manual serve that need. Other teachers are comfortable with a more open-ended style that provides flexibility to discuss issues as they come up. In this case, you will want to just use the class meeting activities as an outline. Either approach is fine.

This manual suggests a variety of methods to keep class meetings fresh and interesting for students and adults alike. Most teachers find these meetings relatively easy to conduct and a rewarding way to get to know their students better.

If you do not feel comfortable leading these meetings, members of your school's Bullying Prevention Coordinating Committee or your school's certified Olweus trainer could lead or co-lead the first couple of sessions. Or a teacher with experience in class meetings could co-lead as well.

More detailed information about conducting class meetings can be found in chapter 6 of the *OBPP* Teacher Guide. Again, it is important to hold the class meetings outlined in the Teacher Guide first, before using the class meeting activities in this manual.

Setting basic ground rules for these class meetings is important so that students feel safe in sharing their concerns and all members of the class feel respected and heard. Suggested class meeting ground rules can be found on page 70 of the Teacher Guide.

What Is the Difference between Curriculum Lessons and Class Meetings?

Class meetings are not the same as curriculum lessons. Although you have information you want to share with students, a class meeting is designed to establish communication among all members of your class. You will want to provide time for students to share their opinions and allow students to guide the discussion when appropriate. Class meetings are not a new concept. Many people in the education field have researched and documented this method for years.

Your role in leading class meetings is more of a facilitator than teacher. This does not mean you will not guide the discussion. You will need to make sure your discussion goals are met through the careful use of probing and open-ended questioning. Class meetings are an opportunity for students to share their feelings and opinions and to suggest solutions as they learn about how to follow the rules, interact as a community, and handle bullying situations appropriately.

Remember, as a facilitator, you should

- be an attentive listener (student contributions are the main focus of class meetings)
- make sure the viewpoints of all students are heard
- make sure everyone has the opportunity to speak and that certain individuals do not dominate the conversation
- remind students who interrupt about the ground rules set up at the beginning of your class meetings

What Steps Should Be Taken to Organize and Lead Class Meetings?

When planning and leading your class meetings, keep the following in mind:

- It works best to have students sit in a circle or half circle so that they can see as well as hear each other. Students could be on the floor or in chairs or desks.
- Class meetings should be held regularly, preferably at least once a week. For upper elementary students, the meetings could last 30 to 40 minutes. Meetings for younger students could last 15 to 30 minutes. With younger students, you may want to have more than one meeting per week.
- It works best to have meetings at a specific time each week. Your school's Bullying Prevention Coordinating Committee may want all class meetings to be held on the same day. Check with the committee before starting your meetings.
- Within any given class meeting, you may want to switch from large-group to small-group activities. This keeps the meetings interesting. Many of the meetings in this manual suggest both large-group and small-group activities.
- Don't allow students to intimidate others during the meetings. Take the lead in reinforcing the message that all bullying incidents will be taken seriously and addressed either by you or the other staff at your school. Also stress that if you hear about any retaliation for what is said by students during a class, there will be consequences.
- If you want to bring up a specific bullying problem in your classroom, be sure all students involved have given permission to do so. In these cases, names may be used, but manage this situation and the resulting discussion so all students are respected and the focus is on positive solutions.

- Be aware that you will likely have students who are being bullied by others in your group. Do not force students to talk about their experiences unless they feel comfortable doing so and unless you are prepared to facilitate this discussion. Be sensitive to the painfulness of bullying and the tremendous impact it can have on students. Do not make light of bullying situations and do not allow other students to do so either.

- Evaluating your class meetings will help to refine them and improve their effectiveness. Use the Class Meeting Activity Log on the *OBPP* Teacher Guide CD-ROM (document 19) for these evaluation purposes.

- In every class meeting, suspend the discussion outline for relevant digressions and questions. Students may have bullying issues that they want to work out in a safe environment.

Why Is Role-Playing an Important Part of Class Meetings?

Several of the activities in this manual involve role-playing. An *OBPP* research study has shown that teachers who systematically used role-playing in their anti-bullying work obtained larger reductions in bullying problems than those who did not. Role-playing

- gives students insights into the different types of bullying and what roles bystanders, followers, and defenders might take in each situation

- helps students develop a better emotional understanding of how the different participants feel in bullying situations and what motivates them to do what they do

- provides a springboard for discussions about bullying and ways to stop it

- provides valuable opportunities for students to practice, test, and evaluate solutions to bullying situations. When students act out positive behaviors, they also model them for others. It can be especially powerful for students to see social leaders in the classroom reject bullying or intervene in a bullying situation.

Chapter 7 in the Teacher Guide provides detailed information about how to conduct role-plays so that students are respected and positive messages are conveyed. Be sure to read through this chapter before doing any role-plays.

What Should You Do If, during a Class Meeting, a Student Reveals That He or She Has Been Bullied?

Whenever you are talking about real bullying incidents during your class meetings, it is helpful to suggest that students not use names or too many details. This is done to protect students.

Occasionally during a class meeting a student may reveal that he or she is being bullied. It is best to ask the student to talk with you privately after the class meeting about this situation. Be sure to follow up with the student to find out what has been happening. You may need to report this incident to your school's administration. Check with your school's Bullying Prevention Coordinating Committee to determine the appropriate reporting procedures.

How Are Class Meetings Linked to Academic Curricula?

Although class meetings are not the same as curriculum, learning is still occurring during these meetings. Learner outcomes are provided with each meeting for this reason. Teachers are also encouraged to extend the learning during class meetings by linking the topics to academic subjects such as health, English, history, social studies, science, and communications.

What Else Should You Keep in Mind When Conducting Class Meetings?

- Use both large- and small-group discussions. If your students are less communicative during large-group discussions, you can always have them break into smaller groups. Typically, as students get to know one another better, their comfort level in large-group discussions increases.
- Allow students to spend the time needed to explore these concepts. Many sessions may have content that extends beyond a single class meeting. If you would like to expand any of the sessions into future class meetings, you are encouraged to do so.
- Many class meetings encourage students to try out strategies and implement ideas that come out of the discussions. Be sure to follow up with these suggestions during future class meetings.

Using These Class Meetings Across Grade Levels

Because the class meetings in this manual are designed for students in multiple grade levels, it is important to consider the developmental needs of your students and adjust how each class meeting activities are presented and how the resulting discussions are led. There are more ideas and alternative discussion questions than can be covered in a single session. This is purposeful in order to allow teachers to revisit concepts and class meetings over different grade levels, without repeating material. In addition, linking class meetings to grade-appropriate student literature or other academic content will allow opportunities for greater variation.

Students within each of the two grade groupings (kindergarten–grade 2 and grades 3–5) have some developmental characteristics in common that are relevant to conducting these class meetings. These are summarized here for each level.

Kindergarten–Grade 2

Students in kindergarten–grade 2 share some of these common grade-level characteristics. They

- are in a time of rapid physical growth and need to move around frequently, so keep "sitting time" to 10 to 15 minutes.
- enjoy participating in social situations and want to be liked by adults and other students, so it is helpful to offer simple reasons for acting in socially appropriate ways (because it's friendly or others will want to play with you, for example).
- are learning social boundaries by observing and may have somewhat inflexible ideas about fairness. Use this as an opportunity to reinforce making fair and kind choices and building their repertoire of possible social responses.
- may have questions or concerns they are not able to verbalize, so adults can model language and help them break down situations into concepts they understand.

Grades 3–5

Students in grades 3–5 share some of these common grade-level characteristics. They

- are able to sit and work for longer periods of time (20 to 30 minutes), however students in this age group still learn best when class meetings involve active and experiential components.
- tend to identify most strongly with a same-sex group, and choose their activities accordingly. Gender content and differences in bullying become more evident. Adults can help counter these tendencies by addressing gender stereotypes and providing activities that promote collaboration and facilitate relationship-building with different classmates throughout the day.
- desire adult approval, which is becoming more balanced with a need for independence and peer support. Adults can build on these developmental trends by encouraging positive involvement of bystanders in bullying, and helping to shift attitudes among students to make helping the more normative.
- have both the cognitive and social skills to understand teamwork or group activities, but need direct guidance and tips about how to do work in groups (refer to pages 13–14 for ideas and strategies for grouping students).
- are increasingly able to use words to appropriately express their feelings and thoughts, and are more able to negotiate and act assertively in bullying situations.
- have friendships that might be shifting, so adults need to be particularly vigilant at this age to provide remedial support and assistance for building social skills for students who have difficulties or who tend to be isolated from peers.

Respecting Differences and Promoting Acceptance for Others

As you prepare and lead the three class meetings on respecting differences and promoting acceptance for others (see pages 142–154 for kindergarten–grade 2, and pages 318–335 for grades 3–5), read through these definitions and ideas.

The Importance of Teaching Tolerance and Acceptance for Others

We live in a diverse society and in a world where teaching children to live peacefully with others is becoming increasingly more important. The *OBPP* philosophy is one of ensuring basic human rights. Promoting empathy for others and promoting tolerance for diversity are closely tied to this value. Teaching about tolerance and acceptance of differences is perhaps one of the most important pathways to peace, not only in our world, but in our schools and communities. Participating in age-appropriate discussions about respecting differences and accepting diversity is an important element of a child's basic education that can reduce stereotypes and prejudice. School administrators, whether in socially or economically diverse districts or not, should ensure that all teachers have opportunities to participate in training about how to approach teaching these important concepts. The more teachers feel knowledgeable about these ideas, the more comfortable they will be approaching this subject and addressing issues of discrimination, stereotyping, and bigotry.

Additional Things to Keep in Mind

- The issue of how to address respect for differences and promote tolerance and acceptance goes well beyond the scope of this manual, but is relevant as a broad bullying-prevention issue in two important ways. First, intolerance of any kind impinges on individual human rights. Second, it contributes to and can create a negative school climate where students are unable to fully focus on learning.

- While some schools may have student bodies that represent diversity in several or many areas (cultural, ethnic, linguistic, religious, socio-economic, or family constellations), many schools have very little diversity.
- Teaching about tolerance is not a topic important only to those in "diverse" school communities. Children and adults should be encouraged to view their school community as part of a more global community as a way of preparing them to live in a peaceful society.
- The class meetings in this manual are not intended as a substitute for teaching children about diversity or respect and acceptance for others, but are instead meant to raise awareness about the roles that stereotypes, privilege, and prejudice play in bullying and bullying prevention.
- Discuss any acts of intolerance directly, concretely, and in ways that are related to students' real-life experiences.
- School provides students with an important window to the wider world—beyond what they can see and experience every day. However, true diversity education is more than acknowledging differences and sampling aspects through a "cultural awareness fair" approach. It is more meaningful and effective to strengthen communication and a sense of connection within the school so that students and adults have a strong base from which they can talk about issues that can potentially divide them, lead to exclusion and bullying, or escalate into stereotypes that marginalize, prejudice, discrimination, and hate.
- Discussions about valuing diversity and differences can become misguided when they focus too heavily on individual uniqueness, too-subtle differences (a special learning need that may not be outwardly visible, for example), or experiences that are too far removed from students' daily life to be genuinely meaningful to them (such as general discussions about cultures around the world or isolated "cultural awareness fairs").
- Be aware of how diversity is demonstrated in textbooks and reading lists in your curriculum. Highlight instances where sensitivity to diversity is lacking and offer supplemental materials where appropriate. In reading classes, use works from a variety of cultures and perspectives.
- Many studies have shown that children as young as age three have picked up terms of prejudice without really understanding their significance.
- As part of normal development, children notice differences and form attachments to others they perceive as like them. Early in life, many children acquire a full set of biases that can be observed in verbal slurs and acts of discrimination.

How to Define the Terms Used in These Class Meetings

It is important to explain terminology to students in age-appropriate terms. The following terms are used in the class meetings on respecting differences and promoting acceptance of others. Definitions are provided here to help teachers relate these concepts to bullying-prevention themes.

- **Stereotype:** An exaggerated belief, image, or distorted truth about a person or group. Stereotypes encourage people to think about others based on inflexible and incorrect ideas. These generalizations do not allow for individual differences. Stereotypes are often portrayed or reinforced through images in mass media, or beliefs passed on by family or community members. Stereotypes about gender (and what is considered "normal" behavior or appearance for boys and girls) are particularly prevalent in our society and play a critical role in acceptance and treatment of bullying behavior.

- **Prejudice:** An opinion, prejudgment, or attitude about a group or its individual members. Prejudices are often associated with ignorance, fear, or hatred. Social scientists believe children begin to acquire prejudices and stereotypes as toddlers.

- **Discrimination:** Behavior that treats people unfairly and unequally because of the group to which they belong. Discriminatory behaviors range from subtle and seemingly harmless slights and exclusion to more obvious hate crimes. Discrimination often begins with negative stereotypes and prejudices.

- **Respect:** Can be defined with synonyms such as "to value," "to appreciate," "to care about," "to be considerate of," or "to show consideration for." Many students are more familiar with the word *respect* when used in a very different context, such as "respect your elders," which implies following, obeying, or deferring to another. Reinforcing the notions of respect as valuing each other is more in keeping with both diversity training and bullying-prevention concepts.

Optional Activities and Resources

1. You may wish to take part in Mix It Up at Lunch Day, a nationwide campaign that supports students who want to identify, question, and cross social boundaries that separate them from each other and help build inclusive, welcoming learning environments. On Mix It Up at Lunch Day, schools and students use creative ways to "mix it up" in the cafeteria, helping kids break out of their usual seating patterns and get to know new people. Information about organizing this activity is found at www.tolerance .org/teens/?source=redirect&url=mixitup.

2. The following Web sites and books can provide resources for your class meetings, including in-depth explorations of the importance of tolerance, and dealing with bigotry and prejudice.

- Anti-Defamation League: www.adl.org/default.htm
- Children's Defense Fund: www.childrensdefense.org
- Southern Poverty Law Center: www.tolerance.org
- Global Classroom Connection: www.classroom-connection.org
- The North Carolina Center for Diversity Education: www.diversityed.org
- Books: *Asperger Syndrome and Bullying: Strategies and Solutions* (Nick Dubin), *Perfect Targets: Asperger Syndrome and Bullying; Practical Solutions for Surviving the Social World* (Rebekah Heinrichs and Brenda Smith Myles)

Ideas and Strategies for Grouping Students

Generally, class meetings are conducted with the entire class sitting in a circle. For some sessions, you will be encouraged to have students work in smaller groupings for at least part of the session and then return back together in a circle to process the activity as a class.

Used effectively, small groups can enhance opportunities for communication and cooperation, support development of interpersonal skills and relationship-building, and foster trust and teamwork—all of which reinforce *OBPP* goals for bullying prevention. Unfortunately, group work can also cause tension and conflict for students when assigned groupings reinforce existing social hierarchies or exacerbate problem behaviors, such as bullying. Students at all levels need guidance from adults to learn to work with others who have different styles or viewpoints, to take leadership without being bossy, or to articulate feelings and ideas in socially acceptable ways. Teachers who are aware of potential issues within a particular group of students are better able to make adjustments so *OBPP* activities run smoothly. While carefully considering how to assign groups may initially take some planning on the part of adults, positive results will carry over into building positive class relationships.

Tips for Forming Groups

As much as possible, opt for variety and balance groups by gender, ethnic group, personalities, learning styles, and social diversity; but be mindful of balancing group dynamics, power imbalances, and shared biases.

1. Avoid groupings that reinforce biases or social hierarchies in your class (boys against girls, for example).
2. Provide structure, support, and guidance for students with learning or social difficulties, impulse control, making social connections, or a tendency to withdraw or be "slow-to-warm-up."
3. To ensure inclusion and opportunities for all students to experience working with all members of the class, students need to be assigned to particular partners or groupings.

4. Offer different options for pairings or groupings to provide students a variety of opportunities to interact with different class members and to minimize being "stuck" in a group with poor dynamics.

5. Practice using a variety of approaches for forming or identifying groups: symbols, colors, shapes, activity (such as reading buddy partner), or randomly assigned by counting off using numbers or words (such as "We, Will, Not, Bully, Others").

6. Once students are familiar with groupings, save time by instructing them to "Get into your anti-bullying rules pairings," or "Let's use our color groups for this meeting."

Tips for Maximizing Group Effectiveness

1. Promote teamwork by beginning group projects with icebreaker questions that help students learn more about each other.

2. Consider what each group member has to offer and what skills each needs to develop.

3. Traditional group roles (leader, captain, reporter, and so on) often go to popular or more verbal students, reinforcing existing social hierarchies among students. Teachers can assign roles that emphasize individual talents, and reinforce more even participation.

   - Non-hierarchical roles can be:
     - content-related (information gatherer, question asker, challenger)
     - product-related (artistic consultant, spell checker, fact checker, quality control manager, artistic advisor)
     - process-related (discussion starter, agenda maker, recorder, documenter, timekeeper, quality control manager, presenter, peacekeeper)
   - Discuss vocabulary and what each role entails in advance.

4. Provide support and concrete ground rules for working through common pitfalls of group work, such as uneven participation, negotiating differences of opinions, and so on.

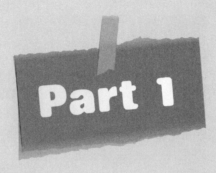

Part 1

Class Meetings for Kindergarten-Grade 2

Category 1

Building a Positive Classroom Climate

(Four class meetings)

Kindergarten–Grade 2

Category: Building a Positive
Classroom Climate

Topic: Team-Building

The Name Game

Background

Young students can benefit from learning friendly ways to greet and interact
with one another. These are important skills that help reduce the likelihood that
students will be bullied or excluded by peers. Greeting rituals foster positive peer
relationships by building awareness about others, helping to integrate new students, and providing a structure for students who have trouble initiating interactions with peers. Use this class meeting early in the school year to help students
get to know each other and to introduce subsequent class meetings.

Learner Outcomes

By the end of this session, students will be able to
- learn names of classmates and facts about them
- practice introducing themselves and others
- give compliments to peers based on observations of their positive traits
  and talents

Materials Needed

- Index cards (5 x 7 inch or larger) for each student and adult
- Current photo (2 x 3 inch bust) of each student
- Basket

- Marker
- Chart paper

Preparation Needed

- Prepare name cards by writing the first and last name of each student on one side of an index card. Place name cards in the basket.
- If possible, use a digital camera to photograph each member of the class. Attach the photos above the names on each card. (This can be done over the first few days of school.)
- Laminate cards if possible.
- Investigate whether there are common cultural practices among your students (such as shaking hands or bowing) or taboos (such as not making physical contact or eye contact) regarding greeting others.

Class Meeting Outline

Opening Activity (15 minutes)

1. **When we try to learn everyone's name and say "hi" or "hello" to each other, we help everyone feel like we are happy they are here. Let's practice this.**

2. Initial class meeting or kindergarten only: Show students a name card. Ask students to identify whose card it is. Repeat the process for each student, selecting cards from the basket one at a time:
    a. **Who is this?** Identify the student by name.
    b. Give the name card to that student to hold, and model a greeting, such as **Good morning, (name). I'm glad you are here today** or **Hello, (name). It's nice to see you!**
    c. Once everyone has a name card, ask each student to name a favorite activity he or she likes to do before putting the card back in the basket.

3. Subsequent class meeting or Grade 1: **Let's practice introducing each other.**
    a. **What could we say?** Prompt as needed. (Examples include "This is ____. He/she likes to _____." or "I'd like to introduce ____." or "I want you to meet ____.") Write students' ideas on chart paper.

b. **Let's try these ideas. Everyone will choose a name card from the basket and introduce that person to the class, using our ideas.** Have students take turns. As each student is introduced, prompt the class to say "Hi!" or "Welcome!" or another greeting.

4.   Grade 2: **Let's get to know each other better. First let's list some things we could learn about each other.** Prompt or offer ideas (see the sample questions below). Divide students into pairs and give each student his or her partner's name card. (See pages 13–14 for ideas and strategies for grouping students.) Sample questions:

   • **What is your favorite (food, color, animal, activity, TV show, book, song)?**
   • **What do you like to do when you are not in school?**
   • **Tell me about your family. (Who lives with you? Do you have brothers or sisters? pets?)**

Discussion Questions (15 minutes)

1. Process the activity.
   a.   Kindergarten: **What are some of your favorite things or places? Did anyone have the same favorite things or places? Who?**
   b.   Grades 1–2:
   • **How can we speak or look to let people know we are listening to them when they're talking?** Discuss how body language, together with words, helps people feel at ease. (Examples of positive listening behavior include looking at the person who is speaking, standing near him or her, or answering in a clear voice.)
   • **What are the different ways people greet one another?** Acknowledge potential cultural differences among students when greeting others such as shaking hands, calling someone by name, or bowing/nodding, as well as taboos such as not making physical contact or eye contact.

Teacher Tips

• Vary this activity according to student age and ability. Young students' observations of peers will focus on superficial or physical attributes, but older students should be encouraged to learn more about their peers' likes and dislikes, special skills, and attributes. Help students practice ways of framing observations in kind and complimentary ways.

• Keep the name cards even after students know each other. Create a card for new students and repeat the introduction activity periodically. Review the cards at the end of the year to see how everyone has changed.

• Make permanent name badges for children to wear for several days when school first starts, when there is a new student in the class, or when there is a substitute teacher or planned class visitor. This will help to promote a "welcoming classroom climate" throughout the entire year.

2. Grade 2 (additional discussion):

- **Use your partner's name card to introduce him or her to the class. Share something interesting you learned about your partner.**
- **Give a compliment about one thing your partner does well by saying: "I like how you . . ."** Have students think of compliments other than hair, clothing, or other physical traits.
- Encourage students to practice ways of giving and receiving compliments.

Wrap-Up

1. **Everyone is welcome in our class! We'll be learning more about each other all the time. One way you can help everyone feel welcome is to say hello to each other on the playground, at lunch, or during free time. Let's try helping everyone feel welcome every day.**
2. Encourage additional questions or comments.

Curriculum Connections

Vocabulary: *compliment, greeting, include, interests, observe, polite, receive, talents, welcome*

Language Arts:

- Read selections from age-appropriate literature about making friends. Discuss whether characters were or were not welcoming, the effect of their behavior, and what could have been done differently. Students can be encouraged to create different endings, compose their own stories, or describe what makes them feel welcome or included when they are with other children.
- Encourage students to brainstorm ways of greeting classroom guests or visitors. Assign a daily or weekly greeter so students have regular opportunities to practice these skills with others.

Arts: Introduce age-appropriate music or dances with welcome or friendship themes.

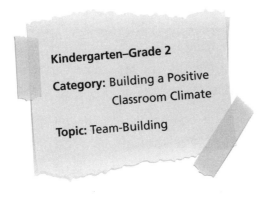

Kindergarten–Grade 2

Category: Building a Positive
Classroom Climate

Topic: Team-Building

We Are All Welcome Here!

Background

Creating a positive classroom climate begins with creating a sense that everyone belongs and is accepted. Factors such as age, gender, social class, race, and popularity can affect whether students feel welcome and included. Students need to be able to trust adults and peers in order to talk freely about their feelings, fears, and problems with bullying. Adults need to model positive behavior for students and be alert to situations when students might feel excluded. Define and use terms such as "welcome," "comfortable," "accepted," and "included" to frame this discussion.

Learner Outcomes

By the end of this session, students will be able to

- identify factors that make them feel welcome, accepted, and included at school
- identify ways students and adults can work together to make their class feel more welcoming and inclusive for all students
- discuss the need to adjust behavior to show respect for the needs of others

Materials Needed

- Chart paper and markers

- Age-appropriate literature such as *The Brand New Kid* (Katie Couric), *Chrysanthemum* (Kevin Henkes), *Oliver Button Is a Sissy* (Tomie dePaola), *Do You Want to Be My Friend?* (Eric Carle), *Swimmy* (Leo Lionni), *Thidwick the Big-Hearted Moose* (Dr. Seuss), or *Chester's Way* (Kevin Henkes)

Preparation Needed

- On a sheet of chart paper, write the heading "I feel I belong when . . ."
- Familiarize yourself with the book you have chosen and the ways that characters in the book are made to feel welcome or excluded.

Class Meeting Outline

Opening Activity (15 minutes)

Teacher Tip

Based on the varying demographics of the children in your class, provide students with guidelines, such as encouraging them to greet everyone in the class, to make the class welcoming and inclusive for everyone. Consider religious, cultural, physical, emotional, and family differences.

1. **When people welcome us to a place, we feel happy to be there. I'm going to read you a story. Think about what makes the person in the story feel welcome and know that other people are happy to have him or her there.** Read the literature selection.
2. Discuss the following questions:
   - **Did the person feel welcome? Were people happy the person was with them?**
   - **What did the other people do to make the person feel welcome?**
3. **What are some things that make you feel welcome and show you that people are happy you are there?** List students' ideas on the chart paper.

Discussion Questions (10 minutes)

1. Process the activity.
   - **What are some things that make people in our class feel welcome?**
   - **What behavior can make people feel left out?**
   - **What can we do in our classroom to make sure that everyone feels welcome and that we are happy everyone is here?**

2. Grade 1: **How did you feel on your first day at this school? What things did teachers or other students do to make you feel welcome? How might each of us help new students feel welcome?**

3. Grade 2: Have students discuss the following question with a partner: **What could you do if some students don't feel welcome or feel left out?** After a few minutes, ask the partners to share their ideas with the group. Compile students' suggestions onto chart paper and post it in the classroom.

Wrap-Up

1. **I want to make sure everyone here feels welcome. We all can help. Every day, I will try to show each of you that I am happy you are here. You came up with lots of good ideas. You can help everyone feel welcome too by** (highlight key student ideas). **Let's all practice this week. We can talk about how that worked next time!**

2. Encourage additional questions and comments.

Curriculum Connections

Vocabulary: *accepted, belong, caring/uncaring, comfortable, different/same, included, welcome/unwelcome*

Language Arts:

- Conduct a "writer's workshop." Ask children to draw or write in response to the story that was read during the class meeting. They might write about how the character felt, what he/she experienced, and their thoughts about that. Some children will be able to make a connection to their own experiences.

- Role-play positive introductions or greetings to build social skills.

Social Studies: Help students research ways that people of different cultures greet each other.

Art:

- Create a large heart-shaped puzzle. Cut it into the same number of pieces as there are students in the class. Ask each student to color one piece with his or her favorite color and write his or her name on it. Each piece is then brought together to complete a beautiful, cooperatively made piece of art. You may wish to post a phrase by the heart that reads: "Each piece unique, together complete."

- Encourage students to create posters with words of welcome in different languages.

- Have students draw a picture, comic strip, or poster that illustrates something that makes them feel welcome at school or in their classroom.

> **Kindergarten–Grade 2**
>
> **Category:** Building a Positive Classroom Climate
>
> **Topic:** Team-Building

Our Kindness Circle

Background

When students view others as like themselves or part of their social circle, they are more likely to feel empathy for them and are less likely to exclude them. This class meeting builds on the previous class meeting, We Are All Welcome Here! Students are encouraged to practice acts of kindness toward peers as a way of building awareness about the needs of others and promoting empathy.

Learner Outcomes

By the end of this session, students will be able to

- discuss ways they can show kind actions to others
- demonstrate giving and receiving a compliment
- Grade 2: give compliments to peers based on observations of their positive traits and talents

Materials Needed

- Nerf or soft foam ball

Preparation Needed

- Identify an open space where the entire class can sit comfortably in a circle on the floor.

Class Meeting Outline

Opening Activity (10–15 minutes)

1. **We've talked about ways we can be kind to everyone so they feel more welcome. Can anyone give me examples of ways we can do that?**

2. Kindergarten–grade 1: **We're going to play a game called the Kindness Game. Here's how we will play:**

    a. **Each of you will share ways that you welcomed someone else or that you were welcomed.**

    b. **Close your eyes (or put your head down) and think quietly for a minute. What did you do to help someone feel more welcome? Or what kind of welcoming thing did someone do for you (at school or some other place)? Once you have a thought in mind, open your eyes and look at me so I know you are ready.**

Teacher Tip

Carefully consider how activities begin so no students are left out. If needed, direct them to roll to specific students, being mindful of those who tend to be excluded, and prompt with an appropriate suggestion for a compliment as needed.

    c. **I have a ball here to help us take turns. I am going to start by sharing something I did to welcome someone. Then I'll roll the ball to someone else in the circle. When the ball is rolled to you, share what you did to welcome someone or what someone did to welcome you. Then, roll the ball to someone who hasn't had a turn yet. We'll keep playing until everyone has had a turn.**

    d. Roll the ball first to a child whom you have observed making other students feel welcome. The first response will often set the tone for more sharing of ideas. Encourage students for positive participation.

3. Grade 2: **Today we're going to practice ways we can give each other compliments. These compliments should be about something someone does well or ways someone shows kindness for others, not about how someone looks. We'll also practice things we can say when someone compliments us—that's another part of showing kindness. Here's how we'll play.**

    a. **I will begin by rolling the ball to someone in our circle. When I do, I will tell that person something I like about him or her as a person.** Focus

Teacher Tip

Older students can use a ball of string or yarn instead of a ball. As each student receives the ball of yarn, he or she will hold on to a portion of the yarn before rolling the yarn ball to someone else. This keeps them connected to each other with the yarn. By the end of the activity, all members of the circle will be connected by a web of yarn.

your compliment on welcoming or kind ways the student behaves, rather than personal things like hair or clothes. **We can give a compliment by saying, "I like the way that you _____" or "I like it when you _____."**

b. **When you get the ball, be sure to thank the person who complimented you before you take your turn.**

c. **Then you will think of a compliment for someone else, and roll the ball to that person. If you need some time to think of your compliment, just say "pass," and we'll come back to you when you're ready.**

d. **We will keep doing this until everyone has had a turn to receive a compliment.**

e. Consider beginning this activity with a student you think may be unlikely to receive positive comments from classmates. Conclude the activity with appreciation for the student's cooperation as appropriate.

Discussion Questions (10 minutes)

1. Process the activity.

    a. Kindergarten–grade 1:

    - **What is one nice thing someone has done to help you feel welcome?**
    - **What were some new ideas that you heard that you might try?**
    - **What can we do for someone who looks like he or she feels left out and not welcome?**

    b. Grade 2:

    - **How did it feel to give compliments?**
    - **How did it feel to receive compliments?**
    - **What is one of the nicest compliments you've ever received?**
    - **What is one of the nicest compliments you've ever given to someone?**
    - **How can a compliment help someone who is feeling left out?**

2. Compliment students on their efforts and encourage them to continue welcoming and including others. Revisit this idea periodically.

Wrap-Up

1. **We all can help make our school a welcoming place. Saying hello, giving compliments, and including everyone in games and activities are all welcoming ways. Everyone feels good and does better when we are kind to one another.**

2. Encourage additional questions and comments.

Curriculum Connections

Vocabulary: *compliments, experience, kindness; words that describe emotions*

Language Arts:

- Read *Have You Filled a Bucket Today?* (Carol McCloud) and discuss ways students can "fill one another's buckets" (improving self-esteem). Students can brainstorm a list of ways to fill a bucket and ways people dip into one another's buckets. Talk about which of the things on the list they would want to give or receive. Refer back to these lists and play a game with thumbs up or thumbs down. Students can put their thumb up if it is a bucket-filling thing and thumbs down for bucket dipping.

- Invite students to draw or write about a time when they helped someone feel welcome at school, even if that person wasn't a friend.

Music:

- Teach students the song "Make New Friends." (Lyrics: Make new friends, but keep the old. One is silver and the other gold. A circle's round, it has no end. That's how long I want to be your friend.) Sing it in a round.

- Work with the group to write a class song, chant, or cheer that has a friendship or teamwork theme.

Physical Education: Stress welcoming students into games and how school rules apply to the playground. Enforcing the rule You can't say, "You can't play" for this age group may be appropriate.

> **Kindergarten–Grade 2**
>
> **Category:** Building a Positive Classroom Climate
>
> **Topic:** Team-Building

This Is Our Island

Background

Research has shown that competitive games can cause increased aggression both during and after play. Many childhood games are inherently competitive (examples include Simon Says, Duck-Duck-Goose, tag, and Red Rover). Collaborative games help reduce aggression and offer children opportunities to practice working together in a fun setting. What matters most is not the game by itself, but how it is presented. Whenever possible, try offering collaborative alternatives to common games (for example, instead of "freeze" tag, play "freeze/unfreeze" tag). Always avoid reinforcing competition between boys and girls. The game in this class meeting is based on a collaborative version of Musical Chairs.

Learner Outcomes

By the end of this session, students will be able to
- help each other and cooperate to reach a class goal

Materials Needed

- Carpet squares for each student or a large, inexpensive plastic tablecloth
- Lively musical recording and player, or any rhythm instrument
- *Optional:* Light snack (pretzels, goldfish crackers, fruit) for celebration (Before serving any food, check your school policy. Also be aware of food allergies among your students. Provide an alternative if necessary.)

Preparation Needed

- Clear a space large enough for the carpet squares or tablecloth. Lay the carpet squares out randomly to form an "island" or cut the tablecloth into an island shape and lay it on the floor.
- Cue up the music. Alternatively, a rhythm instrument can provide a signal when to move and stop.
- *Optional:* Have a snack ready in bowls.

Class Meeting Outline

Opening Activity (10–15 minutes)

1. **How many of you have ever played the game Musical Chairs? What happens when the music stops?**
2. **We're going to play a game that is like Musical Chairs, but a little different. Instead of people being left out when the music stops, we will all cooperate and work together as a team to help everyone stay in the game!**
3. As a group, stand around your "island." **This is our island. Here's how we'll play:**
   - **When the music starts, you will all pretend to swim around the outside edge.**
   - **When the music stops, you will all have to find a space ON the island and to help everyone fit—don't let anyone fall off into the water.**
   - **Here's the tricky part: Each time the music stops, our island will get a little smaller. You will all have to work together to help all of your classmates fit! You can hold on to them if that's okay with them, or scrunch close so no one falls back into the water. Let's try it once.**
4. After the trial with the island full size, continue for six to eight rounds, removing several carpet squares at a time or folding the edges of the tablecloth to make it smaller. Stop when it is clear that students won't be able to all stay on the island if it gets any smaller. If a student "falls off," the student is not out.

Dig Deeper

- Most games at this age are inherently competitive and pit students against each other to find a winner. This inevitably leaves some students feeling left out and "less than" their peers. Whenever possible, work with students to rewrite game rules to emphasize cooperation and common goals.

- Communicate often that all classmates deserve to be treated with kindness and consideration. With very young students, using the term "friends" to refer to classmates is welcoming and promotes inclusiveness. By grade 2 students are forming closer relationships with some peers, so, instead of the term "friends," use the more generic term "classmate" for class meetings.

Encourage classmates to rescue their classmate and to help him or her fit on the island.

5. Congratulate student efforts each round. **Nice job helping (name) so he or she wouldn't fall in!** or **I noticed a lot of cooperation! Everyone is working really hard to help all classmates to stay on the island!**

Discussion Questions (10 minutes)

1. Opt to hold the discussion on the island (restored to full size).
2. Process the activity.

   - **What are ways you worked together to help each other stay on the island?**
   - **How did it feel to cooperate and work together to play this game? Was it more fun?**
   - **It can be a lot easier to get things done if we help someone and work together. What are ways we can work together to help our friends and classmates when they need it?**
   - **How do rules help us cooperate or work together? What do you think it would be like if we didn't have rules?**

Wrap-Up

1. **Working together as a team helps us reach important goals. When we do that, we are cooperating.** Highlight ways students cooperated to help each other in this activity. Point out ways they can use those same strategies to work together in class or during free time.
2. If you wish, celebrate the group's cooperative efforts with a light snack.

Curriculum Connections

Vocabulary: *class goal, collaborate/collaboration, cooperate/cooperation, empathy, patience, support/encouragement, teamwork*

Language Arts:

- Ask students to draw a picture story of a time they cooperated with others to help a person in need.

- Have students read age-appropriate literature with cooperation as a theme: *Frog and Toad Are Friends* (Arnold Lobel), *The Tale of Pip and Squeak* (Kate Duke), *The Giant Cabbage: An Alaska Folktale* (Cherie B. Stihler), *Cooperation* (Kimberley Jane Pryor), *Charlotte's Web* (E. B. White), *Matthew and Tilly* (Rebecca C. Jones).

Social Studies/Science: Use your curricula or draw on current events (using local examples whenever possible) to identify adults and young people who worked together or cooperated to achieve a goal. Examples might include cleaning up an old park or lot, building a house or playground, or helping families in need.

Physical Education:

- Encourage students to rewrite rules for traditionally competitive games to make them more cooperative. Examples of rules include: The group has to work together as a team, no one is excluded, and there is not a winner. (For early elementary grade students, this could be a writer's workshop activity to be done in a writing class rather than during a physical education class. Students will likely require some support with getting started and you may wish to assign pairs for this activity.)

- Practice cooperative versions of races, tag, or ball or circle games. Resources for cooperative games include *Everyone Wins!: Cooperative Games and Activities* (Josette Luvmour and Sambhava Luvmour) or *Cooperative Games and Sports: Joyful Activities for Everyone* (Terry Orlick).

Category 2

Identifying Feelings

(Four class meetings)

Kindergarten–Grade 2

Category: Identifying
Feelings

Topic: Building Empathy and
Perspective-Taking

Our Talking Stick

Background

Teaching empathy to young children relies heavily on positive adult role modeling. Empathy involves two key components, both of which are essential to bullying prevention and need to be nurtured throughout childhood. The first component involves being able to understand what someone else is feeling without being told. Adults promote this aspect of empathy when they teach children to name and recognize feelings, and to observe body language cues in others. The second component involves responding to others' feelings with compassion, based on what they need. Adults reinforce this aspect of empathy when they promote sharing and turn-taking, and teach children ways of caring for all living things.

Learner Outcomes

By the end of this session, students will be able to
- discuss ways they can care for others and all living things
- talk about their feelings
- practice taking turns
- practice perspective-taking

Materials Needed

- Something to use as a "talking stick" (a plain dowel, a short stout stick, or a paper towel tube about 12 inches long)

Preparation Needed

None

Class Meeting Outline

Opening Activity (10 minutes)

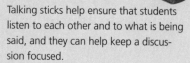

Teacher Tip

Talking sticks help ensure that students listen to each other and to what is being said, and they can help keep a discussion focused.

1. Show your "talking stick" to the group. **For our class meeting today, we are going to use this as our talking stick. Does anyone know what a talking stick is?** (Whoever holds the stick may talk; everyone else must listen and pay attention.)

2. **Our talking stick will help us take turns and practice listening while we have our class meeting.**

3. **Let's practice using the stick: First we'll pass it around and everyone will say his or name.** As the students pass the stick around the circle, welcome or greet each child personally. Once everyone has said his or her name, the stick returns to you.

4. Next ask a few questions aimed at learning more about the students and reinforcing basic empathy concepts. Each time you ask a question, students pass the stick around the circle from person to person, offering their answers. If a child can't think of a response, he or she may pass the stick on but still have the option to respond later. Choose questions from the following list, or feel free to think of your own. Two to four questions are sufficient for one class meeting.

   - **How are you feeling today?**
   - **Name something that makes you feel excited.**
   - **Name something that makes you feel upset.**
   - **What is your favorite season of the year, and why?**
   - **What is your favorite thing to do when you are not at school?**
   - **Do you take care of a pet (or some other living thing)?**
   - **How would you feel if a friend looked very sad?**
   - **What could you do if a friend needed a pencil and you had an extra one?**
   - **What would it be like if you forgot your lunch one day?**
   - **What would it be like if you needed help to get on a swing?**
   - **How would you feel if you lost something, like your jacket?**

- **What could you do if someone told you he or she lost a glove at recess?**
- **How could you help someone if that person's belongings kept falling while he or she tried to put them away?**
- **What if someone needed help reaching something on a shelf that you could reach?**

Discussion Questions (15 minutes)

1. Process the activity. Encourage students to use the talking stick as they participate in the discussion.
   - **What is it like to use a talking stick?**
   - **How can we show each other we're listening when others have the talking stick?**
   - **How can the talking stick help us to learn more about each other?**
   - **What is it like to take turns? Is it easy or hard? Why?**
   - **What has someone done to show you he or she cares about you this week?**

2. Grade 1:
   - **How does it feel to help someone else?**
   - **What ways do you show you care for your family? How do you show you care for pets or other animals? What about our Earth (or environment)?**
   - **How does it feel when someone helps you when you have a problem?**

3. Grades 1–2:
   - **How do you know when another student needs help?**

4. Grade 2:
   - **If someone feels upset, how do you know what help that person might need?**
   - **How do you show a friend you care about him or her?**

Dig Deeper

Talking sticks, feathers, or shells are part of Native North American tribal culture. They are traditionally used in council meetings to show respect for a chief so he can speak without interruption. This ceremonial object is then passed to council members who wish to speak. Talking sticks are carefully decorated to show their importance.

Wrap-Up

1. **Using our talking stick helped us to take turns. That took patience! Taking turns is one way to show we care about each other. Our class meetings help us to practice showing that we care about each other.**

2. Encourage additional questions and comments.

Curriculum Connections

Vocabulary: *care, empathy, help, talking stick*

Language Arts:

- Create a Question of the Day chart to help students learn different things about each other. Write a question (such as What is your favorite season?) at the top of the chart. Make columns for the different answers and have the students mark their responses in the columns.

- Include a few age-appropriate books for talking about feelings in your classroom, such as *My Friend is Sad, I Love My New Toy, Knuffle Bunny: A Cautionary Tale,* and *Don't Let the Pigeon Drive the Bus* (all titles by Mo Willems).

Math: Using results from the Question of the Day, tally most/least common responses and report to the group.

Science: Use classroom pets or a plant to teach students about caring for other living things.

Social Studies/Community Service:

- Explore with students the origins and use of the talking stick in Native American culture.

- Show picture cards depicting people helping each other. Ask the children to tell a story about each picture: what they see and what they think might happen next.

- If your school or community is involved in a caring activity such as supporting a local food bank or helping victims of a fire, find out what your students can do to contribute to this cause.

Art: Have students decorate the class talking stick with colored markings, feathers, or beads.

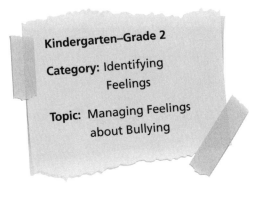

Kindergarten–Grade 2

Category: Identifying
Feelings

Topic: Managing Feelings
about Bullying

A Story about Feelings

Background

Strong feelings play a role in bullying behavior in two key ways. First, young students' competence in identifying and labeling feelings and recognizing body language clues may alert them to potential bullying situations. Second, increasing their abilities to manage their own strong feelings and to regulate their impulses may help students stay focused and in control if they are bullied or acting as helping bystanders. This class meeting helps young children to identify the body language of strong emotions, to label feelings, and to recognize that people may view and respond emotionally to the same situation very differently. This class meeting provides a framework for later class meetings on learning to regulate responses.

Learner Outcomes

By the end of this session, students will be able to

- talk about different body language and facial expressions for happiness, excitement, fear, anger, sadness, and frustration
- observe that everyone does not respond the same way or have the same feelings in different situations

Materials Needed

- Feelings Story on page 41
- Grades 1–2: If students have done this class meeting before, use the Bullying Feelings Story on page 42

Preparation Needed

None

Class Meeting Outline

Opening Activity (10 minutes)

1. **Our faces and our bodies can show others how we are feeling. Sometimes we can tell how someone else feels just by watching that person.**

2. **Do you know how to pantomime (mime)? Pantomime is acting without voices—just using your face and body. We are going to pantomime for each other how our faces and bodies look when we show different feelings.**

Teacher Tip

Students who chronically bully others are generally fairly skilled at reading the facial cues or body language of others. However, they are less likely to use that information to act compassionately when they see the hurtful impact their behavior has on others.

3. Have students stand in a circle. Ask them to stand far enough from their neighbors so that they don't touch if they hold their arms out.

4. **I am going to tell you a story in parts. Pretend the story is about you. After each part of the story, I will pause so you can all use your faces and bodies to show how you would feel. Please be sure not to touch or bump anyone!**

5. Read the Feelings Story, pausing as directed to have the group simultaneously show a feeling based on the story segment.

6. Grades 1–2: If students have done this activity before and can read body and facial clues with a fair amount of accuracy, have them pantomime the Bullying Feelings Story instead.

Discussion Questions (15 minutes)

1. Process the activity for students using the Feelings Story.
   a. Segment 1:
      - **What feelings did you show when I read the part of the story about getting ready for the party?** Based on your earlier observations, choose a volunteer to demonstrate happy emotions.
      - **How can you tell (name) is happy just by looking at him/ her?**

- **What did his/her face look like? How did his/her eyes, eyebrows, mouth look?**
- **What did (name) do with his/her arms and shoulders? body? legs and feet? Were they moving or still?**

b. Segment 2:

- **What feelings did you show when your toy got broken?** Choose two volunteers to demonstrate sad and angry emotions so students can see the difference. Using the format above, ask students:
- **What feeling did (name 1) show? How can you tell he/she was sad?**
- **What did (name 1)'s face look like?**
- **What did (name 1) do with his/her arms and shoulders? legs and feet? Were they moving or still?**
- **What about (name 2)? Was he/she sad too? So, (name 2) showed different feelings. How could you tell (name 2) was angry?**
- **What did (name 2)'s face look like? body? arms and legs?**
- Highlight ways the two students' actions were similar and different.

Teacher Tip

It is important to clarify that strong emotions are not limited to anger. In fact, anger, or misplaced anger, is not a factor in many instances of bullying, and anger management generally is not an effective tool for preventing or addressing bullying.

c. Segment 3:

- **Let's talk about when the dessert fell.**
- **Did everyone feel the same way?** Have students name the emotions aloud. (Some may have thought it was funny; some may have felt embarrassed, some sad, some angry.)
- **How did you know the different feelings?** Highlight the different ways students showed their feelings as well as the fact they reacted differently to the same event.

d. Segment 4:

- Repeat as before for the final segment, calling attention to different responses and ways students expressed the same feeling. Reinforce that people can feel differently about the same event.

2. Grades 1–2: For students using the Bullying Feelings Story:

    a. Briefly review or compare the different ways students responded to each segment. Use prompting questions similar to those suggested for the Feelings Story.

    b. **Let's practice things you could do or say if another student treats you in a way that makes you feel very upset.** (Examples include walking away, telling the student to stop, or saying "No!" and telling an adult.)

Wrap-Up

1. **We all have many of the same feelings, though we don't all show them exactly the same way. We all don't feel the same way in the same situations either. Watching how people show their feelings without words can help us know each other better.**

2. Consider ending this meeting with a calming exercise, such as taking several slow deep breaths.

Curriculum Connections

Vocabulary: *afraid, angry, excited, frustrated, observation, pantomime, pretend, sad*

Language Arts:

- Create a "word wall" of emotions words to which students can refer.
- To help build vocabulary words about emotions, have students create a group Feelings Book. The book should include illustrated contributions from every child.

Science: Have students examine facial expressions more closely by using photographs or picture books that show a range of feelings, such as *On Monday When It Rained* (Cherryl Kachenmeister).

Social Studies: Introduce ways various cultures deal with strong feelings, including dream catchers (Native American) or worry dolls (Latin American). Students may enjoy making their own feelings object.

Music/Art:

- Introduce students to the ways instrumental music can elicit particular feelings.
- Encourage students to use art, music, or dance to express feelings and release tension.
- Have students listen to or sing "Your Face Will Surely Show It" by Jim Gill.

Physical Education: Encourage students' participation in active games as a means of letting off steam, letting go of strong emotions, and relaxing.

Feelings Story

Instructions: Read the four segments of the story to your group, pausing between each segment. At each pause, instruct all students to pantomime simultaneously. Do not have them take turns.

Segment 1

It's your birthday and you are having a party today.
You are going to wear your favorite clothes and have your most favorite dessert.
This morning, before the party, you got a toy you really wanted.
Everyone you like will be coming soon!
PAUSE
Without talking, use your face and body to show how you feel.

Segment 2

The party is very noisy—children are laughing and talking and running around.
A piece on your new toy gets broken.
PAUSE
Without talking, use your face and body to show how you feel now.

Segment 3

At last, it's time for dessert. You got the very first piece!
But it fell on the floor.
Some got on your favorite clothes and made a mess.
Your pet dog starts eating your favorite dessert. Some of the children point and laugh.
PAUSE
Without talking, use your face and body to show how you feel now.

Segment 4

It's time for everyone to leave now.
The friend who broke your toy says, "I am SO sorry I broke your toy! I didn't mean to."
All your friends tell you what a great time they had at your party.
PAUSE
Without talking, use your face and body to show how you feel.

Bullying Feelings Story (Grades 1–2)

Instructions: This story may be used with older students who have participated in the original Feelings Story in previous class meetings. Read the three segments of the story to your group, pausing between each segment. At each pause, instruct all students to pantomime simultaneously. Do not have them take turns.

Segment 1

You arrive at school.

You are really looking forward to today because your class is having a special activity.

You and your class have been looking forward to this activity all week.

PAUSE

Without talking, use your face and body to show how you feel.

Segment 2

As you get near your classroom, a student from another class in your grade bumps into you and knocks your belongings onto the floor.

You think the student did it on purpose, but you're not sure.

Now you have to pick up all your things!

PAUSE

Without talking, use your face and body to show how you feel.

Segment 3

Your class activity was lots of fun, and you are talking about it with some friends on the playground.

Just now, the same student who bumped you this morning bumps into you again, hard.

This time the student calls you a bad name too.

Some other students laugh.

PAUSE

Without talking, use your face and body to show how you feel.

Kindergarten–Grade 2

Category: Identifying Feelings

Topic: Managing/
Expressing Strong
Feelings Assertively

Confidence 101: Taking Care of Myself

Background

Although the primary response for bullying comes first from adults, helping children behave in assertive ways builds confidence to protect themselves and support others. Teaching students assertive rather than aggressive responses, as well as calming strategies when they feel overwhelmed by strong emotions, can help them develop important coping skills in bullying and other situations.

Learner Outcomes

By the end of this session, students will be able to

- practice using assertive tones of voice and body language
- discuss the difference between assertive and aggressive responses
- discuss times when it might be appropriate to use assertive skills
- practice ways to calm themselves when they feel upset

Materials Needed

- Confidence 101 Teacher Tips on pages 47–48
- Confidence 101 Calming Strategies on pages 49–50
- Chart paper and a marker

Preparation Needed

- Create an open space for students to sit on the floor in a circle.
- Review the tips from Confidence 101 Teacher Tips.
- Choose one strategy from Confidence 101 Calming Strategies to teach students as part of the activity.

Class Meeting Outline

Opening Activity (10–15 minutes)

1. **It's important to show others we care about them. It's just as important to care about ourselves, too.**

2. **One way to take care of ourselves is to learn how to act when someone is bothering us and we want that person to stop. Sometimes people don't listen. Sometimes, we don't know what to do or say to stop them.**

3. **We can use our bodies and voices to show others we are confident. When we are confident, we feel strong enough to say "Stop that!" in a way that others will listen.** This demonstration portion of the session should take about 5 minutes.

   a. Demonstrate a passive, nonassertive response for students. Stand slump-shouldered, head down. Show a timid expression, and say "Stop It" or "No" in a weak, quiet voice.

   b. **Did I seem confident? Do you think people would listen?**

   c. **How might I *look* stronger and more confident?** Prompt students step by step if needed: "Breathe! Stand up straight and tall! Plant your feet, like this. Show a calm, confident (not angry) face. Lift your chin up to look at the person's eyes, or, if looking at the person's eyes is too scary, look up at his or her forehead."

   d. **Now what can I do to *sound* stronger? What could a confident voice sound like?** Prompt students step by step if needed: "Use a strong or firm tone of voice. You can use a louder voice, but don't yell. Keep your voice calm, so it doesn't sound either angry or afraid. Say the name of the student bothering you when you say 'No.'"

   e. Demonstrate an active, assertive response using the students' suggestions.

4. **Now it's your turn to practice using confident bodies and voices. For now, we're just going to practice saying the words "Yes, I can!"**

    a. Have students spread out around the space you cleared.

    b. **Let's pretend you're on the playground. Another student says in a mean way: "You can't play here!"** Have students practice using their voices and bodies to say "Yes, I can!" in a confident way.

    c. **Now, let's pretend that you're getting on the bus, and when you start to sit down, a student shouts at you: "You can't sit near us! Go sit over there!"** Have students practice using their voices and bodies again to say "Yes, I can!" in a confident way.

    d. **Now, let's practice saying "I need help!" to tell an adult about a bullying problem.**

Discussion Questions (5–10 minutes)

1. Process the activity.
   - **How did it feel to act and talk in a confident way?**
   - **What might happen if someone was bothering you and you spoke to him or her in that way?**
   - **Do you think this can help students your age feel less scared? How?**

2. **We practiced using the words "Yes, I can!" Do you think those words will work any time someone is bothering you? Let's make a list of some more words you could try.** Make a list on the chart paper.

3. **If you use a confident voice and someone still doesn't listen, what else could you do?** (Examples include telling an adult, asking a friend or two to help, or asking an older student like a reading or playground "buddy" for help.)

4. **We all have strong feelings and sometimes we need to find ways to calm ourselves down. That's another way we can care for ourselves. Let's talk about some ways you can calm down here in our classroom.** Discuss acceptable choices to use at school, such as squeezing clay or a ball, sitting in a quiet spot, walking or running fast at recess or in the gym, drawing, or listening to music.

5. Grades 1–2: **When someone hurts your feelings or says unkind words, you might feel like saying or doing something mean back. What might happen if you made that choice?**

Wrap-Up

1. **Being confident and using words to tell people if they're doing something you don't like is an important way to take care of yourself. Let's practice one more way to help us take care of ourselves. To end our class meeting, I am going to teach you a way to relax and calm yourself down.**

2. Teach students to do one of the calming strategies from the Confidence 101 Calming Strategies list on pages 49–50.

Curriculum Connections

Vocabulary: *acceptable, aggressive, assertive, body language, confident, facial expression, strong*

Language Arts:

- Discuss ways characters in age-appropriate literature respond to being teased or bullied. Highlight strategies discussed in this session. Examples include *Chrysanthemum* (Kevin Henkes), *Bootsie Barker Bites* (Barbara Bottner), *Hooway for Wodney Wat* (Helen Lester), *Arnie and the Skateboard Gang* (Nancy Carlson), *My Secret Bully* (Trudy Ludwig).

- Create a poster using words students generated to stop someone from bothering them. If your student body includes students who speak other languages, consider incorporating words from those languages.

Physical Education/Health: Discuss the role of confident body language in playing a sport.

Confidence 101 Teacher Tips

About Assertiveness

- With younger students, using the terms "strong" and "confident" to describe assertive behaviors is more developmentally appropriate than using the term "assertive." Keep it simple when coaching students about what words to use.
- Responding assertively is not a substitute for seeking out adult help. Rather, it is another skill students can add to their social repertoire.
- Carefully consider the issue of "I messages" before using them to teach assertiveness to children. According to Jane Bluestein ("What's Wrong with I-Messages?"http://www.janebluestein.com/articles/whatswrong.html), teaching students this age to use statements such as "I don't like it when you do . . ." can actually reinforce bullying behavior. Students who bully others generally *know* their behavior is bothersome or unkind. Hearing an I message may actually motivate them to continue their bullying behavior.

About Aggression

- Invading someone's physical space or boundaries can be a form of aggression.
- Responding aggressively either physically or verbally can cause a conflict or bullying situation to escalate.
- Techniques such as hitting a pillow or bop-toys or competitive play may exacerbate aggression.

- Students may offer suggestions for dealing with bullying that cross the line to being aggressive. In this situation, describe the behavior as a poor or risky choice. Encourage them to consider what could happen if someone responded that way.
- Discuss choices that might have harmful consequences, such as yelling and saying mean words to someone, hitting or pushing someone, breaking something, or throwing a tantrum. Be clear about consequences for aggressive behavior, even in retaliation, and discuss acceptable alternatives as better choices.

About Using Literature as a Teaching Tool

- Use age-appropriate literature as a source for role-play situations and discussion.
- Discussing ways that characters felt or acted can help students feel less exposed or vulnerable than talking about their own feelings.
- Choose literature that reinforces good practices in preventing bullying, rather than misconceptions.
- Look for literature that promotes positive involvement from adults and peers, rather than literature that places responsibility for stopping bullying on the bullied student.

Confidence 101 Calming Strategies

Instructions: The following quick-and-simple calming strategies are effective with students in kindergarten through grade 2. Select one strategy from this list to teach to your students during this class meeting. Once students learn a technique, explain that they can do it silently, on their own. Teach a new strategy any time students need to calm down. Refer back to the list or use other methods you know.

1. **Deep Breathing:** Slowly count 1-2-3, instructing students to breathe in slowly as you count. Have them hold their breath for one more second. As you count slowly 3-2-1, tell students to slowly let their breath out. Repeat the exercise twice.

2. **The Countdown:** Count backward very slowly from 10 to 1. Tell students to breathe in and out at each count.

3. **The Scrunch:** Tell students to scrunch or tighten, then quickly relax, muscles in parts of their bodies as you name them: arms, hands, legs, bellies, jaw, then eyes.

4. **The Drain:** Ask students to pretend their bodies are like a sink full of water. The water represents tension or strong feelings. Tell students that just as water goes down the drain, they can let strong feelings drain from their bodies. Ask them to begin relaxing ("draining") from the top of their heads, moving down their bodies to their toes (the "drain"). Prompt students by naming body areas one at a time.

5. **My Favorite Place:** Tell students to close their eyes and pretend they are in their favorite place. Ask them to picture that place in their minds. Prompt students to imagine what colors they see, how the air feels on their skin, what they smell, and what sounds they hear. Use as much sensory detail as time permits.

6. **Blue Sky:** Ask students to close their eyes and imagine a blue sky filled with puffy white clouds. Each cloud represents a stress, or thought, or distraction. Instruct students to clear their minds by "blowing" away one cloud at a time. Young students may physically blow, older students can imagine blowing. Tell them to blow away angry feelings, worries, distractions . . . until all that is left is the beautiful and peaceful blue sky.

7. **Balloons:** Ask students to imagine they are holding balloons. Each one represents a strong feeling or worry. Instruct children to think of their feelings or worries and then slowly let go of each one, allowing it to float to the ceiling or off into the sky.

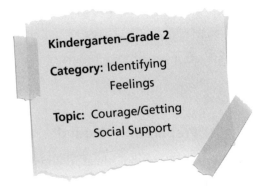

Kindergarten–Grade 2

Category: Identifying
Feelings

Topic: Courage/Getting
Social Support

Being Brave Every Day

Background

It takes courage to stand up to bullying—both to stop it and to report it. Yet courage is a difficult concept for this age group to comprehend. At this age, students' concept of courage may be unrealistic, including notions of fantasy or superheroes. Our culture and the media sometimes represent courage as risky or aggressive behavior. Adults can promote being courageous and helping others through everyday and peaceful acts. One of the most important ways students can show courage is to get help from an adult. Conduct this class meeting after completing the first three class meetings in this category (Our Talking Stick, A Story about Feelings, and Confidence 101: Taking Care of Myself).

Learner Outcomes

By the end of this session, students will be able to
- talk about different ways people can assist others
- discuss realistic ways they can show courage when confronted with bullying behavior
- state that an important way to show courage is to find an adult to help them with bullying problems
- name people they can rely on in different situations when they need help

Materials Needed

- Being Brave Every Day Game on page 55
- Two sheets of construction paper and a marker
- Chart paper and a marker

Preparation Needed

- Using the marker, write YES on one sheet of construction paper, and write NO on the other.
- Place the YES paper on the floor. Place the NO paper on the floor about 8 to 10 feet away.
- At the top of a sheet of chart paper write Ways We Can Be Brave Every Day.

Class Meeting Outline

Opening Activity (10 minutes):

1. **Raise your hand if you have ever tried something you have never done before.** Ask for examples. **How did that feel?**

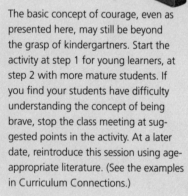

Teacher Tip

The basic concept of courage, even as presented here, may still be beyond the grasp of kindergartners. Start the activity at step 1 for young learners, at step 2 with more mature students. If you find your students have difficulty understanding the concept of being brave, stop the class meeting at suggested points in the activity. At a later date, reintroduce this session using age-appropriate literature. (See the examples in Curriculum Connections.)

2. **How many of you have heard the word "brave"? What do you think it means?**

3. **A lot of people think you have to do something unsafe or risky to be brave, but that's really not true! You can be brave every day without making unsafe choices. I imagine you made some brave choices in the last few days. Tell me ways students like you could be brave every day.** Just a few examples are enough to let you know whether students understand this concept. Guide the discussion as needed and identify any unsafe or risky examples as they come up. If students do not seem to grasp the concept, stop the activity here and end the session with the statement in step 4. Otherwise, continue on with the session.

4. **Making brave choices can feel scary. But you have to be brave to try something new or to stay safe and healthy. Those are positive ways to show you are brave.**

5. **Let's play a game called Being Brave Every Day. I am going to read some choices students your age might have to make to show they are brave. Some are examples of good ways to be brave, some are dangerous. You have to decide which kind of bravery it is.**

    a. **Here is one to try: You have to get a shot at the doctor's office, and you really hate shots. Raise your hand if you think getting a shot, even though you hate them, is a dangerous way to show you are brave. Raise your hand if you think this would be a good way to show you are brave.** If students have difficulty with this, stop the activity here and go directly to Wrap-Up. Otherwise, continue.

Teacher Tip

Reinforce the notion that people can be brave even when they are afraid.

    b. **Let's try some more. If you think the example I read calls for a positive or good kind of bravery, please go stand over there next to YES** (indicate). **If you think it would call for a dangerous kind of bravery, please go stand there next to NO** (indicate). **If you aren't sure, you can stand next to me.**

    c. Read six examples from the Being Brave Every Day Game.

Discussion Questions (10 minutes)

1. Process the activity.
   - **Was it easy or hard to decide whether something showed a positive kind of bravery or a dangerous one?**
   - **How did you decide if something was an everyday act of being brave that you could do safely?**
   - Comment on items students were unsure about. **What made it hard to decide about those examples?**

2. **Raise your hand again if you have ever tried something that you've never done before.** Ask for examples. **Did you feel brave after you did it?**

3. **How can friends help each other when someone bothers them and won't stop (or bullies them)?**

4. Discuss realistic ways that young students can show bravery when confronted with bullying. (For example, they can tell someone, get help, be assertive, or tell themselves "I am strong.") Make a list on chart paper. Post it in a place where you and the students can refer to it. Practice several ideas with the students.

Teacher Tip

Avoid children's literature that portrays courage in the context of magic or fantasy; unsafe, daring, or superheroic acts; or situations that students cannot identify with in real life. Instead look for options that stress courage as peace-making, everyday or "quiet" acts, and overcoming personal challenges.

5. Talk about different ways students can use everyday acts of being brave to help other students. Create a list on chart paper. Leave a marker in a place where students can reach it. Encourage them to add ideas to the chart over the coming week.

Wrap-Up

1. **Being brave does not mean you have to make dangerous or unsafe choices. You can be brave every day just by trying new things. You can be brave and still feel afraid. Remember, telling an adult about problems is one important way to show you are brave, especially if someone won't stop bothering you or a friend.**

2. Encourage additional questions and comments.

Curriculum Connections

Vocabulary: *afraid, brave/bravery, dangerous, everyday, fear, positive, realistic, risky, safe/unsafe*

Language Arts:

- Students can create a class book about everyday acts of courage. Include examples like peaceful acts, doing what you believe in, helping a friend, or telling an adult about a problem.

- Use age-appropriate literature to discuss everyday acts of bravery. Options might include *Arnie and the Skateboard Gang* (Nancy Carlson), *The Cat in the Hat* (Dr. Seuss), *Teammates* (Peter Golenbock), *The Story of Ruby Bridges* (Robert Coles), *The Brand New Kid* (Katie Couric), and *Chrysanthemum* (Kevin Henkes). Note that some of these books portray poor choices that characters made. Discuss with students what the characters could have done differently to make more positive choices.

Social Studies: Have students read about real-life people who have shown everyday acts of courage (including overcoming physical disabilities) or who stood up for their beliefs.

Being Brave Every Day Game

Instructions: Choose six examples from the following lists to read to your students. Choose three examples of positive bravery and three examples of dangerous bravery, and mix them up so they don't follow a predictable pattern. If you wish, create your own examples of positive bravery and dangerous bravery.

Examples of positive, "everyday" bravery:

- You have to ride the bus (or walk to school) by yourself for the first time.
- You decide to try to ride your bike for the first time without training wheels.
- It's your first day in this school and you don't know anybody when you walk into class.
- You're going to your first sleepover tonight, but you're worried because you've never slept away from home before.
- Your family is trying a new kind of food. It looks awful, but your family really wants you to try it.
- When you answer the phone, someone you don't know asks your name and where you live. You feel scared, but you say "No" and get your dad.
- Some older students call you mean names and take your lunch. They say you better not tell—but you tell your teacher anyway.
- You decide to ask an adult to help a friend who's being bullied on the playground.

Examples of dangerous bravery:

- Your friend dares you to ride your sled (or skateboard) down a really big hill.
- A man at the park asks you to help him find his lost puppy.
- Your parents tell you not to cross the street at your house because cars drive by very fast, but your ball rolls out into the traffic and you want to get it.
- Your friend wants you to do something your parents told you never ever to do.
- Your neighbor wants you to play with a real gun when his/her parents aren't looking.
- You see a wild animal in your backyard, so you decide to go pet it.
- Your mom tells you not to answer the door while she is in the shower. The doorbell rings, and you answer it anyway.

Category 3

Communication

(Six class meetings)

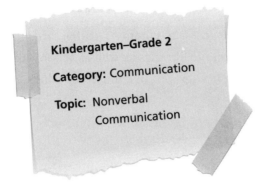

Kindergarten–Grade 2

Category: Communication

Topic: Nonverbal Communication

A Picture Is Worth a Thousand Words

Background

We learn a lot about social situations by observing the facial expressions, body language, and other nonverbal cues of those around us. Learning to use visual cues can help a child in challenging situations, such as bullying. Young children can learn to read body language and other visual cues through guided discussion with adults. This class meeting should be conducted after completing the class meeting called A Story about Feelings on pages 37–42.

Learner Outcomes

By the end of this session, students will be able to
- identify body language and facial cues in pictures
- make inferences about what those visual signs might mean
- brainstorm possible ways to handle difficult social situations

Materials Needed

- Three to six large pictures (photographs) of children expressing feelings such as anger, happiness, sadness, fear, boredom, frustration, and loneliness
- Age-appropriate literature selection that depicts expression of feelings, such as *On Monday When It Rained* (Cherryl Kachenmeister), *Feelings* (Aliki), *Today I Feel Silly: And Other Moods That Make My Day* (Jamie Lee Curtis)

Preparation Needed

- If you do not have access to emotions poster cards (available through most school and public libraries as well as school supply facilities), collect magazine photographs of children or adults expressing various feelings.
- Select and preread your literature selection.

Class Meeting Outline

Opening Activity (10–15 minutes)

1. Begin the session by reading aloud the selected literature sample.
2. **Do you think you can tell what someone else is feeling just by looking at his or her face and body? Let's try.**
3. As you show each picture card or photo, ask questions such as:
   - **How do you think this (child or adult) is feeling?**
     - **How can you tell?** Encourage students to observe facial expression, body language, and situational clues.
   - **What do you think might have happened right before this picture was taken to make the (child or adult) feel this way?**
   - **What do you think will happen next?**

Discussion Questions (15 minutes)

1. Process the activity.
   - **Was it easy or hard to guess what the people in the pictures were feeling?**
   - **Were some harder to guess than others? Which ones? Why?**
   - **Do you think grown-ups have feelings like this too?**
   - **How does this picture make you feel?** Refer to one of the photos depicting a negative emotion.
2. **Sometimes we can tell how other people might be feeling by looking at them. How can this help when you see someone being bullied?**

Teacher Tips

- Consider the children in your class who may have language-based learning disabilities/differences. These children often find it difficult to label feelings and distinguish among or between words like "mad" and "sad," or "bored" and "frustrated."
- Have students give a "thumbs up" or "thumbs down" signal when evaluating how a character in a book reacted to or handled a difficult feeling or situation. Students should think about whether choices were safe, realistic, or appropriate.

3. **What can you do if you can't tell how a person is feeling, but you think he or she is being bullied?** (Responses might include ask the person about it or tell an adult.)

Wrap-Up

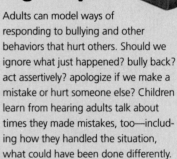

1. **Watching how people use their faces and bodies can tell us a lot about how they feel. It can also help us understand why they act the way they do. Those clues can also help us to know what we can do to help others. Pay attention to others' feelings this week by watching how they use their faces and bodies. See if you're able to help someone!**

2. Encourage additional questions and comments.

Dig Deeper

Adults can model ways of responding to bullying and other behaviors that hurt others. Should we ignore what just happened? bully back? act assertively? apologize if we make a mistake or hurt someone else? Children learn from hearing adults talk about times they made mistakes, too—including how they handled the situation, what could have been done differently.

Curriculum Connections

Vocabulary: *body language, facial expression, feelings, realistic; words describing emotions: afraid, angry, bored, frustrated, happy, lonely, sad*

Language Arts:

- Let students write captions for the pictures showing emotions.

- Ask students to act out alternative endings or solutions to literature selections. They might also use puppets to dramatize an ending or solution.

- Work with students to create story cards or graphic stories about the emotions related to a particular event. The story should have three panels: emotion before the event, during the event, after the event.

Art/Music: Encourage students to draw pictures or use dance or pantomime to depict particular emotions. Use music as an inspiration.

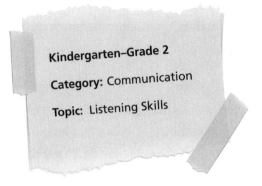

Kindergarten–Grade 2

Category: Communication

Topic: Listening Skills

The Case of the Fractured Fairy Tale

Background

There are important differences between hearing and listening. Hearing is a passive physical process, while listening requires actively engaging our brains to tune in to what's being said and to screen out irrelevant background noises. "Active listening" is an interactive, shared process that allows us to have meaningful communication with others. It is also an essential part of forming relationships and getting along with others. Young students are more skilled in delivering monologues or taking turns telling stories than carrying on reciprocal conversations. Adults need to provide opportunities for practicing different kinds of listening and to model give-and-take conversation.

Learner Outcomes

By the end of this session, students will be able to
- differentiate between hearing and listening
- practice listening without interrupting
- listen to a story with the purpose of describing facts from the story
- express answers to questions about the story verbally

Materials Needed

- Familiar preschool book, short fairy tale, fable, or short story passage (2 to 3 minutes long)

- Two sheets of chart paper and a marker
- A pencil and sticky labels

Preparation Needed

- Use a pencil or sticky labels to alter key words, characters' names, places, or the ending in a familiar story you have selected. For example (changes are italicized):
  a. "Little Red Riding Hood put on her *blue* cape and filled *his* basket with *turnips* to take to *his* sick *wolf*."
  b. "*James* and Jill went *over* the hill to fetch a pail of *blueberries*."
  c. "Cinderella *vacuumed* the house with a *toothbrush*."
  d. "The fairy god*father* transformed the pumpkin into a beautiful *wagon followed by* six white *zebras*."
- Count or mark the number of changes you made in the story for the following activity.

Class Meeting Outline

Opening Activity (15 minutes)

1. **Today, we're going to practice listening to a story. While I read, please listen carefully without talking. I will ask you some questions about it when I'm done.** Some children may blurt out changes they notice before you are finished. If that happens, stop and explain that to really listen, they need to be quiet without interrupting.

2. Read the story with the changes you made. Use a quiet, monotone voice, and do not show any pictures (so students have to rely on listening only). **What was the story about? Have you heard it before? What did you notice that was different or strange about it?** On one sheet of chart paper, list student responses. Label this sheet #1 at the top and turn it so students can't see it.

Dig Deeper

- Model active listening for students. When students talk about their feelings, reflect back what you hear, maintain eye contact, and pay full attention.

- Reading regularly to children has also been shown to improve their listening skills. Encourage students to practice listening or reading for a main idea, facts, or details in a variety of situations to strengthen listening skills and develop reasoning and inference abilities.

3. Instruct the students to listen again. Reread the story with the changes you made. Use your normal voice, inflections, and expressions (but again, do not show the pictures).

4. Post the second (blank) sheet of chart paper beside you. **Now, who can tell me what this story was about? Did you notice anything different or unusual about it this time?** List student responses on the blank chart paper and label it #2 at the top.

Discussion Questions (10–15 minutes)

1. Process the activity. Hang the two sheets of chart paper side by side.

   a. If the students have not already volunteered the name of the story, tell them what it was.

   b. **I made (number) changes in the story. Look at our chart paper. How many did you notice the first time I read it? How about the second time?** If the students missed a lot of changes, you may reread the story now or a bit later.

   c. **What else did you notice about the two times I read the story? What did I do differently?**

   d. **Was one way harder to listen to or to understand? What made it harder to listen and hear the first time?**

2. **Sometimes it's hard to listen when there are other noises around us. What noises might make it hard to listen?** (Responses might include traffic, noises during group activities, when someone is talking when you're trying to listen to the teacher, or loud music.)

3. **What can you do to help you be a good listener and ignore other noises?**

4. **Being a good listener isn't just good for learning in school, it can help us make and keep friends. How do you think being a good listener helps us make friends? How does it help us keep friends?**

   a. **Let's practice: turn to the person next to you and tell each other what you like about your favorite food. Now say back what your partner said. Did she or he get it right?**

   b. **Can you think of a time when you were talking and people didn't really listen? How could you tell they weren't listening?**

   c. **What happened? How did that feel?**

Dig Deeper

All students benefit from basic prompts to remind them to pay attention: making eye contact with the student you are speaking to (get down to eye level), rhythmic reminders such as clapping patterns, or phrases like "1-2-3, eyes on me."

---

5. **When someone is talking to you, what are some ways you can let that person know you're being a good listener?** (When someone is talking, don't talk until he or she is finished, pay attention to or look at that person when he or she is talking, watch his or her face so you can tell what he or she is feeling, nod or smile to show you are listening.)

Wrap-Up

1. **We are learning to become better listeners! When we practice careful listening we learn more and it helps us make friends. Careful listeners make good friends!**

2. Encourage students to practice careful listening this week.

Curriculum Connections

Vocabulary: *careful, changes, details, differences, fairy tale, hear, listen*

Language Arts:

- Read *The True Story of the Three Little Pigs!* and *Squids Will Be Squids* (Jon Scieszka) to encourage students to pay attention to twists on familiar tales and plays on words.

- Work with students to create their own "fractured fairy tales" and fables. The Internet offers several teacher resource sites, including www.teacher.scholastic.com/writewit/mff/fractured_fairy.htm.

Science: Divide the class into two groups to play Telephone or Whisper-down-the-Lane. Give one group a short simple sentence, the other a nonsense sentence. Compare results.

Art:

- Have students draw a picture of the fairy tale you read in this class meeting. Include the changes you made.

- Invite students to create a poster that says "Careful Listeners Make Good Friends."

Music: Sing simple rounds with students to practice listening to different parts and knowing when to join in. Another technique to encourage listening is practicing songs, chants, or clapping games that have syncopated beats or that require pauses.

Physical Education: Teach students simple jump-rope chants or play games that require listening such as Simon Says.

Kindergarten–Grade 2

Category: Communication

Topic: Other Communication
Skills

That's Not Funny!

Background

Laughter can be fun and a good way to release stress. But when laughter is used to taunt others or exclude them, it can be very hurtful. Children this age may not always be aware of the ways that laughter is interpreted by others. They need practice differentiating between laughing with someone and laughing at them. Young students may also not realize immediately when laughter makes them feel bad. They need adult modeling and encouragement to communicate those feelings, even after the moment has passed.

Learner Outcomes

By the end of this session, students will be able to
- discuss the difference between friendly laughter and laughter that is used to hurt feelings or taunt others
- practice ways to identify when laughter hurts their feelings
- tell others when they feel they are being laughed at and their feelings are being hurt

Materials Needed

- Age-appropriate tongue twisters and humorous jokes or riddles

Preparation Needed

- Prepare an open space on the floor large enough for all students to sit in a circle.
- Consult your school librarian for classroom copies of books showing the following aspects of laughter:
    - Healthy or positive humor, jokes, and riddles: *Knock, Knock! Who's There? My First Book of Knock-Knock Jokes* (Tad Hills), *What Do You Hear When Cows Sing? And Other Silly Riddles* (Marco Maestro), *Laugh Out Loud: Jokes and Riddles from Highlights for Children* (Erin Mauterer)
    - Mean laughter, practical jokes, making fun of another: *Arthur's April Fool* or *Muffy's Secret Admirer* (Marc Brown), *Don't Laugh at Me* (Steve Seskin and Allen Shamblin), *Odd Velvet* (Mary Whitcomb), *Crow Boy* (Taro Yashima)

Class Meeting Outline

Opening Activity (5–10 minutes)

1. Invite students to sit in a circle. **We're going to try something a bit different today. Turn in your bodies so you are each looking at your neighbor's back.** Indicate which way. **Carefully place your hands on your neighbor's shoulders.**

2. **(Name someone to go first) will say, "Ha! Ha! Ha!" Then (name second person) will say it . . . then everyone around the circle will say it until we get back to (name first person). Ready? Let's begin.** This part of the activity should quickly result in students spontaneously laughing out loud.

3. *Optional:* **Now let's try doing this backwards.** Prompt the last person in the circle to begin. Continue back around to the first person in the circle. Stop the activity at any point it stops being fun.

4. End the activity. **Everyone turn your bodies back to face the center of our circle.**

Teacher Tip

If there are children in your class who struggle with social pragmatics or are known to be on the autism spectrum, consider the appropriateness of this topic and activity. The discussion and activity in this class meeting could be difficult or frustrating for them.

5. Tell or read a few jokes or silly riddles you've selected from age-appropriate literature. Invite students to tell knock-knock or other jokes or riddles they think are funny.

6. **We laughed a lot. Let's take a few deep slow breaths to calm down.**

Discussion Questions (10–15 minutes)

1. **What was it like when we all started laughing? How did it feel?**

2. **What are some examples of times when laughter isn't fun? What are some examples when laughing can hurt or upset someone?** (Examples include someone copycats you and won't stop, someone tickles you too much, someone laughs at a mistake you made, someone makes fun of you and others laugh.)

Teacher Tips

• When you ask the group to share a joke or story, not everyone has to take a turn. Avoid terms like "funny story" that can lead to telling about practical jokes, pranks, or inappropriate humor.

• Before asking students to tell jokes, give them some guidelines. Remind students that "bathroom humor" is not appropriate for sharing in class. If you recognize one of these jokes as it begins, simply interrupt and say, "That's not appropriate for our classroom. Do you or anyone else have an appropriate joke to share?"

• If a student tells a joke that turns out to be inappropriate in a more serious or bigoted way (makes fun of a particular person or group), say, "We all hear jokes like this, and sometimes people laugh at them. But this kind of joke can hurt people's feelings. Let's talk more about this now." Move directly into the discussion portion of the class meeting.

3. **What is the difference between having fun and making fun of someone?** (Possible answers include having fun makes everyone laugh or feel good. Making fun can leave someone out or make him or her feel sad, it hurts that person's feelings, it feels wrong, you may worry that a grown-up will hear or see you, you do it even if the person tells you to stop, the person isn't laughing. Refer back to body language and facial expressions to encourage students to see if they are hurting someone with laughter.)

4. **Have you ever laughed at yourself?** (Prompt students with examples as needed: you fell down but didn't get hurt, you made a silly mistake, you put your boots on the wrong feet or accidentally wore clothes inside out, you spilled something, you said a wrong name or word.) **How did that feel when you laughed at yourself?** (Students might say funny, relieved, or less embarrassed.)

5. **Would it feel the same or different if someone else laughed at your mistake instead? Why? What could you say or do when that happens?** (Responses might include tell a teacher, get a friend, say something, or laugh with the person if he or she wasn't laughing to hurt you.)

6. **Jokes can make us laugh, can't they? They are one way we share our feelings with friends. We all know what makes us laugh and what we think is not funny.**
    - **Is it fun when someone does something to be funny, like "copycat" another person? Why?**
    - **How does the other person usually feel about being copied?**
    - **How can you tell when a joke or laughing is hurting someone's feelings?**
    - **How can we help if we see someone being laughed at?**
    - **If someone laughs at you in a way that hurts your feelings but says "Just kidding!" or "That was a joke!" does that make you feel better? Why or why not?**

Wrap-Up

1. **Laughter can be fun and make us feel good. It's hard not to laugh when we hear other people laughing. When we make fun of our own mistakes, it can make us feel less embarrassed. But it's not okay to laugh at someone or to make fun of them. That hurts people's feelings and makes them feel left out. Friendly laughter can make each day better. Let's remember to use plenty of friendly laughter every day!**
2. Encourage additional questions and comments.

Curriculum Connections

Vocabulary: *humor, joke, laughter, practical joke, riddle*

Language Arts:
- Use literature to help students explore different forms of humor.
- Ask students to write jokes or riddles to collect for a class book.

Music: Teach the song "I Love to Laugh" from Walt Disney's *Mary Poppins* or songs that include tongue twisters or silly words.

Kindergarten–Grade 2

Category: Communication

Topic: Cyber Bullying

Be Cyber-Safe!

Background

Children are exposed to telephones and cyber technologies at younger and younger ages. Students may know more about using these devices than adults. This can be challenging for adults who are charged with overseeing that students use these technologies safely and appropriately. While there are many positive aspects to cyber technologies, young children may be vulnerable to information that may make them feel confused, scared, or uncomfortable. It is not too early to introduce younger elementary students to issues of cyber-safety, "netiquette" (good manners while online or on the telephone), and cyber bullying, in sensitive and developmentally appropriate ways. The purpose of this class meeting is twofold. First, it provides a way for teachers to learn the extent to which their students use these technologies. Second, it opens a discussion about the safe use of telephones, cell phones, and the Internet.

Learner Outcomes

By the end of this session, students will be able to

- discuss ways that students their age use phones, cell phones, and computers
- provide positive examples of ways cyber technologies help us learn and communicate
- be alert to ways that these technologies can be used in unsafe or inappropriate ways

- state that any inappropriate use of technology should be immediately reported to adults
- state that if someone asks for personal information by phone or online they should not give it

Materials Needed

- Teacher Tally Sheet on page 72

Preparation Needed

- Copy the Teacher Tally Sheet to record student responses.

Class Meeting Outline

Opening Activity (10 minutes)

1. **Lots of boys and girls use telephones, cell phones, or computers. I'll bet some of you have, too. Phones and computers are special ways that can help us to learn and talk with each other.**
2. **I'd like to learn more about what you know.**
   - **What does it mean to go "online" on a computer?**
   - **What does it mean to surf the Web?**
   - **What is email?**
   - **What is a text message? an instant message?**
   - **What is a Web site?**
3. **What else do you know? Raise your hand if you have ever done one of these things.** Use the Teacher Tally Sheet to ask questions and to tally your students' use of cyber technologies.
4. **Lots of you raised your hands for at least one or two of my questions.** Based on your tally, briefly share with students the types of technology/ways they reported using the most.

Teacher Tips

- **Email:** Electronic mail. Email is used to send messages (usually in text form) from one Internet user to another.

- **Instant Messaging (IM):** A tool for communicating that combines the real-time features of chat with the person-to-person contact of email. Internet service providers (see below) may provide free instant messaging services or the software may be downloaded from the Internet.

- **Internet Service Provider:** A company that provides access to the Internet. America Online (AOL) and Comcast are two examples.

- **Text Messaging:** A means of sending short messages to and from mobile phones. Because text messages are typed on a phone keypad, most messages are abbreviations and symbols.[1]

Discussion Questions (10 minutes)

1. Discuss items you feel are most relevant for your students. Make a point to highlight positive ways to use technology and cyber-safety rules.

Dig Deeper

- Consider holding a parent information night on cyber-safety or send home cyber-safety tips. Share what students reported in your class discussion about cyber technologies.

- Connect this session with other training you might do on child assault prevention or "stranger danger."

- For more information about cyber bullying or cyber-safety, visit the following Web sites:

   www.wiredsafety.org

   www.isafe.org

   www.wiredkids.org

   www.netsmartz.org

   www.cyberbullyhelp.com

   a. **There are lots of good things about phones and computers. How can they help us?**

   b. **Sometimes people use phones and computers to play mean tricks, to say or do mean things, or to try to scare others. Sometimes these people are other children or teenagers, and sometimes they are adults. And sometimes, we can't tell who is doing these things.**

   c. **Has this ever happened to you or someone you know? Did anyone try to help? How?** Emphasize that students should show or tell what happened to an adult.

   d. **Things like this can happen to anyone—even grown-ups. If this happens, it is never your fault.**

   e. **Sometimes people on a phone or online may ask you questions about yourself—like your name, your phone number, your age, or where you live. Is it ever a good idea to answer questions like this? Why not?** Emphasize that students should never share personal information on the phone or online—even if they think they know the person.

   f. **How would you feel if someone played mean tricks or said mean or scary things to you on the phone or on the computer?**

   g. **If anything like this ever happens to you, be cyber-safe! Even if you feel embarrassed or scared:**

   - **Walk away from the computer or cell phone but do not turn it off.**

   - **Get an adult right away.**

   - **Tell and show the adult what happened. That's really important.**

Wrap-Up

1. **There are lots of good things about telephones, cell phones, and computers. They can be fun and they also can help us in lots of ways every day. Some people don't use phones and computers in good ways, and that might make you feel scared or uncomfortable or confused. If that happens, tell your parents or another adult you trust right away! We can help.**

2. **Today, we mostly talked about how it would feel and what to do if someone says mean things to you. Remember not to ever use the phone or computer to make mean jokes or say or do mean things to others.**

3. Encourage additional questions or comments.

Curriculum Connections

Vocabulary: *comfortable/uncomfortable, communicate, email, embarrassed, online, surf the Web, text message, Web site*

Health/Language Arts/Social Skills:

- If you have a computer in your classroom, consider connecting to a classroom in another part of the country or world to broaden students' learning about peers in other places.

- If you extend this discussion to additional class meetings, www.netsmartz.org has resources appropriate for students in kindergarten–grade 2.

- Use play telephones to practice polite phone etiquette and to role-play what to do if students receive a "crank" or obscene call or are asked for personal information.

- Help students role-play what they should do if someone says or sends them inappropriate content online or asks for personal information online.

- Problem-solve what to do if students are with a sibling online or on a cell phone and receive inappropriate or mean material. Problem-solve what to do if students happen upon a Web site with inappropriate content.

Art: Have students create posters to highlight what children should do if something online makes them scared, uncomfortable, or confused. Have them display the posters around school.

Be Cyber-Safe!

Teacher Tally Sheet

Instructions: Make a copy of this page. For each question, ask students to raise their hands if they have done the activity in the last week. Tally how many students respond by gender, if you are able, or do a simple total.

In the last week, have you . . .	Girls	Boys	TOTAL
Gotten a phone call?			
Called someone else on a telephone?			
Talked on a cell phone?			
Used your own cell phone?			
Used a computer to play a game?			
Used a computer with a teacher or librarian to go online?			
Used a computer with a parent to go online?			
Used a computer with a brother or sister to go online?			
Used a computer by yourself to go online?			
Sent or gotten an email message?			
Sent or gotten an IM or text message?			

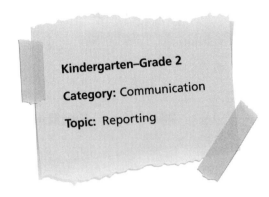

Kindergarten–Grade 2

Category: Communication

Topic: Reporting

Important to Report? You Decide!

Background

Although adults may feel young students over-report the conduct of others, children often report problems because they are unsure about what to do. While children do need to learn to resolve some disputes on their own, it is unrealistic to expect younger elementary students to do so without adult intervention and modeling. When adults ask young children to work things out on their own, the unintended message is "I am not going to help you if you tell me about your problems." Better results can be achieved when adults consistently respond to student requests in a way that teaches them to develop good judgment about when adult help is needed, and what can be realistically handled by students themselves.

Learner Outcomes

By the end of this session, students will be able to
- describe reasons to "report" problems or concerns to an adult
- practice reporting using real-world examples
- practice words and actions to report problems to adults

Materials Needed

- Sample Reporting Situations on pages 76–77
- Age-appropriate literature that can be used to discuss the circumstances for reporting: *The Butter Battle Book* or *The Cat in the Hat* (Dr. Seuss), *Telling Isn't Tattling* (Kathryn M. Hammerseng)

Preparation Needed

- Choose four or five situations from the Sample Reporting Situations

Class Meeting Outline

Opening Activity (10 minutes)

1. **Have you ever seen something happen at school that didn't seem right, and you told a teacher about it? When you told a teacher, you** *reported* **what happened.**

2. **When you report something to a teacher or another adult, you are telling that person what happened. What are some things that need to be reported to adults?** Allow students to respond without judging their examples.

3. **Sometimes it's hard to know what to say or when to report problems to adults. This can happen even though one of our school rules says we should tell an adult when we see or hear bullying happening.**

4. Read *The Cat in the Hat,* another literature selection, or four or five situations from the Sample Reporting Situations.

Teacher Tips

- This lesson may be more challenging for some kindergarteners. You may want to consider repeating this lesson as a review as needed throughout the school year.

- Because students often equate the term "telling" with "tattling," try using the word "reporting" instead of "telling."

Discussion Questions (15 minutes)

1. Process the activity.
   a. If you used *The Cat in the Hat,* ask:
      - **What do you think you would do if this happened to you? Would you tell your mom? Why or why not?**
      - **What do you think about things the Fish said?**
      - **Why do you think the Cat didn't listen?**
      - **What would have been different if the Cat hadn't gotten things cleaned up in time?**
      - **Have you ever had someone ask you to do something you didn't want to do? What did you do or say? Did you report it to an adult? Why or why not?**
   b. If you used the Sample Reporting Situations, ask about each situation:

- Did you agree with the choice (character/ situation) made? Why?
- What other choices could (character) have made?
- Do you think there was a right or better choice? If so, what?
- What would you do if you were (character/ situation)?

2. **When do you think it is a good idea to report a problem?** (Students might say when someone's feelings are hurt, when something is dangerous or unsafe, when someone is left out, or when someone is unkind on purpose.)

3. **Sometimes I hear students call other students "tattletale" if they report something to an adult. What does it mean to call someone that name?** (A student may be called a "tattletale" when he or she tells on someone "just to get that person in trouble.") **Using the word "tattletale" is calling someone a name. That's not okay. It's always the right thing to report bullying.**

4. **How should you report problems to an adult? What can you say and do?** (Responses might include tell the facts, tell what happened, use a strong voice, tell how you feel, or say what you did if you helped.)

Dig Deeper

- It can be difficult for adults to distinguish whether a child's report is legitimate, particularly when the adult didn't witness the event or when a student is a frequent reporter. Some students who frequently report feel uncertain about how to handle problem situations because they lack particular social, cognitive, or communication skills. When in doubt, it is best to take all reports seriously.

- Teachers model when it's "appropriate" to report by their reactions. A simple "Oh" (when something might be handled by a student) says one thing, but thanking the student and acting on the report (such as a bullying situation) says another thing entirely.

Wrap-Up

1. **Everyone should feel safe in our classroom and in our school. Sometimes it's hard to report a problem, but you need to tell an adult when you or someone else needs help.**

2. Encourage additional questions and comments.

Curriculum Connections

Vocabulary: *choice, reporting, tattletale, tell/telling*

Language Arts/Art: Invite students to draw or write a story about what happened when they reported a problem to an adult.

Sample Reporting Situations

Instructions: Select four or five of the following situations to read to the class. For each situation, ask students to decide whether or not it was important for the character to report the problem to an adult.

1. Carolyn always tries to get in line first. Ethan yells, "Hey, Mr. Jackson, Carolyn is butting in line again!"

2. There is a rule that no one is allowed to bring nuts to school because some students have bad allergies. Shonda sees Tim sneak some peanuts into his desk. He tells her that he'll give her some if she promises not to tell their teacher. Shonda tells her friend Maria about it instead.

3. Ray accidentally bumped Megan in the hall. Her lunchbox fell on the floor, but she didn't get hurt. Ray apologized and helped pick up her lunch. When Megan saw Mrs. Williams, the hall monitor, she started crying and said Ray hit her.

4. Ella saw Sophie take something out of Max's backpack before the morning bell. Ella asked Sophie what she was doing. Sophie told her to mind her own business. Ella waited until recess to tell her teacher what Sophie did.

5. Out on the playground, some boys keep grabbing the girls' jump ropes. At first the girls laughed. But the boys wouldn't stop, even after the girls told them to. James saw what happened and told an adult.

6. Rose says, "Teacher, Umberto just sharpened his pencil without asking!"

7. A group of older students always sit in certain seats on the bus. They say those are *their* seats. If other students try to sit there, the older students call them names or push them away. Today, Amy and Ben wait until everyone is off the bus, and then tell the bus driver what's been happening.

8. Kieran told his friend Eric a secret: he still sleeps with a teddy bear. Eric told other students in their class and now a bunch of them are making fun of Kieran. Kieran tells his teacher that Eric bullied him.

9. Jacob saw the new girl in his grade crying outside of school today. When he asked the girl why she was crying, she said some students were making fun of her, but she made him promise not to tell. When he went home, Jacob told his dad.

10. Trinnie heard some students talk about a mean trick they were going to play on Brian, who is blind. When Trinnie told the teacher what the students said, they yelled "Tattletale" and said they were just playing.

11. It's snack time. The teacher tells everyone they are allowed to take two crackers. Aiden sees Jessica take three crackers and immediately says, "Hey, that's not fair, she took three!" Jessica looks embarrassed.

12. Several boys and girls are playing a game with a ball—throwing it back and forth to each other. Everyone is laughing and playing. But when it's Emily's turn to catch the ball, she misses and she yells, "Teacher, they are throwing the ball too hard! It's not fair."

13. Amy always asks Donalyn for her cupcake at lunch. Today, Amy asked Donalyn for her cupcake, but Donalyn said she didn't have one. When Amy saw Donalyn eating a cupcake, she told their teacher that Donalyn told a lie and lying is against the rules.

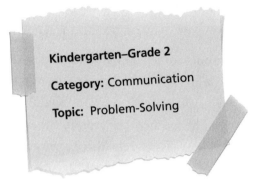

Kindergarten–Grade 2

Category: Communication

Topic: Problem-Solving

Sometimes We Agree, Sometimes We Disagree

Background

Even close friends don't always agree and sometimes get into arguments. When small disagreements aren't settled quickly, they can lead to bigger problems such as teasing, exclusion, or other forms of bullying. Teachers can help build students' skills and resilience for solving interpersonal problems before they escalate, and they can remind children that disagreements are a natural part of life.

Learner Outcomes

By the end of this session, students will be able to

- discuss situations when they agree or disagree with another person
- practice words and actions they can use when they disagree with someone

Materials Needed

- Age-appropriate literature for talking about disagreements and different opinions: *Best Friends* (Miriam Cohen), *Matthew and Tilly* (Rebecca C. Jones), *Best Friends* (Steven Kellogg)
- Tricky Situations on page 81
- Chart paper and marker
- *Optional:* puppets or dolls to act out situations and solutions

Preparation Needed

- Select literature appropriate for your students.
- Grade 2: Select two to four situations from Tricky Situations, or use examples of disagreements drawn from student experiences.

Class Meeting Outline

Opening Activity (10 minutes)

1. **Even friends don't always agree and sometimes they even argue. Today, we're going to read a story about two friends who didn't agree and how they solved their problem.**

2. Read one of the literature selections suggested in Materials Needed or one you have selected.

Discussion Questions (15 minutes)

1. Process the activity.
   - **What did the friends in our story have a disagreement about?**
   - **Why did they disagree?**
   - **How did they solve their problem?**
   - **Do you agree with the way they solved their problem? Why or why not?**
   - **Were there other things they could have tried or done?** Write students' ideas on the chart paper.
   - Act out the story with students (or use puppets, optional) and create an alternative ending that demonstrates a new or different positive solution.

2. **When we hurt someone's feelings, even if it wasn't on purpose, just saying "I'm sorry" may not be enough. Sometimes we have to do something to show we are sorry and still want to be friends. What are things you might do?**

3. Grade 2: Divide students into small groups. (See pages 13–14 for ideas and strategies for grouping students.)

Teacher Tips

- Sometimes it's not possible to work out differences quickly. Let involved students know what behavior is expected of them to maintain peace in your classroom. When students can't seem to get along, you may need to encourage some time apart or help them keep some distance from each other until they cool down and can be together without arguing. School counselors may be needed to help with lingering issues.

- Make it clear to students that they should treat each other in kind and respectful ways, even if they aren't friends.

a. Read aloud one situation at a time from Tricky Situations to the whole group.

b. For each situation, ask the small groups to talk about or show: **What can be done to solve this problem? What words or actions could make things better?**

c. Invite the class to choose three or four of the best ideas, based on how safe, realistic, and kind/considerate they were.

Wrap-Up

1. **We will all have disagreements from time to time. It's important to try to find ways to work them out, so we all can get along and keep our friends. When we don't try to solve small disagreements, they can turn into bigger problems. Remember, adults are here to help you find good ways to work things out.**

2. Encourage additional questions and comments.

Curriculum Connections

Vocabulary: *agree/disagree, argument, problem, solve*

Language Arts/Art: Encourage students to draw a picture or a short comic strip about a time they disagreed with a friend and how they solved the problem.

Tricky Situations

Instructions: Select two to four of the following situations to read to the class. Have students work in small groups to talk about or act out possible solutions.

1. You and your friend Jaymie are playing a game together. You think the game should be played one way. Jaymie says, "No! It's supposed to go like this!"

2. You and another student want to use the swing and you both get there at the same time.

3. Only (number) students are allowed to use the (block or library corner, easels, computer, climbing structure) at one time. You have been waiting for a turn, but now another student gives his/her spot to a friend instead.

4. You and another classmate are coloring a picture together. The other student wants to color the leaves on the trees purple. You get into an argument because you think the leaves should be green.

5. You had just started playing with a particular toy you like when you got up for just a second to get a tissue. Now someone else is using the toy and doesn't want to give it back.

6. Your friend promised to sit next to you at lunch today but now is sitting with two other classmates, and there is no room for you.

7. Some other students are playing a game and you want to join them. They say you can't play because that would be too many players.

8. You and your friend get into an argument about the correct name for a particular kind of dinosaur.

9. You and another classmate want to use the same color to paint faces on drawings at the easel, but there is only one container for the color you want to use.

10. One of your classmates tells you, "I won't be your friend if you don't play *my* way."

Category 4

Hot Spots

(Five class meetings)

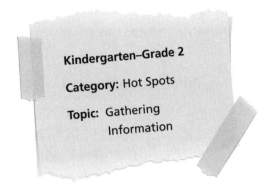

Kindergarten–Grade 2

Category: Hot Spots

Topic: Gathering
Information

What We Know about Bullying

Background

Information about young students' bullying experiences can be hard to obtain. They have an inconsistent understanding about what bullying is, and it is impractical to include them in formal written anti-bullying surveys. Yet, their experiences with bullying and where they feel most vulnerable are vital considerations for school bullying-prevention plans. Using words like "okay/not okay," "friendly/ unfriendly," or "welcome/unwelcome" offers an age-appropriate base to begin conversations about bullying with young students. This session provides information about students' experiences and a concrete method to talk with them about bullying. Conduct this class meeting after students have been introduced to what bullying is and before subsequent class meetings in this category.

Learner Outcomes

By the end of this session, students will be able to
- share experiences about potential bullying behavior
- identify times or places they feel unsafe or experience bullying ("hot spots")
- state what actions they can take if they or someone else is bullied

Materials Needed

- Chart paper
- Markers or adhesive dots for recording votes

• Copy of *OBPP* Our School's Anti-Bullying Rules Poster (*OBPP* Teacher Guide CD-ROM, document 8)

Teacher Tips

• The Question of the Day is a familiar format in many classrooms. It can be a useful tool to encourage students to identify a range of issues. Encourage students to think for themselves and not just vote as their friends do.

• If using colored adhesive dots to distinguish gender, avoid stereotypical pink for girls and blue for boys.

Preparation Needed

• Create a Question of the Day chart. At the top, write "Where are places I feel unwelcome at school?" Create four or five columns with locations that apply to your students, such as Hall, Playground, Lunch, Bus, Classroom, Bathroom, or Other. For non-readers, use three or four columns, and make each heading a different color, add simple symbols, or underline the first letter of the word as literacy aids.

• Consider using one color marker or adhesive dot for boys and a different color for girls. This will help you distinguish if there is a gender difference in bullying hot spots.

• Hang the *OBPP* Our School's Anti-Bullying Rules poster where everyone can see it.

Class Meeting Outline

Opening Activity (10–15 minutes)

1. **We'd like our school to be a friendlier place, where bullying doesn't happen. Where are places in the school that you like to be, where you feel welcome?**

2. **I also want to find out more about places at school where you feel unwelcome because of the way other students behave (or where you have been bullied). Our Question of the Day is Where are places I feel unwelcome at school?** Read each column heading aloud. **Think for a minute about which of these places makes you feel unwelcome. I will ask each of you to say which place you feel unwelcome so I can show it on our chart.**

3. Ask each student in turn to respond to the question.

a. Students may pass if they do not want to answer or feel uncomfortable.

b. As each student responds, place a tally or adhesive dot in the column that reflects her or his response. (Students this age tend to follow their peers, even when told to think for themselves. Instead of getting individual responses in front of the entire class, you may wish to call students to up to your table privately to place their adhesive dots.)

c. Record multiple responses to accommodate students who feel unwelcome in more than one place.

Discussion Questions (10 minutes)

1. Process the activity.
   a. Tally the results at the bottom of each column and comment on patterns you see in the chart.
   b. Review each column and ask:
      - **What kinds of things happen here that make you feel unwelcome?**
      - **Do students sometimes feel unwelcome because they are bullied here? How?**
      - **Why do you think students don't all feel the same way?**

2. Discuss additional concerns or issues students bring up.
   a. Clarify what bullying is using the "everyday language" definition on page 11 of the Teacher Guide.
   b. Discuss ways that bullying is different from other behaviors that may be upsetting.
   c. Discuss behaviors that occur accidentally versus those done on purpose.
   d. Discuss different kinds of hurt (such as emotional hurt from being called a mean name versus physical hurt from being pushed).

3. **Do you remember what our school rules are about bullying?** Refer to the *OBPP* Our School's Anti-Bullying Rules Poster. Ask students to say what they should do if they experience or know about bullying. Go beyond simply reciting the rules and ask students to say what they

could actually do. **Remember, it's really important to tell an adult even if you aren't sure if something is bullying.**

Wrap-Up

1. **We've learned some things today about how students feel here at school. Take a minute to summarize what was learned. All of the grown-ups here care about how you feel. We are working together to try to make our school feel more welcoming and safer for everyone.**

2. Encourage additional questions and comments.

Curriculum Connections

Vocabulary: *accidental/on purpose, bullied, choice, tally, welcome/unwelcome*

Language Arts/Art: Encourage students to draw pictures or write stories about ways they can respond to bullying. Have them include descriptive captions with their pictures.

Math: Help students graph their responses from the chart in this class meeting. Create 3-D graphs using a series of identical jars or cups and filling them with colored objects such as marbles, beads, or coins corresponding to the tallies.

Kindergarten–Grade 2

Category: Hot Spots

Topic: Resolving Problems
in Hot Spots

Making Safe Passages

Background

Transitions at the beginning and end of each school day or moving between activities may involve large numbers of students, few adults, minimal structure, and high levels of noise and activity. While transitions provide positive opportunities to socialize, some students feel overwhelmed by the noise and movement. When transitions involve a mix of young and older students, younger students are more vulnerable to being bullied. Both positive and negative experiences carry over into the classroom and affect students' abilities to focus on learning. Adults must create order during transitions and improve their supervision. Children can also benefit from learning ways to cope with high-stress situations, like transitions. Complete the previous class meeting (What We Know about Bullying on pages 83–86) prior to conducting this session.

Learner Outcomes

By the end of this session, students will be able to
- identify aspects of transition times that make them feel overwhelmed or bullied
- talk about ways to improve transition times so they feel calmer

Materials Needed

- Question of the Day chart (from previous class meeting)

Preparation Needed

- Refer to the Question of the Day chart created during the previous class meeting as a reminder of how many students reported difficulty with hallway transitions.

- Observe your students during transition times over a two- or three-day period to get a better sense of issues that they might encounter in the halls.

Class Meeting Outline

Opening Activity (15 minutes)

1. **We walk through the hallway every day. We walk through it when we come to or leave school. We walk through it to get to lunch or recess. Sometimes our class is together in the hall. Other times you are there on your own or with other students. Adults see many things that happen in the hall, and so do you.**

2. Choose to read aloud questions from the list below or think of questions based on your own observations. Include one or two positive and one or two problem examples. **What could you do if you are in the hallway and**

   - **you see a friend who has been out of school for a few days?**
   - **you see a younger student try to open a door that's too heavy?**
   - **I have told you all to be very quiet, but someone in our group makes a funny noise that makes everyone laugh?**
   - **students from another class make faces at you when adults aren't looking?**
   - **you see a student push someone, knocking his/her belongings onto the floor?**
   - **a bigger student calls you a baby every day when you first get to school?**
   - **it is so noisy and busy that you feel scared and confused?**
   - **someone in line behind you keeps stepping on the back of your shoe on purpose?**

- it's so busy at the end of the day you worry you'll (get lost, miss your bus, get knocked over)?
- you see a new student in the hall who looks confused about where to go?

Discussion Questions (10 minutes)

1. Process the activity.
   - What do you like about being in our hallways? What are things that make you feel happy when you are there?
   - What do you like least about being there? What things make you feel unhappy or worried when you are there?
   - What ideas did we talk about that could make our hallway feel safer?
   - What else can you do if you need help in the hallway? Encourage students to find and tell an adult. Refer to hallway and school bullying rules.

2. If your students walk in lines to activities, encourage them to discuss their concerns and ideas to make those passages better. Role-play situations as appropriate.
   - When we go to (the library, the gym, lunch, or recess), how do we decide who goes first?
   - How does it feel to be first? in the middle? last?
   - Does the way we do this now work? Let's practice ways that might work better.

Wrap-Up

1. Our time in the hallway can be fun. But sometimes it can be very busy and noisy. You thought of good ideas to make the hallway more pleasant. I will help too!
2. Encourage additional questions and comments.

Curriculum Connections

Vocabulary: *afraid, anxious/worried, concerned, confused, crowded, pleasant*

Language Arts: Student literature often deals with hallway problems as part of starting school or being new to school. Choose from the following to read with students: *The Brand New Kid* (Katie Couric), *My First Day of School* (P. K. Hallinan), *First Day Jitters* (Julie Danneberg), *Vera's First Day of School* (Vera Rosenberry), *The Night Before Kindergarten* (Natasha Wing), *The Night Before First Grade* (Natasha Wing).

Academics/Community Service: Collaborate with teachers of older students to establish a system of cross-grade "buddies" related to academic areas like reading, math, or science. Once positive student relationships have been established, if practical, encourage students to use their buddies if they need assistance in the hallway or other hot spots.

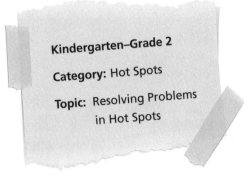

Kindergarten–Grade 2

Category: Hot Spots

Topic: Resolving Problems
in Hot Spots

Come Play with Us

Background

Young children often report that recess is a favorite part of their school day. Recess on the school playground provides them with an opportunity to exercise, let off steam, and socialize. For children being bullied there, recess is a painful experience. Large mixed-age groups, low adult-child ratios, spaces that are difficult to supervise, and not enough activity choices all contribute to playground behavior problems. Teachers and playground supervisors need to know how children feel about their playtime so they can provide adequate supervision and play options. Conduct the class meeting What We Know about Bullying on pages 83–86 prior to conducting this session.

Learner Outcomes

By the end of this session, students will be able to
- identify hot spots for bullying behaviors on their playground
- identify reasons some areas feel safe and others feel unsafe
- identify ways to feel safer on the playground

Materials Needed

- Chalkboard or dry erase board and two different colors of chalk or marker
- Outline of the playground or area your students use for recess

- Question of the Day chart (from the What We Know about Bullying class meeting)

Preparation Needed

- On the board, draw a large outline (or map) of the playground space used by your class. Do not fill in equipment or label special play areas.
- Consider inviting playground supervisors to attend or assist with this class meeting so they have an opportunity to become more familiar with your students and their concerns about recess.
- Refer to the previously created Question of the Day chart as a reminder of how many students reported difficulty at the playground.

Class Meeting Outline

Opening Activity (10 minutes)

1. **Recess can be a lot of fun. What is your favorite thing about it?**
2. Show students the outline of the playground you have made. **This is a map of our playground. But there are some things missing. Can you help me fill in where things like swings and slides are, and where games happen?** Quickly draw items on the board as students tell you, prompting as needed. If your playground does not have equipment or consists of only open space, ask students: **What do you do on the playground? Show me where students play different kinds of games.** Encourage students to indicate different ways the space is used.
3. **Now that our map is finished, I am going to point to different places.** Point to each spot and say:
   a. **Raise your hand if you really like this part of the playground (or spend a lot of time here).** Tally the number of responses and write the totals on the map.
   b. **Now raise your hand if students seem to have a hard time here.** Tally the number of responses and write those totals on the map using a different color chalk or marker.
   c. If a playground supervisor joined you, invite him or her to share observations for these same questions after students have responded.

Discussion Questions (10 minutes)

1. Process the activity. Have students look at the map.
   - **Which places on the playground are most popular? Why?**
   - **Disagreements can happen more often in our favorite places. Why?**
   - **Where do students have the most trouble getting along? Why do you think so?**
   - **How can adults help students more? What help do students need?**

2. **Sometimes, students get upset about things that happen at recess. I will read you some recess problems students might have. Tell me what you could do. There are no right answers, but some choices may work better than others. Think of as many positive choices as possible.** Choose two or three ideas from the following list or add some of your own. **What could you do if**
   - **you are swinging on the swing set, and there are three other students waiting to use it?**
   - **you are playing (a ball game or hopscotch) and others want to join? How do you decide who can join in and who cannot?**
   - **a group of older students are using the slide and have told all the younger kids that it's their slide and no one else can use it?**
   - **a group of students tell other students they can't play with them because they are too little or young?**
   - **whenever you go out to recess, a group of older students chase you?**
   - **one student is always by herself/himself and looks sad?**
   - **you can't find anyone to play with you at recess?**
   - **some students call you and your friends mean names whenever a grown-up is not close by?**
   - **when you tell an adult about the name-calling, the other students say you are lying?**

3. *Optional:* Provide role-playing opportunities to reinforce positive responses and behaviors discussed.

Wrap-Up

1. **Recess should be fun for everyone. It's a time to play with friends and exercise your bodies. But sometimes the playground isn't fun for everyone.** Highlight a few positive ideas students had about ways they

could intervene in playground dilemmas. If there are things adults need to improve, tell students you will be following up.

2. Thank students for their ideas and thank any playground supervisors for joining you and participating. **Let's keep practicing ways to let others know they can play with us.**

3. Encourage additional questions and comments.

Curriculum Connections

Vocabulary: *fair/unfair, popular, recess, taking turns*

Art/Language Arts: Ask students to create posters of playground rules or rules for particular areas of the playground.

Recess/Physical Eucation: Teach students new games they can play at recess, particularly if there is limited or no playground equipment.

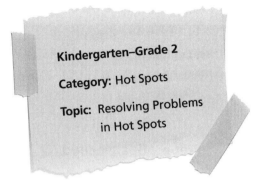

Kindergarten–Grade 2

Category: Hot Spots

Topic: Resolving Problems
in Hot Spots

Let's Eat!

Background

Along with recess, mealtimes are often the highlight of a student's school day. Unfortunately, like hallways, the lunchroom can be a daunting place for young students who may feel overwhelmed by noise levels, time constraints, and the confusion that can occur when large groups of students are together. Young students are more vulnerable to bullying when combined with older students; but taunting and exclusion can occur when they eat in classrooms or with same-age peers. Adults must provide adequate supervision and structure to keep students safe in this area. This class meeting explores what students' mealtime experiences are like. Conduct the class meeting What We Know about Bullying on pages 83–86 prior to conducting this session.

Learner Outcomes

By the end of this session, students will be able to
- identify positive and negative aspects of school mealtime experiences
- identify positive or friendly mealtime behavior
- identify behaviors that may lead to mealtime bullying

Materials Needed

- Sample placemat or placemats
- Colorful construction paper (11 x 15 inch)

- Enough markers or crayons so that all students can share a range of colors
- *Optional:* Materials to laminate finished placemats
- Question of the Day chart (from the What We Know about Bullying class meeting)

Dig Deeper

Ask your Bullying Prevention Coordinating Committee and administrators to observe the use and flow of lunchroom space. Consider ways to make adjustments as needed, such as relocating tables or trash receptacles, changing ways students enter or exit the space, reconsidering age-level groupings, looking at ways to reduce noise levels, and improving adult supervision.

Preparation Needed

- Consult the previously created Question of the Day chart as a reminder of how many students view mealtime as a problem. If students do not eat lunch at school, focus this session on snack time.
- If possible, observe your students as they prepare for and eat snacks, lunch, or other meals provided at school. Is it quiet or noisy, calm or chaotic? How do they know where to sit? What kinds of situations challenge students at these times? How do they socialize with each other? What are interactions with older students like?
- Set out paper and art supplies at tables for work in small groups or in the center of your class meeting circle space.

Class Meeting Outline

Opening Activity (10 minutes)

1. **Many of us are excited to eat our lunch (or snack) every day. We like the food we eat and enjoy having a break to move around or talk with friends and classmates.**
2. Show the sample placemat or placemats you brought. **I'm sure that you all know what a placemat is. How do we use placemats during meals?**
3. **I thought it would be fun to make placemats while we talk about what our mealtimes at school are like.** Have students work in small groups at tables or in the large circle.
4. Instruct each student to select a sheet of construction paper to make a placemat. **First, put your name on either the front or back so you**

know it is yours. **You can decorate your placemat any way you'd like. While you draw, we will talk.** Help younger students as needed. (If you wish to extend this lesson for the older grades, table etiquette rules could be written on the back of the placemat. These rules could be used to help remind students of polite behavior at meal time.)

5. Give students a few minutes to settle into making their placemats. Keep the discussion light and conversational as students work. Talk about favorite foods or what they decided to put on their placemats.

Discussion Questions (10 minutes)

1. As students are finishing up their placemats, ask questions such as the following:
   - **What do you like most about lunchtime (snack time)? Do you think there is enough time to eat your food?**
   - **What do you like least about lunchtime (snack time)? Why?**
   - **What are some things that happen at lunch (snack) that could make someone sad or angry?**
     Talk about common problems such as touching other people's food, making fun of what people are eating, trading foods, bumping people, not staying in your own space, and making people feel unwelcome at the lunch table. Refer to rules that you may have in place to deal with these problems.
   - **What are some ways you can help? What are ways I and other adults can help?**

2. Invite students to show what they created. For students who still need more time, offer some choices for when they might complete their placemats.

3. Ask students if they'd like to use their placemats at school or take them home. If possible, laminate the placements before they are used so they can be easily cleaned.

Dig Deeper

- Because lunchtime can feel rushed or chaotic, find ways to help students slow down and enjoy that time of day. You might conduct special lunchtime rituals such as quieting down before proceeding to the lunchroom. Special events can be planned to practice good social skills at mealtime. Setting the table with a tablecloth, making centerpieces, and inviting guests to share a special meal can be a highlight for students.

- If your school permits, students may be encouraged to help with mealtime chores such as setting tables, decorating dining areas, passing out milk cartons, helping with recycling, wiping tables, or sweeping the floor. Performing such tasks can be a way of developing responsibility for helping to make mealtimes more pleasant.

Wrap-Up

1. **You made some beautiful placemats!** If the placements are to be used at school, briefly state how or when this will happen. **You have many good ideas about ways we can work together to make our mealtimes here at school friendlier.** Summarize three things that adults and/or students will do.

2. Encourage additional questions and comments.

Curriculum Connections

Vocabulary: *placemat, pleasant, table manners*

Language Arts/Social Studies: Discuss the jobs of cafeteria and janitorial staff and the roles they play in making lunchtime possible. Write a group thank-you note to those staff, inviting each student to contribute one thought to the note.

Art: Have students create centerpieces to place on tables for a special occasion lunch.

Community Service/Cross-Grade Activities: Plan a special lunch for cross-grade "buddies." Practice icebreaker questions and table etiquette in advance with both sets of students.

Social Skills/Friendship Groups: Use role-play and teacher modeling to help students practice table etiquette—including acknowledging and greeting people sitting nearby—and ways to carry on a pleasant conversation.

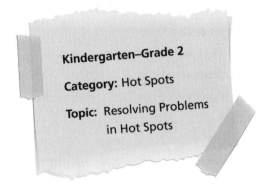

Kindergarten–Grade 2

Category: Hot Spots

Topic: Resolving Problems in Hot Spots

We're on Our Way to School

Background

Regardless of how they travel to and from school, student experiences at the beginning and end of the day can set the tone for how they feel about school. Teachers can help students by being alert to potential problems, by working together to build a sense of community among students on the same bus routes, and by helping individual students identify a safe person they can talk to if they run into difficulty during travel time. Conduct the class meeting What We Know about Bullying on pages 83–86 prior to conducting this session.

Learner Outcomes

By the end of this session, students will be able to

- discuss their experiences traveling to and from school
- identify a safe adult or student they can go to for help while on the way to or from school
- identify a trusted adult at home and at school with whom they can discuss any problems they experience in getting to and from school

Materials Needed

- Chart paper and marker or adhesive dots
- Props such as puppets, chairs, or carpet squares for acting out scenarios

Preparation Needed

- Using chart paper, prepare a Question of the Day. At the top, write "How do I come to school?" Create three or four columns for options you know your students use: School Bus, Car, Walk, Public Transportation, or Bicycle. If most students use the same form of transportation, create columns for the people they travel with: Parent, Brother or Sister, Friends, Someone Else, or Alone.

- Talk to your school's transportation coordinator to find out information about how your students get to school, how long it takes them, how far they travel, and with whom they travel.

Class Meeting Outline

Opening Activity (10 minutes)

1. **Our Question of the Day is How do I come to school?**

2. **How do you get to and from school each day?** Go around the class, using a marker or adhesive dot to record students' responses on the chart. Tally the results at the bottom of each column.

3. **How do most students in our class get here? What way do the fewest students use?**

4. Ask a few additional questions such as:
   - **Can you guess who lives the farthest away from school?**
   - **Who do you think lives closest?**
   - **Who has the earliest bus?**
   - **Who might ride the bus the longest?**
   - **Who travels with the most people (or the most students in our class)?**
   - Use this information to build empathy and understanding among students, but use the information with sensitivity.

5. Grade 2: Divide students into pairs. (See pages 13–14 for ideas and strategies for grouping students.) **Tell your discussion buddy the best thing about how you get to school. Then tell your buddy the worst thing about it.**

Discussion Questions (15 minutes)

1. Process the activity.

    a. **When students have problems on the way to or from school, how do you think they feel about coming to school?**

    b. **If you ever have a problem on the way to school, who should you tell?**

    c. **I want each of you to think of one other "safe" person who you can get help from right away if you need to.** Ask each student to identify someone. (Examples include a friend, older sibling, another student, or an adult they travel with.) If students can't name someone, work with them on this later.

    d. Grade 2: **What did you find out from your discussion buddy?** Invite pairs of students to share either what they like most or what they don't like. Summarize similarities and differences among students.

2. Choose one or two scenarios from the list below for volunteers to role-play. Encourage students to think of as many different ways to deal with the situation as they can. **What could they do to help?**

    - **Tomas just moved here and walks to school alone. He lives near you.**

    - **While waiting to come into the school, some of the older kids called Ashanti mean names that made her cry. You saw it happen.**

    - **Tameka and Ronald are in the same carpool with you. Every day it seems they argue about something.**

    - **Tommy's mom wants him to walk to school with the same kids who bullied him when he was younger. Tommy is your friend.**

    - **Julie always sits next to Samir on the bus and pokes him or puts her finger close to his face to bother him. You ride the same bus.**

    - **Raina and her little brother take the city bus to school with you. When the bus pulls up, Raina realizes she lost some of her bus money.**

    - **You and Latika walk to school together every day. Today a man in your neighborhood stops and offers you a ride to school.**

Wrap-Up

1. **What happens on the way to and from school affects how we feel when we get here. Let's all practice ways we can make our trips the best they can be.** Recap some positive ideas from students' discussion. **We can help make everyone feel welcome here every day. Say something kind to classmates each morning!**

2. Encourage additional questions and comments.

Curriculum Connections

Vocabulary: *advice, early/late, long/short, near/far, safe person*

Language Arts:

*   Read a book like *Junie B. Jones and the Stupid Smelly Bus* (Barbara Park) to encourage students to talk about issues on the bus.

*   Have students draw a picture or write a story about something that happened to them recently on the way to or from school.

Math: You may wish to make a graph (using images of a car, bus, bicycle, walking feet, and so on) of ways that students travel to school, based on information gleaned in this class meeting.

Science/Geography: Display a map of your local area or city. Put pins or markers on the map to locate the school and where each student lives. Use the map to teach or reinforce students' knowledge of their home addresses and phone numbers.

Category 5

Peer Relationships

(Ten class meetings)

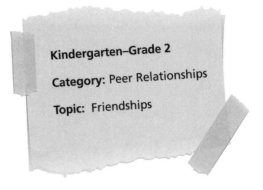

Kindergarten–Grade 2

Category: Peer Relationships

Topic: Friendships

Make New Friends

Background

Many students entering school have had some experience getting along with peers in preschool and daycare, but they may still lack basic friendship-making skills. During these early childhood years, students rely on adults for pointers on how to work and play harmoniously, on how to see things from someone else's perspective, and on how to handle conflicts. Adults must not only model by example but also provide opportunities for practicing friendship-making skills. Conduct this class meeting early in the school year to help students establish relationships with classmates.

Learner Outcomes

By the end of this session, students will be able to

- discuss two strategies to initiate and sustain play with other children
- discuss appropriate responses for handling rejection from peers
- demonstrate taking turns and sharing in a group activity

Materials Needed

- One of the following samples of age-appropriate literature: *How to Lose All Your Friends* (Nancy Carlson), *How to Be a Friend: A Guide to Making Friends and Keeping Them* (Laurie Krasny Brown and Marc Brown), *The Brand New Kid* (Katie Couric), *Share and Take Turns* (Cheri J. Meiners)

- Make New Friends Vignettes on page 107
- *Optional:* Three or four puppets to use for role-play

Preparation Needed

- Select one of the suggested literature options from Materials Needed.
- Gather puppets if you decide to use them.

Class Meeting Outline

Opening Activity (10 minutes)

1. **Having friends is a fun part of life. We need to know what to say or do to make new friends and to keep the ones we already have. Here's a story about being friends.** Read the book aloud.
2. **I'm going to read about some things that might happen to students during the school day. Then, we'll practice so you'll know what you could say or do if you run into these situations.**
3. Present one to three situations from the Make New Friends Vignettes. Invite volunteers to role-play one or two options after each vignette, as time permits. Consider using puppets for role-playing with younger students.

Discussion Questions (10 minutes)

1. Process the activity.
   - **How could you let someone know you wanted to play with him or her?**
   - **What could you say if you don't know someone but want to be friends with that person?**
   - **Sometimes friends have problems getting along with each other. What kinds of problems can happen with friends?**
   - **What could you say to a friend who is mad at you or says something like, "You can't be my friend"?**
   - **When might you need an adult to help you with a friend problem?**
   - **What things can you do to be a good friend?**

2. If time permits, have students role-play more situations from the Make New Friends Vignettes. Encourage them to show positive words and actions they heard in the discussion.

Wrap-Up

1. **Having friends makes our days a lot more fun! You had good ideas about how to make friends and how to be friendly. Let's all practice some of these ideas.**

2. Encourage additional questions and comments.

Curriculum Connections

Vocabulary: *cooperate, friend, greet, lose, share*

Language Arts:

- Add books with friendship themes to the class library for free reading or read-aloud. Examples include *It's Mine!* or *Swimmy* (Leo Lionni), *We Are All Alike…We Are All Different* (Cheltenham Elementary School Kindergartners), *The Very Lonely Firefly* (Eric Carle), *It's My Turn!* (David Bedford), *Emmet's Pig* (Mary Stolz), *Charlotte's Web* (E. B. White).

- Have students draw or write about two ways they are friendly to others.

Music: Teach students the song "Make New Friends." Lyrics: Make new friends, but keep the old. One is silver and the other gold. A circle's round, it has no end. That's how long I want to be your friend.

Physical Education/Recess: Teach students cooperative games (parachute play, relays, jump rope, or hand-rhyme games) that encourage turn-taking, cooperation, and sharing. Whenever possible, teach non-competitive games or non-competitive versions of familiar games such as freeze/unfreeze tag instead of freeze tag. Cooperative games have been shown to reduce aggression in children.

Social Skills/Friendship Groups: Have students practice friendly words, tone of voice, and actions in small groups. Include opportunities such as these: introducing themselves, sharing items (art supplies or snacks), giving and accepting a compliment, starting and continuing a conversation, and joining in play.

Make New Friends Vignettes

Instructions: Select one to three of these vignettes to read to and role-play with students. Consider using puppets for role-playing with younger students.

What can you say or do if:

- you see other students playing with building blocks and you want to join them?
- you are swinging on the swings, and you see someone else who has been waiting a long time for a turn?
- your best friend isn't at school today, and you aren't sure who to sit with at lunch?
- someone just asked you if he/she could play a game with you and another friend?
- you are playing by yourself, and other boys and girls keep bothering you?
- you want to play a game with some other students, but they tell you they already have enough people?
- another student grabs something you're playing with and says, "Hey, I want to play with this, too!"?
- at lunch, a classmate tells you, "You can't be my friend anymore!"?

Kindergarten–Grade 2

Category: Peer Relationships

Topic: Friendships and
           Popularity

What Makes a Friend?

Background

Young children may not yet be able to articulate what it means to be popular, even if they tend to gravitate toward peers they view as more likable than others or peers they want to emulate. Their decisions are often based on superficial qualities, such as how peers look, what clothes they wear, or what possessions they have. Young students need ongoing adult support to broaden their social circles. Cooperative games and age-appropriate literature are both useful tools to help young children improve their friendship skills.

Learner Outcomes

By the end of this session, students will be able to
- demonstrate friendship skills such as asking another student to join in play, playing interactively with minimal adult intervention, sharing, and cooperating
- discuss ways they can make a friend
- discuss how to behave in friendly ways

Materials Needed

- Chalkboard, dry erase board, or chart paper and chalk or markers
- Colored paper strips (1 x 8-1/2 inches) and glue, or small manipulative objects that can link together (enough for three to four per student)

Preparation Needed

- Print Friendly and Unfriendly on the board or on separate sheets of chart paper.

- Older students may do this activity at tables in groups of four to six. (See pages 13–14 for ideas and strategies for grouping students.) Place enough paper strips and glue or linking objects on the tables for students to share.

Class Meeting Outline

Opening Activity (15 minutes)

1. **Making and keeping friends is important. We all need friends. We've known some friends for a long time. And it's also important to know the things we can do to show people that we are friendly and to be a good friend.**

2. **Let's think about all the things we can do or say that show others that we are friendly. Each time we think of something, we will use the paper strips to make a chain (or link these objects).** Demonstrate by naming something and then linking the objects or gluing paper strips together. **Let's see how many more things we can think of and see how long we can make our chain of friendship ideas!** If students have difficulty coming up with ideas, reference literature you have read and how characters were friendly or use examples from the classroom.

3. Have students count the number of links in the finished chain. **Are there things that people say or do that could break our chain of friendship?**
   a. Ask for examples (no names). If students have difficulty with ideas, again use either literature references to specific characters' actions or use examples from school.
   b. **What would our chain look like if we took away a link each time something like that happened?** Decide whether to take the chain apart or simply keep a tally of how many links would be lost.

Discussion Questions (15 minutes)

1. Process the activity.

   - **When we are friendly to each other, how does that make our classroom feel?** (When we're being a good friend, we make connections with each other, just like we connected the chain.)
   - **Why should we be friendly to others?**
   - **What were some of the friendly ideas that you liked?**
   - **What happens when we behave in unfriendly ways?** (We break our friendship chain and that keeps us from making or being friends.)

2. Use the following to make sure students can distinguish between friendly and unfriendly actions. **Is it friendly or unfriendly if someone**

   - **tells you what to do?**
   - **shares and takes turns?**
   - **bosses you around?**
   - **listens to you?**
   - **tells you to do something that isn't allowed?**
   - **gives you half a cookie?**
   - **wants to be friends because you have a new toy they like?**
   - **helps you get up if you fall down on the playground?**

3. **What could you do if someone acts unfriendly?**

4. **Is it okay to have more than one friend? Some people use the words "best friend." We also sometimes call that person a "close friend." Is it okay to have more than one close friend? Why or why not?**

5. **What could happen if you are friendly to another student you don't know?**

Wrap-Up

1. **It's nice to have friends. A good friend is someone you can play with, sit next to, or talk to. A good friend is someone who likes you just the way you are! Even if someone is not your friend, it is good to be friendly and nice to everyone.**

2. Encourage additional questions and comments.

Curriculum Connections

Vocabulary: *friendly/unfriendly*

Language Arts:

- Include age-appropriate literature about friendship and friendship dilemmas in your class library. Some examples are *Franklin's New Friend* or *Franklin's Secret Club* (Paulette Bourgeois), *Frog and Toad* books (Arnold Lobel), *Arthur* books (Marc Brown), *Hooway for Wodney Wat* (Helen Lester), *Chrysanthemum* or *A Weekend with Wendell* (Kevin Henkes), *Arnie and the Skateboard Gang* (Nancy Carlson).

- Create a class poem about friendship, with students contributing different lines. Read the poem aloud during the morning announcements or post it on an all-school bulletin board.

Art:

- Create friendship bracelets where each link in the bracelet represents a friendship quality.

- Give each child one 8-1/2-inch square of white paper. Ask the children to decorate their square showing something they enjoy doing with friends. The squares can be spaced on a wall with other bright colored squares to create a friendship quilt.

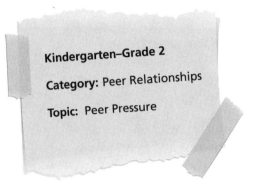

Kindergarten–Grade 2

Category: Peer Relationships

Topic: Peer Pressure

You're Not My Friend If . . .

Background

Students in early elementary grades may not understand the term "peer pressure," but they certainly understand the discomfort that comes from feeling manipulated to do things they don't want to do. It is not uncommon to hear ultimatums like "I won't be your friend if . . ." or "I dare you to . . ." or "You're not my friend because . . ." It is not too early to talk about peer pressure and how it makes students feel. Young learners will need to revisit these ideas many times and have opportunities to practice responses when friendships are challenged. It may help to conduct this class meeting after completing Confidence 101: Taking Care of Myself about using assertive behavior on pages 43–50, which discusses using assertive behavior.

Learner Outcomes

By the end of this session, students will be able to

- discuss how it feels when someone makes fun of another person
- discuss how it feels to have a friend dare them or ask them to do something they don't want to do
- practice responses to challenges, threats, or dares about friendship

Materials Needed

- Kindergarten: Chart paper, Grades 1–2: blank sheets of paper for each pair of students
- Markers, crayons, or pencils

Preparation Needed

- Add your own ideas to the "I'm Not Your Friend If . . ." Situations (see Opening Activity) based on things you have heard from your students.

Class Meeting Outline

Opening Activity (10 minutes)

1. **What are some favorite things you like doing with friends?**

2. **Do friends always get along, or do they sometimes have problems? Have you ever heard of friends saying things like, "I won't be your friend if you don't play *my* way"?**

3. **Have you ever had a problem like this with a friend?** If you have already read some literature on this topic, refer to problems characters had with similar issues.

4. **Here are things boys or girls at our school might say.** Read the statements from the following list. Fill in the blanks using examples you've heard.

   "I'm Not Your Friend If . . ." Situations

   I won't be your friend if . . .
   I bet you can't . . .
   You can't be my friend until . . .
   You're not my friend because . . .
   If you really like me, you'll . . .
   If you are really my friend, you'll . . .
   You can be my friend when . . .
   If you want to be friends, I dare you to . . .

5. Follow each statement with questions such as:
   - **Has that ever happened to you or someone you know?**
   - **How would that make you feel?**
   - **Why do you think people say things like that?**

6. Grade 2: Students familiar with this exercise may work in pairs. Give each pair a sentence fragment from the "I'm Not Your Friend If . . ." list. Have each pair fill in the blank and then write or draw something a student might say or do in response.

Discussion Questions (15 minutes)

1. Process the activity. Ask for student comments. Summarize key points addressed.

2. **Sometimes students dare each other or pressure us to do or say things we don't want to do. What could we do about that?** Read each of the following examples to students and have them practice saying each response (from the right-hand column) aloud.

If Someone Says:	You Could Say:
I won't be your friend if . . .	Maybe we can't be friends.
I bet you can't . . .	Friends don't say things like that.
You're not my friend because . . .	Stop. That's not fair.
If you really like me, you'll . . .	I don't want to do that.
If you're really my friend, you'll . . .	I am your friend, but I'm not going to do that.
You can be my friend when . . .	I don't feel like playing when you talk like that.

Wrap-Up

1. **We all want to please our friends. Even grown-ups have a hard time knowing exactly what to do sometimes. You came up with some great ideas. Remember, if you hear someone tell a classmate they can't be a friend, help them out—stick up for them or tell them you will be their friend, no matter what!**

2. Encourage additional questions and comments.

Curriculum Connections

Vocabulary: *challenge, dare, threat*

Language Arts: Keep sample literature on this topic available. Examples include *Arnie and the Skateboard Gang* (Nancy Carlson), *Arthur's April Fool* (Marc Brown), *The Araboolies of Liberty Street* (Sam Swope), *Miss Hunnicutt's Hat* (Jeff Brumbeau), *I DOUBLE Dare You!* (Dana Lehman), *George and Martha* books (James Marshall), and *Nobody Knew What to Do: A Story about Bullying* (Becky Ray McCain).

Social Studies: Talk with students about people who dared to be different by standing up for what was right (such as Rosa Parks). Avoid the traditional notion of dare as taking on a physically dangerous challenge.

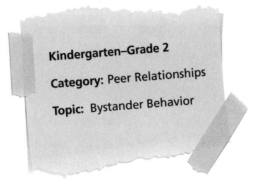

Kindergarten–Grade 2

Category: Peer Relationships

Topic: Bystander Behavior

Stop That!

Background

Bystanders play a key role in helping to prevent and stop bullying behavior. Young students frequently tell adults about bullying because they rely on adults to provide assistance with peer relationships. Adults need to intervene consistently to stop any bullying that they see or that is reported to them. They can also help students by teaching specific words and actions that a protective bystander can use. Practicing proactive responses in a safe situation helps students build confidence and learn skills to use when confronted with actual bullying situations. Before leading this class meeting, conduct class meetings from the *OBPP* Teacher Guide that define bullying behavior, define the term "bystander," and discuss the various roles bystanders might play in bullying situations.

Learner Outcomes

By the end of this session, students will be able to
- discuss the role of bystanders in bullying situations
- use the *OBPP* Bullying Circle to identify their role in a bullying situation
- demonstrate how to get help from adults when they witness bullying
- demonstrate other ways they can help when they witness bullying

Materials Needed

- Age-appropriate literature about bullying and the important role bystanders can play: *Say Something* (Peggy Moss), *My Secret Bully* or *Trouble Talk* or *Just Kidding* (Trudy Ludwig), *Nobody Knew What to Do: A Story about Bullying* (Becky Ray McCain)
- Chalkboard, dry erase board, or chart paper and chalk or markers
- *OBPP* Bullying Circle (see page 24 of the Teacher Guide)
- *Optional:* Two to four puppets to aid student role-play

Preparation Needed

- Preread your literature selection, focusing on points in the story where bystanders could have helped the student being bullied.
- On separate sheets of chart paper or columns on the board, print the words "I can . . ." and "I need help to . . ."

Class Meeting Outline

Opening Activity (10 minutes)

1. **Everyone in this class is a helper. You help at home and you help at school. In what ways do students help each other at school?**
2. **Sometimes students bully others. They might say or do mean things on purpose. Have you ever noticed that but weren't sure what to do about it?**
3. **We've learned that it's always right to tell a grown-up when that happens, but there are other ways that you may be able to help out, too.**

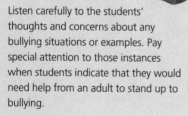

Teacher Tip

Listen carefully to the students' thoughts and concerns about any bullying situations or examples. Pay special attention to those instances when students indicate that they would need help from an adult to stand up to bullying.

4. Show students the book you have selected. **In this book, the characters have trouble knowing what to do. Let's find out what they did. Then we can talk about choices we could make.**
5. Read the book, stopping at key points where bystanders made or could have made some choices about ways to help. Ask either **What did (bystander) do to help?** or **What could (bystanders) have done to help?**

Discussion Questions (10 minutes)

1. Process the activity.

    a. **What did you think about the way (bystanders) helped out in this story?**

    b. **Did their solutions work? Did they have to try different things before the bullying stopped? What are some things they did?**

    c. **Were there some other choices they could have made to help? What ways could you have helped?** Encourage students to think of options before, during, and after the bullying took place. Write these under "I can . . ." Prompt with examples as needed. (Ideas include telling an adult, saying "Stop it," asking the bullied student to come with you, sitting with the bullied student, comforting him or her, saying you're sorry that it happened, including the bullied student in your play group.)

    d. **If you knew about a bullying problem like this, in what ways would you need help from an adult?** Write responses under "I need help to . . ."

2. Select a few options from the "I can . . ." list. Have volunteers role-play bystander responses or use puppets as desired or appropriate with your students. Refer to the diagram of the Bullying Circle to help older students look at bystander actions.

    a. **Why might it be hard to know what to do?**

    b. **Are there ever times when it's better to help after the bullying has stopped? How could you help then?**

    c. **How could your friends help you if you see bullying happen to someone else? How could they help if bullying happens to you?**

Teacher Tip

When role-playing bullying situations, focus on bystander responses instead of the bullying act itself. Role-playing should reinforce positive behaviors in responses to negative bullying behaviors—not reenact and reinforce the act of bullying.

Wrap-Up

1. **When we see or hear bullying happen, it can make us feel confused and scared. Always tell an adult when you know about bullying. Remember ways you and your friends can help out, too. We'll keep working on being helpful bystanders. I will be thinking about the things you put on our "I need help to . . ." list because it is important that everyone feels comfortable in our class. Thank you for your help!**

2. Encourage additional questions and comments.

Curriculum Connections

Vocabulary: *bystander, defender*

Language Arts/Art:

- Use the "I can . . ." list to have students draw pictures or write stories that show students taking action as bystanders.

- Have students create their own stories paralleling the book you read. They should include their ideas about actions bystanders might have taken, and how those actions might have changed the story.

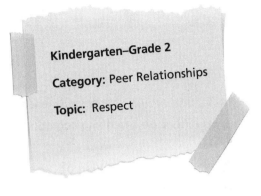

Kindergarten–Grade 2

Category: Peer Relationships

Topic: Respect

Thinking of Others

Background

Showing respect is an important aspect of learning to socialize and live in harmony with others. Young children can be taught basic ways to nurture their relationships while they are still learning to form friendships and to distinguish their own desires from the needs of others. A developmentally appropriate way to approach the concept of respect for others is by framing it as sharing, cooperating, being polite, taking turns, being kind, and helping others.

Learner Outcomes

By the end of this session, students will be able to
- explain that sharing, cooperating, taking turns, being kind, and helping are ways to show respect for other people
- discuss the link between showing respect and having friends

Materials Needed

- Thinking of Others Dilemmas on page 122
- Paper for each student and markers or crayons

Preparation Needed

None

Class Meeting Outline

Opening Activity (10–15 minutes)

1. **When we are being kind to others, sharing with each other, working together, and helping others, we are doing something called showing respect for them.**

2. **We're going to play a game called Thinking of Others. I am going to read some very short stories to you. After I read the story, we'll talk about what you think should happen.**

3. Choose two or three situations from Thinking of Others Dilemmas. After each dilemma, brainstorm possible solutions as a large group.

4. Have students choose one of the dilemmas and write a story or draw a picture that shows what they think would be the best choice to make.

Discussion Questions (10 minutes)

1. Process the activity.
   a. **Was it easy or hard to decide what to do? For those who felt it was hard: What made it hard? For those who felt it was easy: What made it easy?**
   b. **Do you think there was just one right choice or several good choices you could make?**
   c. **What are some of the things you can do to show kindness and caring for your friends and family?**

2. If time permits, choose another situation from Thinking of Others Dilemmas and repeat the activity.

Wrap-Up

1. **Friends come in many shapes and sizes. You will have friends your whole life long if you treat them kindly and with respect. We should make sure to take time every day to show our friends that we care about them. Having friends makes every day better, especially when you know that friends will be thoughtful and caring about you, too!**

2. Encourage additional questions and comments.

Curriculum Connections

Vocabulary: *compassion, consideration, dilemma, respect, thoughtful*

Language Arts: Instruct students to write class friendship poems using the letters in the word "friends" or "respect." Turn these poems into mobiles to hang in the classroom as a reminder to be a good friend.

Cross-Grade/Community Building: Create a hands-around-the-school project using outlines of students' hands cut from colored paper. Write the student's name on the hand and an act of kindness he or she performed. Encourage students to practice enough kind or respectful acts to be able to line the perimeter of the whole school (or cover a whole wall) with hands.

Thinking of Others Dilemmas

Instructions: Select two or three of the following dilemmas to read to the class. For each dilemma, discuss what students could do to show respect for others.

1. You break your friend's toy by accident. What could you do?

2. You find (an action figure or other toy) on the playground. You are pretty sure it belongs to another student in your class who lost one just like it. What could you do?

3. Everyone is trying to get into the building at the same time. A student next to you drops her lunchbox and everything falls out. What could you do?

4. You accidentally knock something off the teacher's desk when no one was looking and it breaks. What could you do?

5. Someone takes another student's hat and is playing keep-away with it. What should you do?

6. A friend lets you borrow his or her library book and it's due today, but you don't know where the book is. What could you do?

7. You put your lunchbox on a shelf in the coatroom. When you go to get it, you see that something leaked out all over someone else's jacket. What could you do?

8. You notice another student crying on the playground. What could you do?

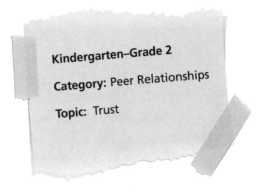

Kindergarten–Grade 2

Category: Peer Relationships

Topic: Trust

Lean on Me

Background

The concept of trust is important in relation to bullying prevention. First, it is essential that children learn to trust their emotional or gut feelings if they feel unsafe and get assistance from adults right away. Second, they need to feel there are people they can depend on to keep them safe by providing social, emotional, and physical support. Trust provides the basis for developing caring relationships, including friendships, and is important for good communication. A fun way to build connections and communication among students is to conduct trust-building activities.

Learner Outcomes

By the end of this session, students will be able to
- discuss what it feels like to depend on one another
- discuss that it takes work and practice to trust each other

Materials Needed

None

Preparation Needed

- Plan pairing students together who are of fairly equal size and physical proportion to help everyone succeed. Also pair students who are of the same gender.

Class Meeting Outline

Opening Activity (10–15 minutes)

1. **How many of you have ever asked someone else to help you try something new, like ride a bike, use skates, climb up high, or jump into a pool? What was it like to depend on that person to keep you safe? Was it easy or hard to depend on him or her? Why? How did you know you could depend on that person?**

2. **When we rely on each other like that, we call that trust. We all need to trust that people will take care of us and do what is best for us. At school, we need to be able to trust teachers, friends, and classmates.**

3. **We're going to try an experiment called Lean on Me. Each of you will work with a partner.** Pair up students according to your plan. Provide the instructions, step by step.

   - **First, sit on the floor, back-to-back with your partner, legs stretched straight out in front of you.**
   - **Now, link your arms together like this with your elbows bent** (demonstrate) **so you stay connected.**
   - **When I say "Go!" keep your arms linked (don't let go) and try to stand up. Ready? Go!**

4. There will most likely be a lot of laughter as the students try to stand up.

5. **This is hard! You will have to work together to stand up.** If needed, prompt students with hints. (Examples: Talk together to decide how to do this. Try taking turns leaning one way or the other so your partner can move to get ready to stand. Once both your legs are steady, carefully push back against each other's back to stand up.)

6. As time permits, change partners and try the exercise again, or try variations, such as standing back to back with arms linked and walking in a straight line (one person will walk forward, the other backward), or standing side by side, arms linked, and skipping around in a circle.

7. If students are excited, provide an opportunity to cool down before the discussion. Have them stand in a circle. Instruct them to take a deep breath and let it out slowly while you count out loud to 3. Repeat as needed, increasing the exhale count to 5, to help students slow their breathing.

Discussion Questions (10–15 minutes)

1. Process the activity with all students in a circle. Encourage students to notice how trusting their partner helped them communicate and take turns.

   - **What did you think about the activity? What did it have to do with trust?**
   - **How many were able to finally stand up with your partner? What things worked?** Share your own observations as well (for example, I noticed that people who talked to their partner found it easier to do).
   - **What was the hardest thing for you and your partner?**
   - **When did you have to depend on each other the most?**

2. **Which people in your life can you trust? Why?**

3. **Most of the time, we don't need to trust a friend or classmate to physically hold us up, but we need to trust that we can depend on a friend or classmate in other ways. In what ways do you depend on or trust your classmates or friends?**

4. **How do you let your friends know that they can trust and depend on you? How do you show them?** (Responses might include tell the truth, take turns, stop when they say no, don't laugh at them, or help them.)

Wrap-Up

1. **We need to trust every day that we will be safe and cared for. We need to be able to trust our friends and be there for each other. Talking, learning, and having fun together helps us learn to trust each other.**

2. Encourage additional questions and comments.

Curriculum Connections

Vocabulary: *depend on, rely on, trust*

Language Arts: Have students write a thank-you note or draw a picture to send to someone they trust.

Music: Listen to *Lean on Me* (Bill Withers) and discuss the lyrics.

Physical Education: Introduce group games that involve depending on and trusting others. Some examples include blindfold tag, scavenger hunts, relays, and tug-of-war and cooperative games like freeze tag.

Art: Make a banner or poster for the classroom that says "Talking, Learning, and Having Fun Together Helps Us Learn to Trust Each Other."

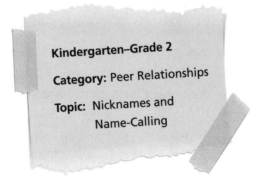

Kindergarten–Grade 2

Category: Peer Relationships

Topic: Nicknames and
Name-Calling

The Trouble with Names

Background

Our name can be a source of pride and distinction, or a source of lifelong aggravation or embarrassment. Names and nicknames, most often chosen by others, can be used with affection and respect or can be fuel for teasing and bullying. Students may tease others about an unusual name, what someone's name rhymes with, and family nicknames. When unwelcome, this kind of teasing can be especially hurtful because it attacks one's personal identity. Adults must take responsibility to stop unwanted and inappropriate use of nicknames in their school.

Learner Outcomes

By the end of this session, students will be able to

- explain the difference between positive and negative nicknames
- explain how using some nicknames can cross the line to be name-calling
- practice possible responses to name-calling and unwanted nicknames

Materials Needed

- Age-appropriate literature about names and nicknames: *Crow Boy* (Taro Yashima), *Chrysanthemum* (Kevin Henkes), *Franklin's Nickname* (Paulette Bourgeois), *The Adventures of Pinkie: A Nickname*

(Maddy Rose), *Sticks and Stones!* (Pierrette Dubé), *The Name Jar* (Yangsook Choi), *Angel Child, Dragon Child* (Michele Surat)

- Chart paper

Preparation Needed

- Select and preread one of the literature selections for content questions.

Class Meeting Outline

Opening Activity (15 minutes)

1. **Many of us have special nicknames that our families have given us. Do any of you have nicknames that you like and want to tell us about?** Invite students to share, but allow them to pass if they don't wish to share.

2. **Why do you think we have nicknames? Sometimes our family nicknames have a funny story or come from something we did as a baby. Those may feel okay to us in our families but might make us feel embarrassed if someone else uses them.**

3. Show students the book you have selected. **Here is a story about nicknames. Let's see how our character feels about his/her name/nickname.**

4. Read the book to the students.

Teacher Tip

Take advantage of opportunities to discuss gender or cultural differences in naming, use of nicknames, or put-downs about gender, heritage, or abilities.

Discussion Questions (10 minutes)

1. Discuss the book.
   - **How did (character) feel about his/her name/ nickname?**
   - **What did you think about how he/she handled this?** Ask students to give a "thumbs up" or "thumbs down." **Why?**
   - **What would it be like for a student at our school to have that name/nickname?**

Dig Deeper

Rules about names and nicknames vary tremendously across cultural and family lines. What is considered acceptable to some could be considered offensive to others. Be aware of the range of tolerance for these names in your group. Setting a limit for what's okay in school versus out of school can be one way to prevent concerns regarding differences in cultural norms or childrearing practices. Create rules for your students regarding the use of nicknames.

2. **We talked about nicknames you like. Are there others that you like, too?** Invite sharing. **How about some you don't like? Why?** Invite sharing, but recognize that some students may not want to share aloud.

3. **Do students ever use nicknames to tease or bully other students? What are some of the nicknames you have heard used to bully others?**

4. **What should you do if students use nicknames to tease or bully you or someone else?**

   a. Discuss useful steps:

      1. *State the facts* ("My/his/her name is _____." "I need my glasses.")

      2. *State the rule* ("Using that nickname without my/his/her permission is not allowed." "Name-calling is against our rules." "That is bullying.")

      3. *Speak up!* (Tell an adult about name-calling that you hear. Tell the student you don't agree or don't like what he or she is saying.)

   b. Write the steps on chart paper and help students give examples.

      5. **Let's make some rules about using nicknames so we can decide when it is okay to use them, or when it might be name-calling or bullying.** Ask for student input into the development of classroom guidelines for use of nicknames.

Wrap-Up

1. **Names are an important part of who we are. When someone makes fun of us or our name, it hurts our feelings and can be bullying. When someone uses a nickname that we like or agree to, it can make us feel good. It's also one way we show each other we are friendly toward each other. Let's always be sure someone feels good about the name we use for him or her.**

2. Encourage additional questions or comments.

Dig Deeper

- Make it a practice never to call a child by a nickname unless he or she specifically asks you to (and then it should fit within acceptable school guidelines). If you hear a student being called a nickname, privately ask the student what it means and if it's okay that other students use the nickname. Adults should be discouraged from using student-given nicknames, as they may have hidden negative connotations.

- Students who bully others may use personal physical traits as a topic for name-calling, although other students with those same attributes may not be targeted. Students who bully often know which terms to use to aggravate vulnerable peers and enjoy watching their reactions.

Curriculum Connections

Vocabulary: *birth name, choice, name-calling, nickname,*

Language Arts: Use an extension of an acrostic poem, highlighting positive characteristics of each child in the class.

Math: Have students do a tally of the most common names for boys/girls in their grade.

Kindergarten–Grade 2

Category: Peer Relationships

Topic: Creating Healthy Boundaries

A Bubble of My Own

Background

Students have varied needs for personal space. Some students are comfortable with close contact, while others become irritable if a peer sits too close or touches them. Learning to recognize and respect our own and others' personal space is an important social skill. Bullying prevention relates to personal space in several important ways, which will be explored in this class meeting. This session should be preceded by Confidence 101: Taking Care of Myself on pages 43–50 and A Picture is Worth a Thousand Words on pages 57–59.

Learner Outcomes

By the end of this session, students will be able to
- acknowledge that individuals have different needs for personal space
- identify and show respect for their own and others' personal boundaries
- practice ways to use assertive behaviors to maintain personal boundaries when they feel uncomfortable

Materials Needed

- Kindergarten: Small bottle of bubbles for blowing and a simple wand
- Grades 1–2: Sidewalk chalk for each student

Preparation Needed

- Grades 1–2: Make plans to conduct this activity outside on a paved area.

Class Meeting Outline

Opening Activity (15 minutes)

1. **Imagine that each of us has a space around us like a bubble.** Blow a few bubbles toward each student, above each student's head. **Can you picture yourself inside a bubble like this? We'll call this our personal bubble. This is the space that we like to have around us, that makes us feel comfortable and not crowded.**

Teacher Tip

Become familiar with existing school or districtwide programs that address personal space and safety concerns so that you can use the same terminology when discussing boundaries. Review them with students before beginning this discussion.

   a. **Most of us like to let some special people inside our bubble with us, to be close to us. Who are some of the people you like to be close to and share your bubble with?** Ask students not to use names—guide them to talk about the relationships (parents, family, friends). **What do you like about being close to them?**

   b. **How do you like to share that bubble space? What do you like to do?** (Share a hug, snuggle with our families, hold hands with or sit close to a friend.)

   c. **Are there special times you like to share your bubble? When?** (For example, when you are tired or hurt, when it's bedtime, when you just want to spend time with people you care about.)

   d. **Are there times when you don't like to share? When?** (Examples include when you feel like being alone, when you're mad or tired, when someone is annoying you, or when someone gets too close.)

2. Grades 1–2: With older students, explore the notion of personal space further with the following activity.

   a. **Everyone, start out standing in our circle close enough together so each person is touching shoulders with his or her neighbor.**

b. **Now, take one step at a time backwards, until you feel you are not too close, but not too far away from other students.**

c. **When you get to that spot, stop and raise your hand and I will give you a piece of chalk.** Give students chalk and show or help them to draw a circle on the ground around themselves to define their personal space.

d. **This is your personal bubble. Write your name in it so you remember which one is yours.**

e. **Notice that some people in our group have big circles, some have small circles, and some have medium-sized ones.** If this is hard for some to visualize, they can walk around and look.

f. **You can experiment with a partner having him or her walk slowly toward you. When your partner gets to the edge of your bubble, ask him or her to stop.**

g. **Now, take turns inviting the people in the bubbles near you to come into your bubble, one person at a time.** Make sure everyone is invited and invites someone else, so no one is left out.

Dig Deeper

Young children, along with students who become easily over-stimulated by social contact, may benefit from having a small, cozy designated space in the classroom where they can go to be alone, collect their thoughts, or calm down. This area should be different from a time-out space used for discipline.

Discussion Questions (10–15 minutes)

1. Process the activity with all students in a circle.
   - **How did it feel to have your own bubble of personal space?**
   - **How can knowing and respecting each person's bubble help us to get along?**
   - **What are some ways we can show our classmates that we respect their bubble of personal space?**
   - **How can we use our bubble to make us feel safe if someone bullies us or does something to make us feel uncomfortable or scared?**

2. **Sometimes people may get too close to us or they may come inside our bubble when we don't want them to. That can make us feel uncomfortable and even unsafe. It doesn't feel right having them so close to us, even though we may know them. Has that ever happened to any of you?**
   a. Quickly pair students and ask them to practice assertive but respectful ways of protecting their personal space. As one student approaches, the other might use words such

as: "Please don't get so close," "Stop! I need to have more room," or "No, please move back."

b. **You should also come tell me or another adult you trust if someone makes you feel unsafe.** Invite comments about unsafe actions, including bullying, or issues that might come up around child assault prevention, if students have covered that.

Wrap-Up

1. **We all need to have our own private bubble of personal space. It's up to us to invite people to come in or not. It's okay to say "No," "Don't," or "Stop" when people make you uncomfortable by getting too close. Remember, you can get help from a grown-up, too. When you want company in that bubble, having people close to us can make us feel good inside.**

2. Encourage additional questions and comments.

Teacher Tip

Be aware of ways cultural differences among students affect traditions and taboos regarding personal space, touching, eye contact, greetings, and privacy. Teach your students to respect those differences.

Curriculum Connections

Vocabulary: *boundaries, healthy/unhealthy, personal space*

Science: Tell students about ways animals establish boundaries and defend their territories.

Social Studies: Research ways that families in different cultures (past and present) set boundaries about eye contact, greeting others, personal space, touching, and displays of affection like hugging, holding hands, and kissing. Discuss these cultural differences with students.

Health/Physical Education: Discuss child assault prevention and similar personal safety issues as needed and appropriate. Relate these lessons to bullying prevention.

Kindergarten–Grade 2

Category: Peer Relationships

Topic: Gender Issues in
Bullying

Girls Can, Boys Can

Background

From infancy, children begin learning that boys and girls are expected to behave in very different ways. Children are bombarded by messages about gender expectations in literature, in the media, and from family members and friends. Students in early elementary grades have already incorporated gender biases into their behavior, beliefs, and interactions. Students can learn that such stereotypes can be limiting and harmful. This class meeting and the next (We Can on pages 138–141) deal with gender-based bullying that is common at this age. After completing both sessions, teachers are encouraged to remain focused on the important role that gender plays in shaping school and classroom climate, and to continue addressing these issues with students on a regular basis.

Learner Outcomes

By the end of this session, students will be able to
- identify problems associated with expectations about "acting like a girl" or "acting like a boy"
- discuss how some attitudes and words about gender can be hurtful
- identify ways that their own ideas about gender are shaped by the world around them

Materials Needed

None

Preparation Needed

- Select six to eight statements from step 3 of the opening activity. If you wish, add statements that reflect gender biases you have observed in your class. Be sure to select an equal number of stereotypes about boys and about girls.

Class Meeting Outline

Opening Activity (10 minutes)

1. **We have talked as a class about ways that we are the same and different from each other. One of the ways we are the same or different is that some of us are boys and some of us are girls.**

2. **I'm going to say some things about girls and boys.**
    - **If you agree or think what I say is true, stand here.** Indicate a spot.
    - **If you don't agree or think what I say is false, go stand there.** Indicate a spot.
    - **If you're not sure, stand over here.** Indicate a spot.

3. Read six to eight of the following statements, and include an equal number about boys and girls. Allow time for students to move from one spot to the other. Observe and note which responses fall strongly along gender lines or reflect gender stereotypes.
    - **Boys are stronger than girls.**
    - **Girls are smarter than boys.**
    - **Boys hit, girls say mean words.**
    - **Girls are teased more than boys.**
    - **Only girls should play with dolls.**
    - **Boys are better at sports.**
    - **Girls are better at helping people.**
    - **Boys are better at math.**
    - **Girls are better at reading.**
    - **Only boys should play with cars and trucks.**
    - **Dance classes are only for girls.**
    - **Boys can run faster than girls.**

Teacher Tips

- While this session deals with gender and gender bias, it is not generally developmentally appropriate to teach these terms at this age. However, if your students use or raise the term, simply explain that gender means whether you are a girl or a boy.

- Some of your students' families may have strong feelings about this topic, which may be reflected in your students' own opinions. This class meeting is designed to encourage open discussion among students, so they may express their opinions in a non-judgmental atmosphere.

- Girls are nicer than boys.
- Boys are better than girls at keeping secrets.
- Girls should always set the rules in games.
- Big boys don't cry.
- There are parts of the playground that only boys should play in.
- There are parts of the playground that only girls should play in.
- Most books are for girls.
- Only boys are interested in dinosaurs.

Discussion Questions (10–15 minutes)

1. Process the activity. Share your own observations to start the discussion if needed.

   - **What do you think about the statements I read? How did they make you feel?**
   - **Do you think that there are things boys can do that girls can't or shouldn't do?**
   - **Are there things girls can do that boys can't or shouldn't do?**
   - **Did boys and girls in our class mostly agree or disagree with each other?**

2. **Some people think that boys and girls shouldn't have the same toys, or kinds of clothes, or play the same kinds of sports or games. Do you agree or disagree with that? Why?**

3. **A lot of people have ideas about what girls and boys can or should do. Why do some people think this way? Where do these ideas come from?** (Examples include TV, commercials, traditions, or what you are told as a child.)

4. **Boys often like to do things that some people think only girls should do. What examples can you think of?**

5. **Girls often like to do things that people think only boys should do. What are some examples?**

6. Invite students to share things they like to do that might be traditionally associated with the opposite gender.

Dig Deeper

Gender bias is common in children's literature, even among esteemed award-winning books. Fewer books have female main characters, and girls are often shown as passive, dependent, weak, overly sensitive, or indecisive. Boys are often depicted more appealingly as active, decisive, leaders, independent, and physically strong or aggressive. Pay close attention to possible gender bias in literature you use. When you can, discuss these biases directly with students.

Wrap-Up

1. **Boys and girls have lots of choices and skills. None of us like to be told we can't like or do things because we're a girl or a boy. Let's all try to pay closer attention to the ways we think about and treat boys and girls in our school.**

2. Encourage additional questions and comments.

Curriculum Connections

Vocabulary: *beliefs, boy/girl, choices, true/false, (optional: gender, bias/stereotype)*

Language Arts:

- Add books to your library that explore and challenge traditional gender role stereotypes, such as *William's Doll* (Charlotte Zolotow), *Oliver Button Is a Sissy* and *The Art Lesson* (Tomie dePaola), *Ira Sleeps Over* (Bernard Waber), *Anna Banana and Me* (Lenore Blegvad), *Prince Cinders* (Babette Cole), *Amazing Grace* (Mary Hoffman), and *Mermaid Janine* (Iolette Thomas).

- Fairy tale "fracturing" is one approach to alter biased images or gender-role perspective. Reverse the gender of well-known fairy tale characters when reading to students.

- Encourage students to create their own versions of well-known fairy tales through drawings or group writing activities.

- Encourage students to write about unfair events they have experienced. Assure them that these essays will not be shared with others, unless they give their permission.

Social Studies/Media Literacy: Look through toy catalogs with students to explore and critique ways boys and girls are portrayed.

Kindergarten–Grade 2

Category: Peer Relationships

Topic: Gender Issues in Bullying

We Can

Background

It is important that all children have the opportunity to flourish and grow, free from the influence of negative stereotypes of all kinds. Because stereotypes about gender are so prevalent and can become ingrained at an early age, adults need to address these biases proactively to help young students view the roles of boys and girls and women and men less rigidly. Building on concepts presented in the previous class meeting, this session provides further opportunities to explore how gender stereotypes develop and the role they can play in bullying.

Learner Outcomes

By the end of this session, students will be able to

- identify gender-related words and beliefs that can be hurtful to others
- identify stereotypes about boys and girls that lead to put-downs and bullying

Materials Needed

- Chalkboard, dry erase board, or chart paper and chalk or markers
- *Optional:* Two to four puppets to facilitate role-playing

Preparation Needed

- On the board or chart paper, write the heading "We can . . ."
- Add put-downs observed in your class to the list in step 3 of the opening activity.

Class Meeting Outline

Opening Activity (15 minutes)

1. **We've been talking about ways some people think boys and girls should behave.** Review examples and key points from the previous discussion if needed.

2. **Sometimes people make fun of or bully others because of how they expect boys and girls to behave. Is that fair? Is it ever fair to bully? It's not okay to bully in our school. We have rules about that because it hurts people's feelings.**

3. **What is a put-down?** Explain that put-downs are words someone says to make another person feel bad about himself or herself. Read examples of gender-based put-downs from the list below.
   - **Sissy!**
   - **Only (girls/boys) can play here!**
   - **Girls wear pink, not boys!**
   - **Why don't you cut your hair like other boys?**
   - **Private! No (girls/boys) allowed!**
   - **Girls are so stupid!**
   - **What's the matter, do you need your (sister/mommy) to help you?**
   - **You run like a girl.**
   - **What a wimp!**
   - **That outfit makes you look fat (or gay).**
   - **Why do you wear boy's clothes all the time?**
   - **Boys can't be (teachers, nurses, baby sitters)!**
   - **Girls can't be (firefighters, doctors, plumbers, president of anything)!**
   - **Boys don't play with dolls.**

4. **Let's practice things we can say or do when someone makes put-downs like this.** Choose two to four of the examples for role-play. Invite several students to act out responses to each put-down. If they wish, they can use puppets to show the class. You may need to actively suggest words and guide students to act out what they could do or say if (1) someone said that put-down to a friend, or (2) someone said that put-down to them. Remind them not to use aggression or inappropriate words in their responses.

5. Write all positive choices on the "We can . . ." list.

Discussion Questions (10 minutes)

Dig Deeper

- Gender roles are "socially and culturally defined prescriptions and beliefs about the behavior and emotions of men and women."[2]

- Many school materials and student literature contain examples of gender bias.

- Periodically take note of ways your responses to students or ways you assign roles/jobs may reflect gender biases so you can model positive examples for students.

1. Kindergarten–grade 1:
   - **Raise your hand if you have ever heard anyone say any of these things. How did that make you feel?**
   - **Do you think more boys or girls use put-downs like these?**
   - **Why do you think students use put-downs like these?**
   - Use the "We can . . ." list to review the positive choices students came up with. Discuss any that seem unsafe or unrealistic and consider erasing them from the list.
   - **Which of these solutions do you think you might try?**

2. Grade 2:
   - **Why can these kinds of put-downs be so hurtful?** (Responses might be you can't change who you are, it's only their opinion, girls and boys can like the same things, or it makes us feel bad to be a girl/boy.)
   - **Were any of these examples of bullying? Do you think students know that the words they are saying are hurtful? Are they being hurtful on purpose?**
   - **Let's talk about each of these choices on our "We can . . ." list. What was good about this response?** (Was it safe? Was it aggressive or bullying back? Was it realistic or would it work?) **How can girls and boys work together to stop these put-downs?**

Wrap-Up

1. Highlight solutions on the "We can . . ." list.
2. **I am going to post this list in our classroom to remind us about how important it is not to use put-downs. Remember, it's not okay for someone to tell you that you can or can't do something just because you are a girl or boy. It's not okay to use mean words like some of the ones I read to you. If anyone does that, tell that person to stop. You should also talk to an adult and ask for help.**
3. Encourage additional questions and comments.

Curriculum Connections

Vocabulary: *accidental/on purpose, put-down*

Language Arts: Continue to use age-appropriate literature and writing examples as opportunities to explore gender bias.

Art: Have students make self-portraits on the theme What will you be when you grow up?

Physical Education: Make a special effort to include girls in games traditionally played by boys, and include boys in activities and games played more often by girls. Encourage individual strength and efforts regardless of gender.

Category 6

Respecting Differences and Promoting Acceptance

(Three class meetings)

Kindergarten–Grade 2

Category: Respecting Differences and Promoting Acceptance

Topic: Promoting Understanding

Who Are We?

Background

Bullying prevention goes hand in hand with promoting acceptance of others and emphasizing the ways we are all connected. Learning to value the ways that they are similar and not focus on the ways they are different helps students develop empathy and move away from an egocentric view of the world to one that is more inclusive. The class meetings in this category build on each other; it is recommended that they be conducted sequentially. Additionally, because the class meetings in this category require a level of established trust among students in your class, you should conduct the meetings from *Building a Positive Classroom Climate* (pages 17–31) and *Communication* (pages 57–81) before the meetings in this category.

Learner Outcomes

By the end of this session, students will be able to
- discuss ways that the students' similarities and differences can make their class stronger
- discuss how learning about each other brings them together

Materials Needed

- Interesting facts about students in your classroom
- Chalkboard, dry erase board, or chart paper and chalk or markers

Preparation Needed

- From the facts you gather about your class, prepare a list of ten to twelve questions to use in the opening activity. Use information that applies to one or more students and that students would know about themselves, but not necessarily about each other. Examples of facts might include birth month, state or country where they were born, favorites/dislikes, number of siblings, birth order, who they live with and family types (generations at home, single- or two-parent family, foster or adoptive, etc.), whether another language is spoken at home, whether they have had their tonsils removed or lost one or more teeth, special interests or talents.

- Prior to conducting any class meetings in this section, read through "Respecting Differences and Promoting Acceptance for Others" on pages 9–12.

Class Meeting Outline

Opening Activity (10–15 minutes)

1. **Every one of us is a person, a human being. That makes us more alike than we are different. But no one is exactly like us (even if you are a twin)! Each one of us has something special to offer that makes our class better.**

2. **We're going to play a game. We'll see how we are alike, and how we are different from each other. Ready?**

   a. **I am going to ask you some questions. When I ask something that describes you, stand up. If it does not describe you, stay seated.**

   b. **Here's a practice question: Who was born in June? Stand up.**

   c. Instruct students to sit down between each question. Refer to the list of questions you have prepared; go through as many as you can in the time allotted. Before moving on to a new question, encourage students to notice who is standing up.

Teacher Tips

- Consistently remind students of ways that accepting others helps create a welcoming classroom.

- Teach students to show respect for others in all ways, weaving this ideal throughout daily curricula and positive role modeling.

3. Grades 1–2: A variation of this game for older students could be "Just Like Me." When a common attribute is named, students can say aloud, "Just like me!"

Discussion Questions (10–15 minutes)

1. Process the activity.

a. **What did you learn about a classmate that you didn't know before? How are we the same? How are we different from each other?** Invite students to give a few examples of each.

Dig Deeper

Observe student interactions and note subtle and overt ways they express intolerance and stereotypes about others. Common stereotypes at this age relate to race, social class, and gender roles. Use these observations to enrich class meeting discussions.

b. **What are some special talents you have?** Be sure to highlight something special about each student, even if the student is not able to think of something him- or herself.

c. **How can we find out more about each other?** Make a list of students' ideas on the chart paper.

2. Grade 2: **Each of you has something you can do very well.** Refer to a few special talents you highlighted in the opening activity, such as musical or athletic ability, or the ability to speak another language. **But we have other kinds of talents, too.**

a. Choose a few of the following, and add other non-traditional talents that might apply to students in your class, particularly those who might otherwise go unnoticed. **Tell me, who in our class**

- **can make us laugh?**
- **can make us feel good about ourselves?**
- **is a really good listener?**
- **takes his/her time and notices details?**
- **has a special way with animals?**
- **can tell a really good story?**
- **is especially kind to others?**

b. **These are all special talents, too. We might not notice these things right away. But they can make our class a better place to be.**

Wrap-Up

1. **We learned a lot of interesting facts about each other. We found out ways we are similar and ways we are different. We can learn a lot by talking to each other and getting to know one another. When we really know each other, we learn to accept one another, just the way we are.**

2. Encourage additional questions and comments.

Curriculum Connections

Vocabulary: *accept, alike/different, describe, details, facts/information, human being, similar/similarity, stereotype, talents*

Language Arts:

- Picture books such as *Frederick* or *A Color of His Own* (Leo Lionni) or *What I Like about Me* (Allia Zobel Nolan) provide concrete ways to talk about unique (or non-traditional) talents.

- Other examples of age-appropriate literature that focus on embracing differences and valuing connections between people include *Whoever You Are* (Mem Fox), *I'm Like You, You're Like Me: A Child's Book about Understanding and Celebrating Each Other* (Cindy Gainer), *All the Colors of the Earth* (Sheila Hamanaka), *The Skin You Live In* (Michael Tyler), *The Little Yellow Leaf* (Carin Berger), and *The Crayon Box that Talked* (Shane DeRolf).

Social Studies:

- Connect this class meeting to curriculum units you have in place about families or cultural diversity.

- Learn more about various cultures represented in your class and school. Talk about customs, food, greeting words, special clothing, and meanings of student names to increase understanding among students.

Art: Invite students to draw self-portraits to display in the classroom. More advanced students could write eight to ten self-describing words around their self-portraits.

Kindergarten–Grade 2

Category: Respecting Differences and Promot-
ing Acceptance

Topic: Promoting Respect

R-E-S-P-E-C-T

Background

Living harmoniously in a diverse and changing society requires embracing differences and valuing others as human beings who have rights. Respecting human
rights is an important premise of bullying prevention. We all benefit by treating others with respect and consideration. The process of promoting acceptance
among students will entail dealing directly with potentially sensitive issues about
race and gender, cultural or socioeconomic backgrounds, differences in abilities
and personalities, and religious beliefs. Young students naturally notice differences.
This can lead to positive beliefs and attitudes when adults model positive and non-
judgmental responses and deal directly with stereotypes and prejudice. Complete
the class meeting Who Are We? on pages 143–146 prior to conducting this session.

Learner Outcomes

By the end of this session, students will be able to
- demonstrate ways they can show respect for others
- discuss actions that show disrespect for others
- name an adult they can talk with if they are treated disrespectfully

Materials Needed

- Age-appropriate literature selection about friends showing respect for
  each other in spite of their differences, such as *Amos and Boris*

(William Steig), *Frog and Toad Are Friends* (Arnold Lobel), and *George and Martha* or *George and Martha One Fine Day* (James Marshall)

- Chart paper and markers

Preparation Needed

- Obtain and preread the literature selection you chose so that you can add content-specific questions about the book during the discussion.

Class Meeting Outline

Opening Activity (10 minutes)

1. **Last time, we learned about many ways we are the same. We found out about ways we are each a little different from everyone else and some special talents we have.**
2. **Today I'm going to read you a book about some friends who are very different from each other. Let's see how they show they appreciate and care about one another.**
3. Read your literature selection to the class.

Discussion Questions (10–15 minutes)

1. Process the activity.

Teacher Tip

Respect: Define respect as *valuing each other.* This stays true to both diversity training and bullying prevention concepts. Use synonyms such as *to value, to appreciate, to care about, to be considerate of,* or *to show consideration for.* Otherwise, many students will associate the word "respect" in the context of "respect your elders," which implies following, obeying, or deferring to another.

- **What were ways that (the characters) were the same? How were they different?**
- **Do you think (the characters) were friends?**
- **Did their differences affect their friendship? How?** (They disagreed, got frustrated with each other, or talked about their differences.)
- **How did (the characters) show they appreciated and cared about each other?** (They listened, they laughed *with* each other and not *at* each other, they helped each other with a problem.)
- **Were there times you thought (the characters) weren't nice to their friend? Give some examples.**

- **Do people have to be just the same as you are to be your friend?**
- **How does liking people just the way they are help us get along better with our classmates or others?**
- **How can we show that we appreciate others?** (Responses could include smile, say hello, be kind, compliment them, tell them you like them, or invite them to play.) Write students' responses on the chart paper.

2. Grades 1–2: Extend the discussion by focusing on the concept of respect. See Teacher Tip for suggestions about how to define respect in an age-appropriate way.

- **What are some ways we can show appreciation and respect for each other?**
- **How can you tell when someone is being disrespectful?** (Responses could include they criticize, they leave someone out, or they make fun of something that is different about another person.)
- **If someone shows you disrespect or if you see someone showing disrespect to someone else, remember to tell me or an adult at home. I care about you, and will help.**

Wrap-Up

1. **When we appreciate (respect) each other, we will get along better. We feel good when other people care about our feelings, are kind to us, and like us just the way we are. It's never okay to criticize or be mean to someone because he or she is different from you. We can all get along and feel welcome here in our classroom.**
2. Encourage additional questions and comments.

Curriculum Connections

Vocabulary: *appreciate, considerate, criticize, judge, respect/disrespect, value*

Social Studies/Language Arts: Read *We Are All Born Free: The Universal Declaration of Human Rights in Pictures* (Amnesty International, Contributor) to encourage discussion about respecting differences by protecting human rights.

Music: Work with students to create a class chant or rap about respect. (Though the song content is not age-appropriate, the cadence of Aretha Franklin's song "Respect" may provide a catchy model to begin.) Other song titles that would work nicely with this section are "The World Is a Rainbow," "Love in Any Language," and "Don't Laugh at Me."

Social Skills/Friendship Groups: Model and role-play with students ways to show caring, as well as considerate and respectful ways of talking and disagreeing with peers.

Art: Students in grade 2 could make puppets based on the literature read aloud and use them to role-play the respectful behavior they learned from the story.

Kindergarten–Grade 2

Category: Respecting Differences and Promot-
ing Acceptance

Topic: Bias, Stereotypes,
and Privilege

Do You See What I See?

Background

Young students' experiences with diversity are often based on whom they know
at school and home. Students develop biases about "good" versus "undesirable"
differences from messages they get from the media, adults, peers, and others in
their communities. They soon learn that how people look, how they act, where
they live, what they wear, or even what they represent is "good" or "bad."
Young students need adults to model respectful behavior and acceptance. Honest,
age-appropriate discussions are needed to confront stereotypes and prejudice
directly. This class meeting should take place after students have gotten to know
each other. Complete the class meetings Who Are We? on pages 143–146 and
R-E-S-P-E-C-T on pages 147–150 prior to conducting this session.

Learner Outcomes

By the end of this session, students will be able to
- talk about their observations of differences using positive and respectful language
- talk about ways that judging someone based on appearance can be
  hurtful

Materials Needed

- Three to six picture cards (preferably photographs) depicting children, adults, or families engaged in everyday activities like cooking, cleaning, eating, and playing. Include pictures of people of different races or ethnicities, some with disabilities, some from non-traditional families, and various body types (thin or overweight), well dressed and not-so-well dressed.
- Chalkboard, dry erase board, or chart paper and chalk or markers

Preparation Needed

- Select three to six picture cards for the activity. Note: Prepared sets like these are readily available in most school resource rooms or through school or public libraries.

Class Meeting Outline

Opening Activity (10 minutes)

1. **I brought some pictures for us to look at today. Please look at each one. Then tell me what you think the people you see are like.**
2. Show students the picture cards one by one.
    a. For each, ask questions such as:
       - **Would you like to play with or go visit this (boy or girl)? Why?**
       - **Would you want to be friends with them? Why?**
       - **What do you think this (boy, girl, person, or family) is like?**
    b. Try not to ask probing questions unless students don't respond. As needed, ask questions such as:
       - **Do you think they are happy?**
       - **What do you think they do for fun?**
       - **Do you think they'd like living here in our neighborhood?**
       - **How do you think they would treat you?**

Dig Deeper

According to the Anti-Defamation League, children who are taught to consider and value other people's feelings and to show empathy are less likely to be prejudiced.[3]

3. Write students' observations on the board or chart paper. Be sure to model positive descriptive words and address negative stereotypes and bigoted language directly. (See Dig Deeper.)

Discussion Questions (15 minutes)

1. Process the activity. Ask questions such as the following:
   - **Can you tell what someone is like just by looking at that person? Why or why not?**
   - **How can you learn what someone is really like?**
   - **What things can't you tell about someone just by looking at him or her?**
   - Encourage students to think of positive qualities about themselves that others may not know. Ask for volunteers to share their ideas.
2. Grade 2: Continue the discussion with these questions:
   - **What would it be like if someone decided not to get to know you because of how you look?**
   - **How would that feel? Would it be fair?**

Dig Deeper

- Dealing with bigoted language can be a challenge for many teachers. Biases about social class and gender are most common among students this age. Because students this age tend to be concrete thinkers, simple responses such as the following are best: "Some people believe that (one color skin, hair, type of family, etc.) is better than others, but that is not true." Or "Using words like that hurts people and is not okay in our school."

- Explore biases or stereotypes that students may have raised in this class meeting and talk about where these misconceptions about people come from, helping students understand that "hate hurts."

Wrap-Up

1. **All students are welcome here. It doesn't matter how they look or if they are different from us. If we judge someone before we get to know them, we might miss making a good friend.**
2. Encourage additional questions and comments.

Curriculum Connections

Vocabulary: *assume, belief, different/differences, fair, judge, respect*

Language Arts/Social Studies:

- Age-appropriate literature can help initiate sensitive discussions about prejudice. Use it to illustrate different points of view and to encourage discussion about accepting and respecting differences, standing up for what is right, or supporting human rights. Some examples to include in your class library are *The Black Book of Colors* (Menena Cottin), *Andy, That's My Name,* or *Oliver Button Is a Sissy* (Tomie dePaola), *Thank You, Mr. Falker* (Patricia Polacco), *Stand Tall, Molly Lou Melon* (Patty Lovell), *Chrysanthemum* (Kevin Henkes), *Fireflies!* (Julie Brinckloe), *My Name Is Yoon* (Helen Recorvits and Gabi Swiatkowska), *The Other Side* (Jacqueline Woodson), *White Socks Only* (Evelyn Coleman), *The Story of Ruby Bridges* (Robert Coles), *Teammates* (Peter Golenbock), *Don't Laugh at Me* (Steve Seskin and Allen Shamblin), *Fly Away Home* (Eve Bunting), *Crow Boy* (Taro Yashima), *Wabi Sabi* (Mark Reibstein), *The Ugly Duckling* (Hans Christian Andersen), *Sleeping Ugly* (Jane Yolen), and *Abuela's Weave* (Omar Casteneda).

- Use magazines like *National Geographic Kids* to teach the class about people from other countries and their cultures. Pay special attention to ways articles link to diversity in your classroom and students' own communities.

- Use resources such as *The Kids' Multicultural Cookbook* (Deanna F. Cook) to try recipes from around the world. Ask students to share their favorite recipes. Look for similarities and differences in ingredients and preparation.

Music: Have students listen to folk music and musical instruments from a variety of cultures.

Art: Encourage students to try art activities such as those suggested in *The Kids' Multicultural Art Book: Art & Craft Experiences from Around the World* (Alexandra M. Terzian).

Physical Education: Teach children games from other cultures using resources such as *Kids Around the World Play! The Best Fun and Games from Many Lands* (Arlette N. Braman).

Category 7

Serving the Community/Reaching Outward

(Two class meetings)

Kindergarten–Grade 2

Category: Serving the Community/Reaching Outward

Topic: Raising Awareness

We Can Help Others

Background

Young students may not always be sure if behavior is teasing or bullying, but they do understand how unkind behaviors make them feel. Adults can encourage perspective-taking and empathy by modeling ways to care for those who are mistreated. Adults can also help students think about ways to help create a peaceful school environment. This class meeting should be conducted after discussing how negative behaviors make students feel (category 2: *Identifying Feelings*) and about school hot spots (category 4: *Hot Spots*).

Learner Outcomes

By the end of this session, students will be able to

- discuss ways that unfriendly and unkind behaviors affect all students at school
- identify ways to share anti-bullying messages within their classroom and school

Materials Needed

- Chalkboard, dry erase board, or chart paper
- Three different colored markers or chalk

Preparation Needed

- On the board or chart paper, draw a large, simple map of the school that includes areas students use such as hallways, lunchroom, library, and playground.
- Decide with other teachers doing this same class meeting how classes might work together to make these areas more welcoming.

Class Meeting Outline

Opening Activity (15 minutes)

1. **We're going to work on a project together to find ways that we can make our whole school feel more welcome and friendly.** If this will be a joint project with other classes, briefly state that here.
2. **Whenever we do a big project like this, we need to do some thinking and planning first. That's what we're going to do today.**
3. Refer to the map you drew of the school. **Here is a map of the places you use every day in our school.** Orient students to how the map represents spaces they use.
4. **In which places do you think students feel the most welcome? the least welcome?** Use one color marker to draw a star in areas where students generally have positive feelings, use another color to draw an X where students generally have negative feelings, and the third color to draw a question mark where students have mixed feelings.
5. **Remember when we talked about places at school where some students didn't feel welcome—sometimes because they were physically hurt, left out, or called names?** (If the term "hot spots" was used to discuss these areas, use it here as well.)
6. **Let's look at each place on the map where we marked an X. For each one, let's think of words or actions we could use to make other students feel happier to be there.** (Some ideas might include: smile and say something pleasant to others, help others if they drop something, include others in activities, or help others if they are having a hard time.)
7. **Now let's look at those areas we marked with a question mark. What could be done to help people feel more comfortable in these areas?**

8. In each spot, write students' suggestions, probing as much as possible to get them to stretch their thinking and be specific.

Discussion Questions (10 minutes)

1. Process the activity.

   a. **We still need to do some work in our school to make sure everyone feels safe and welcome. We can help others and make our school better when we work together.**

   b. **Let's look at the ideas you mentioned in our discussion.** Review the ideas you wrote on the map.

   c. Take a vote to see which areas in the school students think need the most help. Circle the top three on the map.

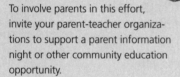

Teacher Tip

To involve parents in this effort, invite your parent-teacher organizations to support a parent information night or other community education opportunity.

   d. **Next, let's think of a way we can share our ideas with other students in the school (outside of our classroom).** Propose ideas for a project such as posters or placards, bulletin boards, a "quilt" of student art, or a positive slogan to place on a banner or button. Based on feedback with possible partners in other classrooms, help students in kindergarten and grade 1 choose one project idea for the whole class to work on; students in grade 2 can choose several ideas that small groups of students can work on together.

2. Tell students how their ideas will be shared with other partners in this project.

Wrap-Up

1. **Thank you for sharing your thoughts and for wanting to help. Together, we can make sure our school is a friendly place where everyone feels welcome. In our next class meeting, we're going to do more work on our project using your good ideas.**

2. Encourage additional questions and comments.

Curriculum Connections

Vocabulary: *action, aware, banner, initials, peaceful, poster, quilt, responsibility*

Language Arts:

- Provide literature in your class library or pictures that tell about people working together to solve a problem in their community. Examples include cleaning up a deserted lot, creating a community playground, or collecting clothing or food for a relief effort.

- Create word pyramids with students: the top word names an area of the school such as the playground or lunchroom; words that branch out beneath describe positive ways to interact there (such as share, take turns, say please and thank you, or clean up your space).

- Students in grade 2 could use the dictionary to find an opposite positive feeling word for each unwelcome feeling listed on the opening activity map.

Community/Cross-Grade: With other teachers, define areas that each class or grade can target to deliver bullying-prevention messages (posters, buttons, cookies, banners). Use this as an opportunity for multi-class or cross-grade projects.

Kindergarten–Grade 2

Category: Serving the Community/Reaching Outward

Topic: Reaching Out

Reach Out and Teach Someone

Background

When students share what they have learned about bullying prevention with others, it not only reinforces those concepts for them but also emphasizes that they are part of a larger community. Community outreach at this age level will be most meaningful if done within the school building itself and then discussed at home with family members. The class meeting We Can Help Others, on pages 156–159, is a prerequisite for this class meeting. If this project is a collaborative or cross-grade effort, it will take more than one class period or may be extended into an art period. This project might be used to prepare an all-school assembly to introduce the *Olweus Bullying Prevention Program* to new students and to review the rules and expectations for positive behavior for all students if all classes become involved. This can be an educational, exciting experience for younger students and an inspiring event for older students, parents, and the educators and staff at school.

Learner Outcomes

By the end of this session, students will be able to
- develop positive messages about ways to prevent bullying
- work together with classmates to develop a project on bullying prevention
- share bullying-prevention messages with others in the school

Materials Needed

- Art supplies for the project selected

Preparation Needed

- If desired, collaborate with other teachers to coordinate project(s).
- Make arrangements to display the finished project(s) around the school building.
- Set out materials.

Teacher Tip

Keep the project as simple as possible! Choose materials that require minimal setup and cleanup.

Class Meeting Outline

Opening Activity (15–20 minutes)

1. **Today we're going to work on our project to help make our school a friendlier place.**
2. **Here is what we will be doing.** Explain the project and show the materials.
3. Assign students to work individually or in small groups according to the project chosen. (See pages 13–14 for ideas and strategies for grouping students.)
4. If students are not able to finish their work within the time allowed, offer options for them to complete the work during another period, at home, or in another class meeting.

Teacher Tips

- Plan a celebration or unveiling of student efforts. Invite family members and key community leaders to view the work and take pride in the completed project.

- Contests that judge and select winning ideas are popular in many schools. Use this project, however, as an opportunity for students to work cooperatively, where everyone's voice and message matter. This approach is more in keeping with the *OBPP* philosophy about building a collaborative community.

Discussion Questions (10 minutes)

1. Process the activity.
   a. **Let's take a minute to take a look at what we've done!** Walk around and compliment what students have done.
   b. Invite students to comment on ways they worked together.
2. **You've all worked so hard on this project! I'd like to invite families and others in our school to see the good work you have done and to celebrate with us.** Give students two or three options for a celebration event

and then have them vote. Possible ideas include holding a celebration breakfast, an evening "artists' opening," or an unveiling event during school.

Wrap-Up

1. **You've all worked really hard on our project. This project will help everyone make our school a friendlier place.**
2. Encourage additional questions and comments.

Curriculum Connections

Vocabulary: *community, cooperate, share*

Language Arts:

- As a class, prepare invitations for families and others to view students' completed project(s). Pre-readers can draw pictures on preprinted invitations. Older students can copy invitation text from an original or use the classroom computer to generate text and design and print out invitations.

- Students in grade 2 could document the project process: If a digital camera is available, take pictures and assign students to write narrations for each. If no camera is available, assign different groups to draw and write commentary on different aspects of the project. Publish and post these with the final project (like an art show), compile into a class book, or post on a bulletin board.

Category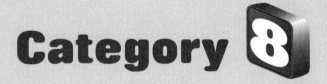

Using Current Events

(One class meeting)

Kindergarten–Grade 2

Category: Using Current Events

Topic: Understanding Media Messages

News Flash: Is It True?

Background

Many teachers incorporate current events into their regular curricula through student newspapers, magazines, news postings, and announcements. Even very young children are exposed to messages from a wide range of print and other media, including television, videos, the Internet, and radio. These messages shape their views about bullying and related topics about gender roles, appearance, and acceptable behavior. At an age when students are still learning to distinguish reality from fantasy, it is not too early to use media to teach them to distinguish whether what they hear and see is fact, fiction, or opinion. This class meeting should be conducted after students have had some experience using age-appropriate news sources.

Learner Outcomes

By the end of this session, students will be able to
- identify different ways to get news
- discuss different ways news is presented
- decide whether headlines are true, false, or opinions

Materials Needed

- News Flash: Is It True? on page 168
- Chart paper and marker

- Samples of recent age-appropriate student news sources such as *Time for Kids, Weekly Reader, Ranger Rick,* or *Scholastic News Online*

Preparation Needed

- Students should know how to identify a headline or main feature story before beginning this session.
- Read through the News Flash: Is It True? headlines and decide which ones you will use. Or create headlines using other sources, such as those listed in Materials Needed.

Teacher Tip

Use familiar samples of age-appropriate student news media (see Materials Needed) to illustrate and explain the concept of headlines to students. Help students practice finding headlines and saying what the main story is about.

Class Meeting Outline

Opening Activity (10–15 minutes)

1. **We are all curious about what's happening in the world around us. We all learn a lot of interesting things from the news. How do you learn about the news?** Display news media you use in the classroom and highlight media that students use at home.

2. **We've learned some amazing things from our news.** Refer to past examples, such as animals that have done remarkable things or people who have accomplished wonderful things. Include familiar local and other news as appropriate.

3. **We're going to play a game called News Flash. Who knows what a news flash is? It is a short sentence or headline that quickly tells us something.**

4. **I will read you a news flash and you will tell me whether it is true (or a fact), or whether it's not true or** `Grade 2:` **whether you think it's an opinion or belief.**

5. **Let's start with an example. News Flash!: (Your name) is a new student at (your school).**
   - **Is that true? Stand up if you think it is. Stay seated if you think it's NOT true.**
   - **How do you know it's not true?**

Teacher Tips

- While this session is focused on using media in current events, the underlying skills of learning to differentiate fact from fiction and understanding what an opinion is can help students in dealing with verbal bullying, gossip, and rumors.

- Even the youngest students seem to know what is happening with their favorite musicians, athletes, or actors! Be aware of current entertainment news that your students may be interested in and include that in discussions as appropriate.

6. **Let's try some more.** After you read each headline you chose, remind students: **Stand if you think it's true, stay seated if you think it is not true.** Grade 2: **Raise your hand if you think it's an opinion or if you need more information.**

7. Pause between items to allow students to briefly say why they thought something was true or not true (or an opinion). Note items that were difficult and review concepts later as needed.

Discussion Questions (10–15 minutes)

1. Process the activity.

   a. **Were any of these tricky? Which ones?**

   b. **What made it hard to decide whether something was true?**

   c. **Did we all agree whether something was true or not true (or an opinion)? Why do you think so?**

   d. **How can you find out whether something is true or not true?**

   e. **Have you ever heard something about another student that you weren't sure was true?** Remind students not to repeat names. **What did you do to check the facts?**

Dig Deeper

All About Explorers (www.allaboutexplorers.com) is a Web site that teaches elementary-aged students how to evaluate Internet sources to determine if something is fact or fiction. A teacher section contains lesson plans for helping students determine fact from fiction in reports.

2. Grade 2:

   a. **Have you ever heard something about another student that sounded like an opinion?**

   b. **If you think something might be an opinion instead of a fact, how can you get more information?**

Wrap-Up

1. **It's important to learn about what is happening in our world to people, places, and living things. You learn about the news here at school, and when you are at home, too. Sometimes it's hard to know if something is true or not true. Always be sure to ask lots of questions and to check the facts if you aren't sure.**

2. Encourage additional questions and comments.

Curriculum Connections

Vocabulary: *headline, news flash, true/not true;* Grade 2: *fact/fiction, opinion, true/false*

Language Arts:

- Read *The True Story of the Three Little Pigs!* (Jon Scieszka) and the traditional version of the same fairy tale. Compare points of view of the pigs versus the wolf and how that changes our views about what happened.

- Rewrite or retell a common fairy tale or nursery rhyme from a different point of view: such as "Miss Muffet" from the spider's point of view or "Goldilocks" from the three bears' viewpoint. Ask students to identify ways that different points of view may change how we view the facts.

Science/Social Studies: Select a picture from a newspaper or student news magazine, or use pictures students bring from home. Have students identify the headline or write a news flash for the picture.

News Flash: Is It True?

Instructions: Choose three to six items to present to your students. Include items you have created based on content from news media familiar to your students. Mix up true and untrue items. **Grade 2:** Mix in opinions with true and untrue items.

Birds Use Wings to Fly (true)

Dolphins "Talk" to Each Other (true)

Butterflies Fly Thousands of Miles Each Winter (true)

Scientists Say Water Is Not Wet (not true)

Live Dinosaur Discovered in (our state) (not true)

(Cartoon character) Starting as Principal of (name of our school) (not true)

Grade 2:

Dogs Are the Best Pets (opinion)

Everyone Should Eat Spaghetti (opinion)

Chocolate Ice Cream: Everyone's Favorite Flavor (opinion)

Winter Is the Best Season of the Year (opinion)

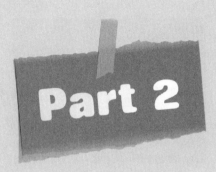

Part 2

....

**Class Meetings
for Grades 3-5**

Category 1

Building a Positive Classroom Climate

(Four class meetings)

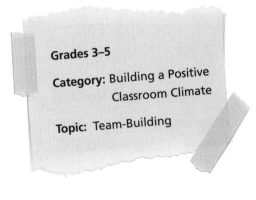

Grades 3–5

Category: Building a Positive
Classroom Climate

Topic: Team-Building

Human Scavenger Hunt

Background

Students in grades 3–5 are becoming more selective about whom they choose as friends. These relationships are now more centered on common interests with peers who are their same age and gender. Helping students create a broader and more inclusive circle of friends expands their social support systems and makes them less likely to be isolated when shifts in friendships occur. Learning more about classmates helps students practice perspective-taking and increases empathy, both of which are important in preventing bullying. This session encourages students to go "outside their comfort zones" to talk with classmates with whom they might not normally interact and to learn things they might have in common.

Learner Outcomes

By the end of this session, students will be able to
- understand more about classmates
- practice ways of initiating conversations and asking polite questions
- define empathy and awareness about peers' individual needs
- discuss things they have in common with peers

Materials Needed

- Human Scavenger Hunt Game Cards on page 175

- Human Scavenger Hunt Worksheet on page 176 and a pencil for each student
- Two containers (one for each set of game cards)

Preparation Needed

- Copy the Human Scavenger Hunt Game Cards and cut into two sets as instructed. Place each set in a separate container. (Note: There are spaces at the end of each column to create your own cards based on things you know about your group, or based on ideas submitted by students.)
- Copy one Human Scavenger Hunt Worksheet for each student.

Class Meeting Outline

Opening Activity (15 minutes)

1. **How many of you have ever been on a scavenger hunt or know how it works?** If there are students unfamiliar with this, ask others to help explain that it is a game where you have a list of things you have to find.

2. **We're going to do a human scavenger hunt. Instead of finding objects, you will have to find out facts about your classmates.** Give each student a worksheet and pencil.

   a. **To play, I will draw two slips of paper—one from each of these containers. One slip will tell you WHO to ask, the other slip will tell you WHAT to find out.**

   b. **The idea is to talk to as many different students for each fact as you can, not just the people you know best.**

   c. **Once you find a person to ask the question, write that person's name and answer on your worksheet. For now, leave the column labeled "Same as Me?" blank.**

   d. **Let's practice once.** Draw a slip from each container, read the WHO slip first, wait a moment; read the WHAT slip next. Allow students about a minute to find someone and ask the question.

Dig Deeper

- For students with limited language proficiency or social skills, model and practice this activity in advance so they are able to participate.

- Small-group projects can sometimes cause tension among students and can reinforce existing social hierarchies. Help promote teamwork by beginning any group project with icebreaker questions, such as those offered in this session, to give students an opportunity to learn more about each other.

e. **Let's begin. Here's the first item on our hunt!** Allow about a minute for each "hunt" item, watching to see if students need more or less time. Make sure each student finds at least one person for an item before moving on to the next. Expect students in grade 3 to finish about five items; students in grade 5 should find more in the time allotted.

Discussion Questions (15 minutes)

1. Process the activity.

   a. **On your worksheets, count up the number of *different* girls who answered your questions. Write that number on the line next to the word "Girls." Then count up the number of *different* boys who answered your questions. Write that number on the line next to the word "Boys." Add those two numbers together and write the total on the line next to the word "Total."** Congratulate students on their efforts.

   b. Grades 4–5: **Who got more answers from boys than girls? Who got more answers from girls than boys?** Comment on gender patterns that surface. Did boys tend to talk to boys and girls talk to girls? If so, ask students why that happened.

   c. **How many of you were able to find someone to answer all the questions? If not, what made it hard?**

   d. **What things did you find out about each other that you didn't know? What answers surprised you?**

2. **Look at your worksheets again. You'll see a column on the right labeled "Same as Me?" Put an X in spaces where you found something in common with (or the "same" as) the person you talked to. Count up your X marks and raise your hand if you had at least three Xs.** Make a personal note of students who did not raise their hands and observe them more closely over the next week. Students with little in common with peers may be more isolated from them, or even excluded. **How many of you learned that you have something in common with someone you don't know well?**

Wrap-Up

1. **The more we know about each other, the more we understand each other. Sometimes it is surprising to find out how many things we have in common, and to learn about ways that we are unique, or different.**

Learning about each other can help us to get along and to work better together as a class. The more people we know, the more choices we have if we need someone to turn to when we need help or are looking for a friend.

2. Encourage additional questions and comments.

Curriculum Connections

Vocabulary: *common, different, gender, scavenger, similar, unique*

Language Arts: Instruct students to make a list of six questions they would like to ask classmates about themselves.

Math: Have students tally responses about similarities they have with peers (for example, the number of students who have a pet, who have a sister, who like computer games). Help them graph the results. Incorporate the use of fractions or percentages (for example, What fraction of our classmates have a relative who lives outside of our state?)

Science: Over the next week, observe whether girls seem to prefer certain activities while boys seem to prefer others. Chart the results.

Human Scavenger Hunt Game Cards

Instructions: Copy the cards and cut them apart. Select the cards that are appropriate for your group. You will need at least six to eight Who to Ask cards, and six to eight What to Ask cards.

WHO to Ask:	WHAT to Ask:
Someone who is the opposite gender	Do you have a pet? If so, what kind?
Someone who has a different color eyes from yours	Do you have brothers or sisters? If so, how many?
Someone who lives on a different street	What is your birthday (month and day)?
Someone in a different reading group	What is your favorite snack food?
Someone wearing red	What is your favorite color?
Someone wearing sneakers	What do you like to do after school?
Someone with the same color hair as yours	Does any of your family live in another state or country? If so, where?
Someone with long hair	Do you like to play computer games? If so, what is your favorite?
Someone wearing jeans	What is your favorite song?
Someone who is taller than you are	What do you like to do in the summertime?
A girl	Do you like to read? If so, what do you like to read?
A boy	Can you play a musical instrument? If so, what instrument?
Someone with different color hair than yours	Do you have a favorite hobby? If so, what is it?
Someone who is shorter than you	Can you speak another language? If so, which language?

Human Scavenger Hunt Worksheet

WHO	WHAT	Same as Me?

I asked:

_____ Girls

_____ Boys

_____ Total

Grades 3–5

Category: Building a Positive Classroom Climate

Topic: Team-Building

Cooperative Relay

Background

Many students are involved in team and group activities that tend to be competitive in nature. While competition can teach certain skills or motivate us to do better, research shows that it can also result in increased aggression that can last well after the competition has ended. Competition can also reinforce tendencies of students in middle childhood to be somewhat arbitrary or rigid about following rules. In contrast, cooperative games help students this age to build connections and a sense of teamwork that promotes collaboration rather than competition.

Learner Outcomes

By the end of this session, students will be able to
- practice working together as a team to achieve a goal
- practice assisting others who need help
- build awareness about the consequences of not being kind to each other

Materials Needed

- Six to eight objects. Include sturdy or easy-to-pass objects (such as a large sponge, soft ball or hacky sack, cereal box or shoebox, shoe, hat, roll of masking or duct tape, lemon or orange) and more fragile or less-easy-to-pass objects (such as a feather, small inflated balloon, paper plate, paper cup, small empty milk carton, hardboiled egg in shell).

- Two containers large enough to hold all objects
- Kitchen timer with a bell/buzzer

Preparation Needed

- Gather objects into one container, leaving the other container empty.
- Familiarize yourself with the activity rules.

Class Meeting Outline

Opening Activity (10–15 minutes)

1. **I have a basket of mystery objects here** (do not show items). **I will tell you that no two are alike and that some are more sturdy or fragile than others.**

2. **How many of you have played relay races before? A relay is a game or race where team members work together to finish the game or complete the task.**

3. **This relay is different because we are all going to be on the same team, and speed is not our goal. Instead, we will see if we can pass each object without damaging it. Here are the rules:**

   a. **You'll be (sitting or standing) in a circle** (or in a line for grade 3) **and you'll pass each object from one person to the other from this basket to this empty one, *without using your hands.***

   b. **Instead of hands, use your forearms and elbows.** Demonstrate by holding an object between your forearms or elbows.

   c. **Every person has to help pass each object.**

   d. **You can help if someone drops an item or is having trouble, as long as you don't use your hands.** If an item is dropped, students don't need to start over. The object may be picked up and passed along from where it was dropped.

   e. **Work as carefully as you can to move each object. When you hear the timer, stop wherever you are.**

4. Arrange students in a circle or line, either sitting or standing (passing objects while in a circle and standing is most challenging). Place the empty basket in the center of the circle (or far end of the line).

5. **I will start the relay by giving an object to (name first person). Everyone hold up your right hand. Pass the object to the person on your right, until it gets to the last person. This person is in charge of carefully putting it in the other basket.** If you think your students won't be too confused, you can increase the challenge for older students by either starting new objects with different people or beginning with a new object before the first has reached the basket.

6. Set the timer for 10 minutes. **Ready? GO!** Start with an object like a ball or sponge that is relatively easy to pass without damaging it— then gradually give students more fragile or difficult items.

7. End the game when the timer goes off, even if students haven't finished passing an object. It doesn't matter whether students moved all the objects.

Discussion Questions (10–15 minutes)

1. Process the activity: Arrange objects from the "finish" basket on the floor to examine as a group. Ask students about each object:
   - **Does this look the way it did when we started?**
   - **What happened to it? Did you expect this might get damaged when it was passed? Why or why not?**

2. **Which objects were more difficult to pass or took more cooperation to pass than others? Why?**

3. **What are examples of the ways you and your classmates helped each other?**
   - **What were good things about being able to help others?**
   - **Did some kinds of help work better than others? Explain.**
   - **What did you learn about teamwork and cooperation from this activity?**

Wrap-Up

1. **There are many chances for our class to work together as a team. The more we practice ways of working together, the better our results will be. You worked together and helped each other in many different ways today. Let's think about other ways we can make our class better by cooperating and working together.**

2. Encourage additional questions and comments.

Curriculum Connections

Vocabulary: *collaborate, cooperate, effective, fragile/sturdy*

Language Arts: Have students work in pairs to talk about a time when they were part of a team or group (sports, scouts, youth activity). Ask pairs to write about things that made the team strong. They should also give examples of ways team members cooperated and worked together, versus examples of things that made working on a team a frustrating or disappointing experience.

Physical Education: Use cooperative games to build teamwork. Emphasize the collaborative aspects of teamwork and elements of good sportsmanship, rather than focusing on "star" players or winning.

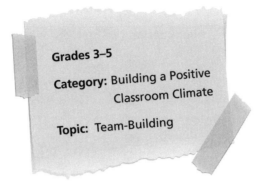

Circles of Caring

Background

Attempting to build self-esteem by spotlighting individual achievements can overemphasize the importance of "me" to the detriment of "us." This common practice can contribute to separation between students. By reinforcing cohesiveness, adults help students begin to view each other as part of their circle of caring. As a result, students are more likely to feel responsible for each other and are less likely to bully peers. They also are more likely to include peers in activities or to respond in helpful ways when a classmate needs assistance.

Learner Outcomes

By the end of this session, students will be able to
- discuss how they are all part of a community
- use the concept of "circles of caring" to identify sources of social support
- discuss how people adjust their behavior depending on their relationships with others

Materials Needed

- Circles of Caring on page 185
- Pencil for each student
- Chalkboard, dry erase board, or chart paper and chalk or markers

Preparation Needed

- Draw a Circles of Caring diagram (without the labels) on the board or chart paper.
- Make copies of the Circles of Caring worksheet, one per student.
- Identify a chant, song, cheer, or rap that has a friendship or teamwork theme to use as a closing.

Class Meeting Outline

Opening Activity (10–15 minutes)

Teacher Tips

- Use vignettes or concrete examples to role-play ways of greeting or interacting with people in each Circle of Caring.

- Be sensitive about what might constitute "family" for your students. This activity may allow discussion about who might fit into that second circle and how students define family. Be careful not to assume that family is "who you live with" or even "who provides care for you."

1. **Today we're going to talk about relationships. We all have relationships with people at school and with friends, family, and others.**

2. Show students the Circles of Caring diagram you created. **We are going to use this diagram to help us think about the different kinds of relationships we have with others.**

3. **We are each in the center of our circles.** Write Self in the center circle.

4. **What kind of relationships might be the next circle closest to us? For most people, our families are the next closest to us. We sometimes refer to this circle as our "immediate" or "inner circle."** Write Family in the second circle.

5. **Who might be next in our circle of caring? For many people, friends would be the next closest to us after our family.** Write Friends in the next circle.

6. **Other schoolmates or acquaintances are next. An acquaintance is someone we don't know very well, but we still know who that person is.** Write Acquaintances and Classmates in the last circle.

7. **Last are people in the circle farthest from our immediate or inner circle. Who might that include?** Write Strangers and People We Haven't Met Yet outside the circle. **These might be people we will have a relationship with someday. We can still care about people we put in this spot.**

8. Give each student a Circles of Caring diagram and a pencil. **For the next 3 minutes, I want you to write who you'd place in each of these circles.**

Discussion Questions (10–15 minutes)

1. Process the activity as a whole group or in groups of two to four students.

   - **Was it hard to decide who you wrote in some categories? which ones?** Grade 5: **How did you decide?**
   - **How many of you included cousins, aunts, uncles, and grandparents when you wrote your family into the diagram? You don't necessarily have to live in the same house with someone you're related to in order to think of that person as family.**

Teacher Tip

In a separate discussion, consider ways to interact with people in the stranger category. Include topics such as when it is safe/unsafe to talk with a stranger, child assault prevention tips, and cyber-safety.

   - **What is a friend? If you aren't friends with some of your classmates, does that mean that you don't care about them?**
   - **Are there times when it might be a good idea to include someone who is not a friend in an activity? How could you do that even if that person isn't your friend?**
   - **Does including someone in an activity or reaching out to someone mean you have to be his or her friend?**

2. Grades 4–5:

   - **Why is it important to show caring for people we don't know very well?**
   - **What do you think makes us care about people we have never met?** (For example, people affected by natural disasters or war or poverty.) **What are examples of times when you helped someone you didn't know?**

3. Grade 5:

   - **In your opinion, is it a good thing or a bad thing that we treat people in our different circles differently?** Write students' responses in two separate columns on chart paper: Positive/Advantages and Negative/Disadvantages.
   - **Is it easier to care for people in some circles? which ones? Why do you think that is?**
   - **Does caring for people who are outside of our circle of caring feel different from the way we care for family or friends?**

Wrap-Up

1. **We all feel closer to some people than to others, and it's normal for our friendships to change over time. Including someone in your circles of caring doesn't mean you have to be good friends. But everyone in our class should treat each other with kindness and respect. We all need to rely on each other for help and to work together to accomplish our goals. Together we are stronger.**

2. End by having students stand in a circle for a class song or cheer.

Curriculum Connections

Vocabulary: *acquaintance, betray, concentric circles, criteria, differentiate, empathy, family, friend, interact, relationship, responsibility, trust*

Language Arts: Have students fill in a Circles of Caring diagram for a character from an age-appropriate literature selection such as *Molly's Pilgrim* (Barbara Cohen), *The Hundred Dresses* (Eleanor Estes), or *Wringer* (Jerry Spinelli). Discuss ways the main character's interactions varied with people in different circles.

Community Service: Help students choose and organize a community service project that helps people they don't know. Examples include collecting toys, books, or clothes for disaster relief or a local Head Start program; raising money for a cause such as the Heifer Project (www.heifer.org); performing songs at a local senior center; helping to clean up a park; or volunteering at an animal shelter. Resources that provide ideas about ways students can get involved in charitable efforts include Reach Out and Give (Cheri J. Meiners and Meredith Johnson), www.dosomething.org, and www.networkforgood.org.

**STRANGERS AND PEOPLE
WE HAVEN'T MET YET**

**ACQUAINTANCES
AND CLASSMATES**

FRIENDS

FAMILY

SELF

Grades 3–5

Category: Building a Positive Classroom Climate

Topic: Team-Building

Class Murals

Background

A skill that will serve students well throughout their lives is being able to work cooperatively. While group work is a part of student life, these settings can be a source of frustration and conflict both for students who possess good social skills and for those who have difficulty with social interactions. All students can benefit from practice working with others, learning to take leadership without being bossy, and negotiating the ups and downs of group participation. This session provides a framework for students to improve their listening and problem-solving skills, practice different leadership roles, and collaborate with others. This activity may require more than a typical class meeting, but portions can be conducted as part of cross-curriculum work or as homework, rather than in multiple class meetings. You may wish to involve the school's art teacher in this class meeting.

Learner Outcomes

By the end of this session, students will be able to
- work together as a team to complete a project
- discuss ways to resolve difficulties encountered in working as a group
- contribute to a positive classroom climate

Materials Needed

- Chart paper
- Index cards (3 x 5 inch) or slips of paper (one per student)
- Large, "mural-sized" sheets of paper (one for each group)
- Markers or paints
- *Optional:* Camera to document phases of the work project

Preparation Needed

- Write the following heading on chart paper: The Way We Want Our Class to Be.
- Plan how you will divide students into work groups of four to six students each. In each group, include students who have different talents or interests (information gatherers, artistic consultants, quality control managers, recorders/documenters, and peacekeepers/diplomats). (See pages 13–14 for ideas and strategies for grouping students.)
- Search the Internet for examples of "community murals" to inspire students. Print out several examples to share with the class or show them on available computers. Sites that provide information about the process involved in creating the murals may be interesting or helpful to you or students.

Class Meeting Outline

Opening Activity (10–15 minutes)

1. **How many of you know what a mural is or have ever seen one?** If students don't know, explain that a mural is a kind of wall painting.
2. **Here are some examples I thought you might like to look at.** Show examples of community art murals from Web sites and tell a little about them. (Many are developed to bring communities together, to make changes, or to celebrate something.) Give students time to discuss what they like about the different examples.
3. **We are going to create our own murals that show how we want our class to be. This project will take us some time and will need teamwork and cooperation. We'll be doing this in several parts, sometimes working as a whole class, sometimes in small groups.** If this project is going to

be done as a cross-curricular project, explain to students how that will work.

4. **Let's begin by thinking about words or phrases that describe how we'd like our class to be.** Write students' responses on the chart paper.

Discussion Questions (10–15 minutes for steps 1–4; 10–15 minutes for step 5, once project is completed)

1. Process the planning activity.

    a. **You had a chance to look at different kinds of murals. Some show one main theme or idea, others incorporate more than one. How do you think we should do our mural (one idea or several)?**

    b. Call attention to the list students created about how they would like their class to be. Have them vote on which concept(s) or idea(s) they would like to work on.

2. Divide the class into their preassigned work groups. **Each group will create its own mural. I want you to try out new ways of working together that feel fair and cooperative. Each group will have**
    - **information gatherers**
    - **artistic consultants**
    - **quality control managers**
    - **recorders/documenters**
    - **peacekeepers/diplomats**

3. Spend a few minutes talking about what each role entails, specifically what students should do to carry out their job description. (See Ideas and Strategies for Grouping Students on pages 13–14 for general descriptions of these roles.) Give students a few more minutes to brainstorm how they will work together in their groups or designate a time for them to meet together to do this.

4. Announce to the class when their next work periods will be and/or what portions, if any, they will be assigned as homework.

5. Process the activity upon completion.
    - **What do you think of our finished murals?** Invite students to say a few words about their murals.
    - **How did group members show they listened to each other? How were everyone's ideas used?**
    - **What ways did your small groups work well together? What things made working together challenging sometimes?** Evaluate or problem-solve the group process. **What kinds of**

behaviors led to problems? What are examples of how you solved (or tried to solve) problems?

- Grades 4–5: What kinds of help did you need to make sure things went smoothly?
- Grades 4–5: What did you like about these different kinds of jobs? Did you think they were fair? Did they help students cooperate?

Wrap-Up

1. Be sure to display the murals around the room. If possible, display photos documenting the process as well.
2. After each meeting or phase of this project, compliment students on their efforts. Provide specific feedback about ways you've noticed they worked together productively and cooperatively. Be sure to invite their feedback. End the project with a celebration.

Curriculum Connections

Vocabulary: *collaboration, inspiration, mural, resolve, role;* words used to describe group roles; words used to describe "ways we want our class to be"

Language Arts: Have students write narratives to go with pictures taken to document the process of creating the mural. Assign students different photos to write about.

Social Studies/Math/Science: Incorporate cooperative roles for group projects in other subject areas using the tips and ideas on pages 13–14. Ask students to evaluate how the roles work and whether some roles work better for some projects than for others.

Art: Discuss various community mural projects: how the project got started, what was involved, what kind of help people got, how they worked together.

Category 2

Identifying Feelings

(Four class meetings)

Grades 3–5

Category: Identifying Feelings

Topic: Building Empathy and Perspective-Taking

Lend a Hand

Background

Empathy is often viewed as understanding what someone else feels or experiences. This involves the ability to read body language and correctly label feelings. A second aspect of empathy that is particularly relevant to bullying prevention requires acting on our interpretations of those feelings in a way that is welcomed by the other person. Individuals who bully often know quite well what someone else is feeling—and know what "buttons to push" to get the reaction they want—but they use that information to cause distress in others. Students this age have the capacity to understand things from a different perspective, so the focus of developing empathy for them must shift to nurturing their impulses to treat others with compassion.

Learner Outcomes

By the end of this session, students will be able to
- define empathy
- describe how feelings differ depending on one's point of view
- practice compassionate responses to others
- demonstrate ways to make authentic amends when they hurt someone

Materials Needed

- Four to six large pictures of people showing different emotions (such as happy, sad, angry, afraid, dejected or lonely, confused, frustrated, proud)

Preparation Needed

None

Class Meeting Outline

Opening Activity (10–15 minutes)

Teacher Tips

- Prior to beginning this activity, you may want to check students' understanding of vocabulary related to personal feelings or emotions. Ask students to name words that describe feelings or emotions. Record all words on chart paper and hang in the classroom, serving as a word bank for future use.

- Use photographs or realistic drawings, rather than symbolic images such as a "smiley face." Include multicultural images of boys and girls, of individuals alone, and of people interacting with each other. If possible, include one photo of someone assisting someone else. (If you or colleagues do not have photos or drawings such as these at your school, you can find them in the children's section of public libraries or school supply outlets.)

1. **We're going to look very closely at some pictures today. When you look at each one, notice your very first reaction when you see it.** Hold up one card at a time for the class to view.

   a. **How do you feel when you see this picture?** Encourage students to use words describing emotions.

   b. **Sometimes, just looking at pictures can make us feel an emotion inside our own bodies. Did any of you feel something? Where in your body did you feel that emotion most?** Mention as appropriate: sadness, joy, and pride are sometimes felt in the chest or as a lump in the throat; anger can be felt in the "gut" or stomach; helplessness or rage might be felt in the upper back or shoulders; fear can cause a dry mouth or prickly sensations in the back of the neck, arms, or legs.

2. **It is amazing. Even when we don't know the people, our own bodies help us understand what they feel, even if they don't tell us. That special way of knowing how someone else feels is called empathy.** Students may be interested to know that newborn humans and even animals show primitive forms of empathy. One example they might understand is the way babies' crying is contagious: when one infant starts crying, others often quickly follow suit, and they react more strongly and consistently to human cries than other kinds of noise!

3. **Empathy is more than just feeling part of what someone else feels. It also makes us want to help others, even if we don't know them. We need to practice taking actions to show that we care about each other.** Choose one to two of the following to ask students: **What would you do if . . .**

   - **you saw another student you didn't know crying in the hall?**
   - **you saw two younger students arguing?**
   - **you saw someone drop his or her lunch and it was ruined?**
   - **you saw someone's papers fall all over the floor?**
   - **someone told you he or she just failed a test?**
   - **you found out a friend just won a prize or game?**
   - **your friend got the highest score in the class on a test?**
   - **you heard someone say something nice about your teacher?**
   - **you saw some older students being very kind to a younger student?**
   - **you saw someone slip and fall at recess?**
   - **someone said a mean name to the person standing next to you?**
   - **you saw some students playing a practical joke on another student?**

Teacher Tip

Older students may prefer photos pulled from current events or other photos that evoke strong feelings. Examples include a rescue, people dancing or celebrating, people grieving from a disaster or war, people arguing or fighting, people hugging or showing affection, animals in trouble, people receiving awards, and people assisting others.

Discussion Questions (15 minutes)

1. Process the activity.

   - **Can you think of any examples where you have felt empathy for someone else? How did you respond to that person? What did you do?**
   - **How has someone else shown empathy to you? What did that person do?**
   - **Were that person's actions helpful to you?**
   - **Has anyone ever responded to you in a way that wasn't helpful or wasn't what you needed? Like giving you a hug when you didn't want to be hugged? How did that feel?** Students need to be taught how to match their responses to what the other person needs and will welcome.

2. **How can empathy help us when we see or hear bullying?**

3. **If someone seems upset or if you think that person has been bullied, how can you show that person that you care (show empathy)?** (Responses might include listen and ask interested questions, spend time with the person, ask how the person is feeling, or ask what you could do to help.) Introduce and reinforce the idea that empathic responses should be meaningful to the recipient and may be different from what would be meaningful or helpful to us.

4. **What do you think it would be like if we didn't have empathy for others?**

5. **Do you think it's easier to feel empathy for someone you know or like? Why?**

6. **Do you think we expect boys to show empathy more than girls do or less than girls do? Why do you think so? Do you think it's okay for both girls and boys to show their feelings and to help others or show they care for them? Why or why not?**

Wrap-Up

1. **It's hard to imagine what our world would be like if people didn't feel and show empathy and caring for each other! Think for a minute about someone who has shown you empathy. Find a way to tell that person you appreciated what he or she said or did. Let that person know you are glad he or she cares!**

2. Compliment students when they show empathy for others.

Curriculum Connections

Vocabulary: *emotions, empathy, "gut reaction," image, interesting*

Language Arts: Discuss examples of characters in literature who did or did not show empathy for others. Students might read *Just Kidding* or *Sorry!* (Trudy Ludwig), *Horton Hears a Who!* (Dr. Seuss), *Wringer* (Jerry Spinelli), *Hey, Little Ant* (Phillip Hoose and Hannah Hoose), *The Liberation of Gabriel King* (K. L. Going), *Babe: The Gallant Pig* (Dick King-Smith), and *Charlotte's Web* (E. B. White). Read-aloud choices include *Not a Genuine Black Man* (Brian Copeland) and *The Little Prince* (Antoine de Saint-Exupéry).

Science: Involve students in an activity where they can care for animals or help them research how to help animals in trouble.

Social Studies/Community Service:

- Initiate an "Acts of Kindness" campaign where students are encouraged to help others.

- Involve students in planning a "Thank You" campaign for community volunteers or other community helpers. Suggestions include firefighters, police officers, EMTs, librarians, hospital workers, nurses, veterinarians, shelter and food pantry workers, teachers, and child care workers.

Grades 3–5

Category: Identifying Feelings

Topic: Managing Feelings about Bullying

Keeping Our Cool

Background

Many students in grades 3–5 are learning to see things from another person's perspective, to regulate their own impulses, and to control displays of emotions in public. These skills help them in bullying situations in several ways. First, they are better able to understand the negative effects bullying has on others. Second, they are better able to keep their cool if they are bullied or when they are defending someone else. This session focuses on the ways that bullying brings out different emotions depending on one's point of view, and it offers students some strategies to stay calm under pressure.

Learner Outcomes

By the end of this session, students will be able to
- identify emotions associated with different roles in bullying situations: the student who is bullied, the student doing the bullying, and the bystander
- discuss the harmful emotional effects of bullying and why stopping bullying is important
- promote tolerance by identifying differences in how people perceive different acts
- discuss and practice strategies for staying calm under pressure

Materials Needed

- Sentence Starters[4] on page 201
- Small bowls or envelopes, one per student group
- Pencils for each student
- Chalkboard, dry erase board, or chart paper and chalk or markers

Preparation Needed

- Copy and cut enough Sentence Starters so each group of four to six students has a complete set. Place each set of statements in a bowl or envelope, one per group.
- On the board or chart paper, create a diagram (see below) with ample space under each heading to write in student responses.

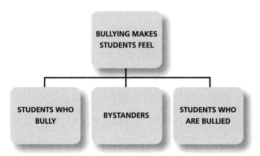

BULLYING MAKES STUDENTS FEEL

STUDENTS WHO BULLY | **BYSTANDERS** | **STUDENTS WHO ARE BULLIED**

Class Meeting Outline

Opening Activity (15 minutes)

1. **Each of us has our own feelings or thoughts about things. We call these our opinions or points of view. Personal opinions about bullying can affect how we feel and act, so it's important to understand more about people's different points of view.**

2. Divide the class into groups of four to six students. (See pages 13–14 for ideas and strategies for grouping students.) Give each group a set of Sentence Starters in a bowl or envelope.

   - **Take out all the Sentence Starters. Each strip has an incomplete sentence on it.**
   - **Read aloud all the sentences as a group.**

Dig Deeper

While strong feelings play a role in bullying behavior, these emotions are not limited to anger. In fact, anger, or misplaced anger, is not a factor in many instances of bullying, and anger management generally is not an effective tool for preventing or addressing bullying situations.

- **Quickly pass these around your group. As you do, each of you will write one word on the strip that you think best completes the sentence. Write the first word that pops into your head. If someone else has already written it, write a different word.**

3. Give students 1 to 2 minutes to complete the sentences. Encourage them to go with their first or "gut" reaction rather than to think hard. If some students have difficulty writing, someone in the group can write as others toss out ideas.

4. Using the diagram you created, ask each group to report. Write responses in the appropriate space on the diagram. Probe for ways someone in each category might feel, if students do not volunteer items for each. **What did your group write for:**
   - **Students who bully are . . . ?** (mean, powerful, popular, angry, strong, funny, etc.)
   - **Students who are bystanders are . . . ?** (scared, don't care, weak, uncertain, caring, strong, calm, etc.)
   - **Students who are bullied are . . . ?** (weak, scared, sad, angry, strong, crybabies, brave, etc.)
   - **Bullying makes students feel . . . ?** (powerful, sad, angry, scared, caring, etc.)

Discussion Questions (15 minutes)

1. Process the activity with all students in a circle.
   a. **What do you notice about your impressions of bystanders? about those who are bullied? those who bully others?**
   b. **What do you notice about how we think bullying makes people feel? Do you think all people feel the same way? Why?**
   c. **Do you think all bystanders feel the same way? Why or why not?**

2. **Why is bullying so harmful to the way people feel about themselves and each other? How can stopping bullying make us feel better about ourselves and each other?**

3. **People view things differently. Something that one person thinks is funny, someone else may think is bullying. Something one person feels is hurtful, someone else may think is no big deal.**
   a. **Without using names, give examples of things you have noticed like that.**

b. **Why do you think people have such different ways of think-ing about the same actions or words?**

c. **What can we do to show thoughtfulness to students who are bothered by some things that might not bother someone else?** Build students' sense of empathy by encouraging them to adjust their behaviors to the needs of the most sensitive members of the class, rather than viewing them as "overly sensitive" or lacking a sense of humor.

4. **Whether we are a bystander or whether we are being bullied, it helps to stay calm or keep our cool under pressure. Why might that be important?**

a. **What can you do to keep your cool or get con-trol of your emotions before you speak or act?** Practice positive suggestions as a whole group.

b. Practice as a group: **Take a few slow, calming breaths. How does that feel?**

c. Practice as a group: **Here are things you can think in your head to help you stay focused or calm under pressure:**

- **I am in control of my feelings.**
- **I am strong. I can do this.**
- **I am brave. I can do something.**
- **That's not true about (me, bullied person).**

d. **What could students who bully others think in their heads to stop themselves before they bully someone?** (Some examples might include: Would I like this if it were happening to me? What would my teacher or parents say if they saw me do this? Is this the kind of person I want to be?)

Dig Deeper

Students build confidence to respond to bullying when they are able to compe-tently identify and label their own feel-ings, to recognize body language clues in others, and to maintain control over their emotions in challenging situations.

Wrap-Up

1. **We know ways bullying behavior can hurt us—it affects each and every one of us in some way. When bullying happens, it can bring up strong and confusing feelings for many of us, even grown-ups. Those feelings can sometimes make it hard for us to know what to do. We can all learn to keep our cool and stop bullying at our school.**

2. Encourage additional questions and comments.

Curriculum Connections

Vocabulary: *believe, control, diagram, pressure, statement*

Language Arts: Suggest that students keep track of their feelings in a journal. They can also write about what triggers their emotions and how they are working to manage strong feelings in different situations.

Arts: Teach students to use drama, music, dance, and fine arts as a means of self-expression and as a creative release for strong feelings. Identify students for whom this would be a useful outlet.

Health/Physical Education: Teach students non-competitive games as a way of reducing aggression and promoting teamwork. Also encourage them to use exercise and physical activity to reduce and release stress.

Sentence Starters

Instructions: Copy the cards and cut them apart. Each group of four to six students will need one set of cards.

Students who bully are (describe):

Students who are bullied are (describe):

Students who are bystanders are (describe):

Bullying makes students feel (describe):

Grades 3–5

Category: Identifying Feelings

Topic: Expressing Strong
Feelings Assertively

Standing Tall and Speaking Up

Background

Between grades three and five, elementary-aged students are developing thinking, reasoning, and social skills that make this an ideal time to practice ways to act assertively and stand by others who may be bullied. To be effective, students still need adult assistance to learn to differentiate between assertive and aggressive body language. They also need opportunities to practice acting assertively in bullying situations. Additionally, adults' actions and assurances are needed to help build students' awareness of shifts in classroom and school norms that signify that standing up for what's right is "cool."

Learner Outcomes

By the end of this session, students will be able to

- demonstrate the differences between assertive and aggressive body language
- demonstrate ways to use assertive responses to stand up for peers in potential bullying situations
- discuss a range of responses they can use to deal with bullying and other difficult social situations

Materials Needed

- Standing Tall and Speaking Up Vignettes on page 207, one vignette per group (or create your own vignettes from student writing samples or your own experiences)
- Chalkboard, dry erase board, or chart paper and chalk or markers

Preparation Needed

- Make a copy of Standing Tall and Speaking Up Vignettes and cut cards apart.

Class Meeting Outline

Opening Activity (10–15 minutes)

Teacher Tip

Student stories and writing samples can provide a good resource for role-plays and discussion. Be sure to ask students' permission to use their stories and change identifying details as needed.

1. **Has anyone heard of the words "assertive" and "aggressive"? People who are** *assertive* **use strong, confident ways of talking and behaving. When you are assertive, you stand up for your beliefs in a positive way. Being assertive can help you with lots of situations in life, including bullying. When people are** *aggressive***, they try to force others to do what they want. Often they act in ways that are unkind or pushy.**

2. **First let's review how to be assertive without crossing the line to be aggressive. Pretend that I am a student who is bullying. I would like someone to please come up and demonstrate using assertive body language and voice tone to say "Stop that!"** Use 1 to 2 minutes to complete this demonstration, including the points below.
   - **What did (name) do with her/his voice to sound assertive? How did she/he hold her/his body? place her/his feet? use her/his arms?**
   - Point out subtle differences: **When you stand your ground, that's assertive. If you move forward into someone else's "bubble" of personal space, that becomes aggressive. Responding back with bullying actions or name-calling is always aggressive, not assertive.**

- If the student uses an aggressive tone or body language, either tell the student what to do differently or get input from the class: **That was close. What could (name) have done differently to be assertive, not aggressive?** Ask the student to try again.

3. Divide students into groups of four. (See pages 13–14 for ideas and strategies for grouping students.) Give each group one of the vignette cards. Assign one student in each group to play the character who bullies, one to play the character who is bullied, and two to be bystanders.

4. **Now you will work in small groups to practice being assertive in a bullying situation. You will not act out the bullying. Just practice using assertive words or actions. You will act out your situation two times.**

    a. **The first time, if you are playing the bullied character, use assertive words and body language that your character could say to the person who is pretending to bully you. You can say "Stop that!" or try something else that is assertive, not aggressive. The bystanders in your group will just watch and will not help.**

    b. **The second time both bystanders will be defenders. This time, *you* will be assertive with the character who is pretending to bully. You can either say "Stop that!" or try something else, as long as you stay assertive, not aggressive.**

5. After students have gone through the vignette twice, have them switch roles and repeat the scene until each student has had a chance to play every role (bullying student, bullied student, nonassertive bystander, assertive bystander). Each round will take about a minute or less. The emphasis is not on acting out a solution, but practicing quick assertive responses. Each time, encourage students to try new assertive behaviors.

6. Grade 3: Rather than dividing the class into groups, you may want to role-play one or more vignettes as a class.

7. Grades 4–5: You may want to choose one of the vignettes and demonstrate the activity before dividing the class into groups.

Discussion Questions (15 minutes)

1. Process the activity with all students together in a circle.

- When you were the bullying character, how did it feel when just the bullied student responded to you assertively? How did it feel when the bystanders took action? What was different?
- If you were the bullied student, how did it feel using assertive behavior on your own? How did it feel when the bystanders stepped in?
- If you were the bystanders, how did it feel to just watch? How was it different when you were able to help out?
- If this were an actual situation, would you have done anything differently?

2. **We just practiced ways to be assertive. Now let's list as many options as we can that a bystander could do or say in this situation.** Choose one of the vignettes (preferably not one used for the activity) to read aloud. Record student responses, prompting with questions such as these:
   - What else could you do to stop the bullying?
   - How might you help the bullied student?
   - What choices might you have besides speaking to the person who bullies?

3. **Without using names, can you tell about a time when you were assertive and it worked for you?** Ask several students to share their experiences.

4. **Have you ever seen someone reacting to bullying in an aggressive way? Without using people's names, can you tell us what happened?**

5. **People who bully others tend to avoid picking on people who look confident. Why do you think that is?**

Wrap-Up

1. **Using assertive behavior can help stop bullying. It can make us feel more confident when we are in tricky social situations. There isn't one solution that will work every time, so you need to try different solutions. It isn't always easy to be firm, especially if you feel scared or uncomfortable. But you have practiced good ways to stand tall and speak up! Remember, it is always important to tell adults about bullying—even if you or others also speak up to try to stop it.**

2. Encourage additional questions and comments.

Curriculum Connections

Vocabulary: *aggressive, assertive, particular, passive, situation, social*

Language Arts: Have students use the Standing Tall and Speaking Up Vignettes to create storyboards that show bystanders responding assertively to resolve the situation.

Social Studies:

- Identify current events that demonstrate ways that aggression can cause or lead to further or escalated aggression.

- Encourage students to investigate ways that diplomats and peacemakers defuse aggression.

Standing Tall and Speaking Up Vignettes

Instructions: Copy the cards and cut them apart. Give each group of four students one card. Assign students to be the character who bullies, the character who is bullied, and the characters who are bystanders. Bystanders should pretend they just saw or overheard what happened.

A student makes fun of a girl in your grade because she has really short hair and wears baseball caps. The student tells her, "You look like a boy."

A popular student calls a younger student a "baby" and has convinced a group of other students to only talk baby-talk to the younger student. If other students don't do what the popular student says, they risk being ignored or called losers.

A student makes fun of a boy whose best friend is a girl.

On the bus, an older student always gives other students a hard time, coming up behind them and pulling on their hair or flicking their ears, then acting innocent if the person being picked on says anything.

One student laughs and whispers mean words every time she/he walks past a particular student who doesn't have many friends.

A student in your class likes to copy other students or follow them around, telling jokes that aren't funny, and generally act like a pest.

A student makes fun of a new boy who doesn't speak English very well. The new boy seems to think the student is trying to be friendly, so he laughs too.

A student in your grade uses mean nicknames to make fun of another student who is overweight. Today, you notice the overweight student rushing teary-eyed into the bathroom.

207

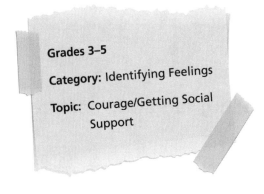

Grades 3–5

Category: Identifying Feelings

Topic: Courage/Getting Social
Support

What Courage Is Needed?

Background

Courage is crucial to prevent and respond to bullying. Bystanders need courage to ask for adult help or to support a bullied peer. Bullied students need courage to report problems to adults or to respond assertively. Even students who bully need courage to change their behavior and make amends for hurting others. Unfortunately, students are bombarded by the idea that courage requires unrealistic acts, physical strength, and even aggression. Adults need to promote a new definition of courage that includes peaceful acts, social responsibility, and resolving bullying situations without aggression or retaliation. Adults can also build students' sense of responsibility for others by encouraging them to make excellent choices and be good citizens.

Learner Outcomes

By the end of this session, students will be able to

- state two ways they can show "everyday" acts of courage
- describe ways that showing courage might vary depending on the situation
- practice realistic responses to show courage in bullying situations

Materials Needed

- Four sheets of construction paper

- Chalkboard, dry erase board, or chart paper and chalk or markers
- What Courage Is Needed? Vignettes on page 212
- Notepad and pencil

Preparation Needed

- On the four sheets of paper, write the following in large letters, one heading per sheet: No Courage, A Little Courage, Some Courage, A Lot of Courage. Post one sign in each corner of the room.

Class Meeting Outline

Opening Activity (15 minutes)

1. **When you hear the word "courage," what words or images pop into your mind?** Write students' responses on the board or chart paper. Consider and briefly comment on the responses: Do they involve risk-taking or aggression? Do they reflect stereotypes about ways boys or girls are expected to act? Are they things students could not realistically do? Are they useful for dealing with bullying or peer pressure?

2. **It takes courage to make good choices. Every single one of us can make positive choices, and be a strong citizen every day.**

3. **I'm going to read some examples of situations you might come across at school. For each example that I read, decide how much courage it would take for you to act assertively. Think for yourself—you may have very different feelings than your classmates.** Point out each of the four signs you made. Remind students that they don't need to decide what they should or would do, but how much courage it would take to act.

4. **Once you decide, go stand by the sign that best describes how much courage it would take for you to act in that situation.** Read five to six of the What Courage Is Needed? Vignettes. Use your notepad to tally students' responses for each example.

Dig Deeper

- Courage is a difficult concept for elementary students to grasp. Even by the late elementary grades, youngsters tend to feel invincible and label aggressive, high-risk acts as courageous. Societal pressures about ways girls and boys should act confuse students about courage by valuing aggression and toughness for boys, and niceness and passivity for girls. Counteract these stereotypes and provide students with examples of realistic everyday actions that demonstrate courage.

- You may want to remind your students that they can model courageous behavior for others and help their friends to be courageous as well.

Discussion Questions (15 minutes)

1. Process the activity with all students gathered together in a circle.
   a. **What did you notice about the choices that people made? Did everyone feel the same way?**
   b. **How did you decide how much courage it would take you to act in a particular situation? On what did it depend?** Be sure to discuss how age, group size, gender, relative popularity, and other factors impact courage.
   c. **What situations would take the most courage for you?**
   d. **Are there ever times when you think the courageous thing to do would be to walk away from a situation?** Encourage students to give an example that supports their point of view.
2. **What are unhealthy or risky ways that courage is shown on TV, in the movies, in videos, or in other places?**
3. Introduce the concept of quiet, peaceful, or everyday acts of courage. **What are examples of this kind of courage?** Compile a list of everyday acts of courage with the students and post it in the classroom.
4. Grades 4–5: **You can be courageous when you make a good choice or do what's right in a social situation.** Choose one or two of the What Courage Is Needed? Vignettes to discuss in more depth.
   a. **What are realistic ways students can show courage in this situation?**
   b. **When it comes to courage, what would it mean to be a good person or make a good choice?**
5. Grades 4–5: Use the What Courage Is Needed? Vignettes in conjunction with the Olweus Bullying Circle on page 24 of the Teacher Guide. Discuss how much courage it would take people in each of the roles to shift their position one spot closer to being a "defender."

Wrap-Up

1. **Being courageous doesn't always mean taking physical risks. There are lots of courageous things you can do every day. Deciding how to act in a bullying situation takes a lot of courage, no matter who you are. It takes courage whether or not you know in your heart what is right. Do your personal best to be a good person and stand up for others.**
2. Encourage additional questions and comments.

Curriculum Connections

Vocabulary: *challenge, courage, excellent, good citizen, hero*

Language Arts: Have students read literature that reinforces overcoming fear, doing the right thing, and quiet acts of courage. There are many examples for this age group, including *Babe: The Gallant Pig* (Dick King-Smith), *Bridge to Terabithia* (Katherine Paterson), *Dancing in the Wings* (Debbie Allen), *Number the Stars* (Lois Lowry), *Wringer* (Jerry Spinelli), *Iggie's House* (Judy Blume), *Through My Eyes* (Ruby Bridges), *Teammates* (Peter Golenbock), *Thank You, Mr. Falker* (Patricia Polacco), *Nobody Knew What to Do: A Story about Bullying* (Becky Ray McCain), and *The Hundred Dresses* (Eleanor Estes).

Math: Teach students how to design a short survey and use it to interview others in their grade about people they consider courageous. Help them analyze and graph the results.

Media Literacy: Ask students to gather examples from the media that reinforce unhealthy concepts of courage and discuss ways they might counteract those messages.

Social Studies: Encourage students to research and report on a peacemaker, humanitarian, or social activist who demonstrated "quiet acts of courage." Ask students to identify traits in these individuals that they would like to follow.

What Courage Is Needed? Vignettes

Instructions: Choose five to six of the following vignettes to read aloud and discuss with your students.

1. It is the first time you have taken the bus to school. You're nervous, but you have to get on the bus.

2. A group of older students always hangs out at the corner in front of your house and bothers you whenever you get near. You have to walk by them to go to your friend's house.

3. Someone you don't like is being bullied at your lunch table. You feel you have to say something to make it stop.

4. You see a group of students grab your friend's lunchbox and play "keep away" with it. You get the lunchbox and hand it to your friend.

5. Two students are watching you in the hall and are pointing and laughing. You ignore them.

6. A teacher blames you for something you didn't do. You ask to talk to the teacher about this after lunch.

7. A student you want to be friends with dares you to do something you know is wrong. You decide not to do it.

8. Another student wants to be your friend and invites you to come over to his or her house after school. You like the person, but your friends think this person is weird. You decide to go over to his or her house anyway.

9. You just started a new after-school activity and you don't know anyone. No one in this new group has said hello or even noticed you. You decide to talk to the person sitting next to you.

10. Your classroom teacher assigned you to be in a group with a student who has bullied you for years. You decide to tell the teacher about the bullying in private.

11. Someone calls you a really bad word and threatens to hurt you if you tell. You feel afraid and decide to tell your parents.

12. You see one student take something from the teacher's desk and hide it in another student's desk. You decide to write a note to the teacher, explaining what you saw.

Category 3

Communication

(Six class meetings)

Grades 3–5

Category: Communication

Topic: Nonverbal
Communication

Watch Closely!

Background

People communicate in many different ways: words and tone of voice; gestures and body language; and creative expression such as dance, music, and visual arts. This class meeting allows students to explore how people use nonverbal communication to express or mask their feelings. Reading nonverbal cues correctly is important to understand others, to nurture relationships, and to build empathy. This skill also may help students to assess and avoid bullying situations. This class meeting builds on skills taught in kindergarten–grade 2 and should be conducted after completing the Lend a Hand class meeting (see pages 191–195).

Learner Outcomes

By the end of this session, students will be able to

- read and label nonverbal cues associated with specific emotions
- discuss ways that verbal and nonverbal communication may sometimes give conflicting messages about how someone is really feeling
- use descriptive words to describe emotions

Materials Needed

- Watch Closely! Chart on page 218
- Two small baskets or bags
- Chalkboard, dry erase board, or chart paper and chalk or markers

Preparation Needed

- Copy the Watch Closely! Chart with sample statements and feelings.
- Cut apart the Phrase and Emotion cards. Place the Phrase cards into one basket, and place the Emotion cards into a second basket. Shuffle the contents of each basket a bit.

Class Meeting Outline

Opening Activity (10–15 minutes)

1. **Have you ever noticed when *what* someone says and *how that person says it* don't match? For example,** (say in a monotone voice) **I'm having so much fun.** Then, repeat the phrase using an excited, animated tone. **Did anyone notice a difference between how I sounded each time? How were they different?**

2. **Today we're going to play a game called Watch Closely!**

   a. **When it's your turn, you will choose one Phrase card from this basket and one Emotion card from this second basket. Sometimes the Phrase and Emotion may match up, but sometimes they won't. Don't show or tell anyone what you chose.** Offer to assist students who might have difficulty reading.

   b. **When you are ready, read the phrase using the emotion on the card you chose. The rest of us will watch and try to guess the emotion you are showing.** If needed, choose one student to demonstrate a practice round and have the class guess what emotion she or he showed. Ask the demonstrator if the class was correct and state the emotion.

   c. **When you are done, put the Phrase card back in here** (indicate first basket) **and the Emotion card back in here** (indicate second basket). It is fine for students to role-play an emotion more than once. Shuffle items in each basket occasionally to ensure students have opportunities to demonstrate different combinations, or remove the cards demonstrated more than twice.

3. Begin the activity. One by one, invite students to select their cards and say their phrase, pausing between each for the class to guess which emotion is being displayed. Continue until everyone has had at least one turn.

Discussion Questions (15 minutes)

1. Process the activity with students gathered together in a circle.

   a. **What was it like to say the phrase when it didn't match the emotion?**

   b. **When you were watching, how did it feel to hear words that didn't match the emotions shown?**

   c. **How could you tell what emotion someone was acting out? Let's make a list of clues you used to figure that out.** Write responses on the board or chart paper. (Examples include facial expressions, tone of voice, gestures, and body language.)

   d. **What are ways that people use different body language to communicate the same emotions?** (For example, some people may show sadness through their eyes and others by slumping their shoulders.)

2. **How could you use nonverbal communication, or communication without speaking, to get someone's attention?** Ask for some demonstrations.

3. Grades 4–5: **Some people can hide how they really feel. Their words may say something very different from their true emotions. Have you ever noticed this?**

   a. **How did you feel? What, if anything, did you do?**

   b. **How can you find out more about what someone is feeling when the words he or she is saying and the emotions he or she is showing don't seem to match?**

   c. **How can you let someone know how you're feeling without telling that person?**

   d. **Why do we use nonverbal communication?**

   e. **When might it be useful to hide your true feelings?** (Examples include when you are bullied and you don't want to cry; if you feel scared and are trying to be assertive or act confident; if you want to keep something private.)

Wrap-Up

1. **Today we practiced different ways we use nonverbal communication. We practiced how to tell when someone's words and emotions don't match. This week, I want you to watch other people closely. Pay attention to how people you know communicate their emotions with words and actions.**

2. Encourage additional questions and comments.

Curriculum Connections

Vocabulary: *body language, clues, communicate, facial expressions, frustrated, gestures, irritated, nonverbal, phrase, proud, sarcastic, statement, thrilled*

Social Studies/Language Arts/Art: Explore different ways that people communicate their thoughts and ideas through written words, art and music, or movement. Discuss how it may be more or less difficult to understand the intended meaning of some forms of communication than others.

Art/Drama: Use improvisation or charades to practice using and reading body language and nonverbal cues.

Watch Closely! Chart

Instructions: Copy the cards and cut them apart. Be sure to keep the Phrase cards and the Emotion cards in separate piles.

Phrase	Emotion
I am so tired.	Excited
Hi.	Welcoming
I can't wait for school vacation next week.	Sad
I brought my favorite lunch today.	Angry
I forgot my homework.	Proud
That didn't bother me at all.	Frustrated
I'm not worried.	Thrilled
Sorry.	Caring
Thanks a lot.	Disappointed
I think I failed that test.	Worried
Thanks for helping me.	Embarrassed
You can use it whenever you want.	Shy
Sure, I know how to do that.	Irritated
Of course it's okay.	Sarcastic

218

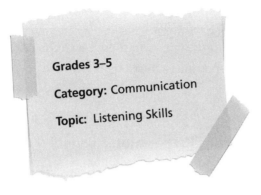

Grades 3–5

Category: Communication

Topic: Listening Skills

Are You Listening?

Background

Being able to listen well serves a purpose at every age. Students need to be interested, ready, and focused in order to listen actively and learn. Focusing not just on someone's spoken (or signed) words, but being aware of the spoken messages, emotions, and nonverbal cues is also an essential part of developing and maintaining healthy relationships. To be a good friend, students need to learn and practice actively listening and relaying back information to the speaker in a way that demonstrates their understanding and engagement. Students this age need adults to teach and reinforce these skills, to improve both their learning and social interactions.

Learner Outcomes

By the end of this session, students will be able to
- identify skills necessary to be an active listener (or listen like a friend)
- rate their own active listening abilities

Materials Needed

- Chinese Ting symbol on page 224
- One sheet of construction paper
- Chalkboard, dry erase board, or chart paper and chalk or markers
- Listening from the Heart Tip Sheet on page 225

- **Grade 3:** Do You Listen from the Heart? Quiz on page 226, or blank sheets of paper for each student
- **Grades 4–5:** Do You Listen from the Heart? Quiz on page 227, or blank sheets of paper for each student
- Two chairs

Preparation Needed

- Mount the Ting symbol on a sheet of construction paper, and laminate if possible.
- Copy the grade-appropriate version of the Do You Listen from the Heart? Quiz for each student.
- Copy one Listening from the Heart Tip Sheet to post in class.
  Grade 3: Show only the first four tips and cover up the rest. The tip sheet will be used again for the next class meeting in this category.
- Place two chairs in your circle so that all students can see.

Class Meeting Outline

Opening Activity (15 minutes)

1. **We hear with our ears, but listening is different. For example, you are listening to my words, but your ears still hear other things happening in our room or around us. As we get older, we learn what things to pay attention to and what things to tune out or keep in the background.**

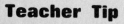
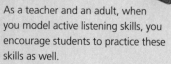

Teacher Tip

As a teacher and an adult, when you model active listening skills, you encourage students to practice these skills as well.

2. **In China, symbols (word drawings) are used to stand for ideas. The symbol called "ting" means "to listen." It looks like this:** Show students the symbol you mounted on construction paper. **The Chinese believe that to listen, you must use your ears, eyes, and an open heart. Can you find the ear, the eyes, and the heart in this symbol?** After a moment, point to or label the parts on the symbol (as shown on page 221). **Grade 5:** Also indicate the horizontal line for "undivided attention" just above the open heart.

3. **How do we listen with our eyes? What do we mean by listening with our heart (or an open heart)? Careful listening shows we understand what**

others say or feel. We call this kind of careful listening
"listening from the heart." Grade 5: Introduce the term
"active listening" instead, if you feel it is appropriate.

4. **I'd like a volunteer to come sit with me here** (refer to
chairs). When the volunteer joins you, say: **Please begin
talking to me about anything you like. For example, you
can tell me about your weekend, a trip you took, an activity you're involved in, or family events.**

5. Listen to the student using poor attending skills for 1 minute: slouch
back in your chair, cross your arms and legs, do not make eye contact,
look at your watch, adjust your clothing, look around distractedly.
Ask the class: **Do you think I was listening from the heart? Why not?**

6. **Let's try this again.** (To volunteer) **Please repeat what you were saying
before.** Listen again using effective attending skills for 1 minute: lean
in, use an open posture and uncrossed legs, make eye contact, nod,
use an interested expression, and ask one or two clarifying questions.
Restate briefly, if desired. Ask the class: **Was I listening from the heart
this time? What was different? Why is it important to listen from the
heart?**

7. Show the Listening from the Heart Tip Sheet. **Here are tips we can use
to help us listen from the heart.** Grade 3: Review first four items only;
Grades 4–5: review all.

   - **Watch: Use your eyes to show you are paying attention, watch
     facial expressions, look at the person, don't look around.**
   - **Lean In: Lean your body toward the person a little and nod
     your head so the person knows you are listening.**
   - **Listen Quietly: Listen to the words a person is saying, don't
     interrupt, don't talk at the same time, listen for facts about
     what the other person is saying.**
   - **Notice Feelings: Listen to how someone's voice or expres-
     sions tell you about that person's real feelings. Notice if that
     matches his or her words.**
   - **Ask, Don't Tell: Wait until someone stops talking and ask
     questions to understand what the person meant, don't give
     advice or tell about something that happened to you unless
     the person asks.**
   - **Summarize/Restate: When the person stops talking, say what
     you think you heard, ask the person to explain parts you
     didn't understand.**

- **Don't Judge: Don't jump to conclusions, don't say someone is wrong, listen to his or her point of view.**
- **Practice Silence: Listen quietly, don't think about what you want to say until the person stops talking.**

Discussion Questions (10–15 minutes)

1. Process the activity.
   a. **What did you learn about listening today?**
   b. **What are examples of ways you show you listen from the heart?**
   c. **How can listening from the heart help us be better friends?**
2. **How many of you think you know how to listen from your heart? Let's find out. Here's a quiz that will help you think about how well you listen from the heart. I won't collect these or see your answers, so answer truthfully.** Distribute the quiz and allow students a few minutes to read and record their responses. Read items aloud to students you feel will have difficulty on their own. If time is short, consider assigning the quiz as homework due by the next class meeting.
3. **This quiz helps us think about how well we listen when others talk to us. Most people, even grown-ups, have to practice listening from the heart.** Go over the quiz questions and what they mean (not student answers, though you might invite students to share what they learned from taking the quiz).
   a. Grade 3: **If you answered "yes" or "sometimes" to any of the questions on your quiz, these are ways of listening from the heart that you need to practice.**
   b. Grades 4–5: **If you answered "yes" or "sometimes" to any of the odd numbered questions and "no" to the even numbered questions, these are ways of listening from the heart that you need to practice.**

Wrap-Up

1. **Please practice listening from the heart this week with your family, your classmates, and friends. Notice whether it makes a difference in how people talk with you. Listening from the heart is something you can do for the rest of your lives.**
2. Encourage additional questions and comments.

Curriculum Connections

Vocabulary: *active listening, attend, communicate, judge, listen, restate, silence, summarize, undivided attention, watch*

Language Arts/Social Studies:

- Use familiar public service announcements (PSAs) such as NBC's "The More You Know" TV spots and PSAs found at www.stopbullyingnow.hrsa.gov to focus on general listening skills. Ask students to identify the main points and what they learned, and to analyze what makes the messages easy to remember.

- A book that could be used to support concepts in this class meeting is *Because of Winn-Dixie* (Kate DiCamillo). This book is also available in Spanish.

Art: Invite a member of your local community to demonstrate or teach students to write other Chinese characters using calligraphy techniques.

TING

Instructions: Cut out the following symbol and tape it to a sheet of construction paper.

Listening from the Heart Tip Sheet

Lean In

Listen Quietly

Notice Feelings

Watch

Ask, Don't Tell

Practice Silence

Summarize/ Restate

Don't Judge

Do You Listen from the Heart?
Quiz for Grade 3

Directions: Read each sentence in the quiz. If you do this a lot, write Y in the space on the right. If you do it sometimes, write S in the space on the right. If you almost never do this, write N in the space on the right.

Y = Yes
S = Sometimes
N = No

	Question	Answer Y, S, N
1.	When someone talks to me, I look around.	
2.	If someone tells me a funny story, I tell a funny story that happened to me.	
3.	When I am with my friends, we talk at the same time.	
4.	I don't listen if someone tells me I'm doing something wrong.	
5.	If someone tells a story I've already heard I don't listen.	
6.	When I am in a group, I do most of the talking.	
7.	When someone talks to me, I listen to what the person says but not how he or she says it.	
8.	If I don't like someone, I ignore them.	

Do You Listen from the Heart?
Quiz for Grades 4 and 5

Directions: Read each sentence in the quiz. If you do this a lot, write Y in the space in the column on the right. If you do it sometimes, write S in the column on the right. If you almost never do this, write N in the column on the right.

Y = Yes
S = Sometimes
N = No

	Question	Answer Y, S, N
1.	When someone tells me a story, I jump in with my own story.	
2.	I notice people's feelings when they talk.	
3.	I often interrupt when I listen.	
4.	I show I am listening with my body language.	
5.	When someone tells me a problem, I think about how to solve it.	
6.	I ask people to explain when I don't understand what they say.	
7.	I pretend to understand even when I don't.	
8.	I don't give advice until someone asks me for it.	
9.	If someone I don't like talks to me, I roll my eyes or stop listening.	
10.	I pay attention when someone talks to me.	
11.	When someone tells me something sad, I tell the person to cheer up.	
12.	When I disagree with someone, I listen to his or her point of view.	

Grades 3–5

Category: Communication

Topic: Other Communication
Skills

How Do You See It?

Background

Students this age can be talkative with their peers, but they may not listen atten-
tively or carry on a mutual conversation. Many students need help learning when
to speak and how to listen without interrupting. Others need help practicing the
art of give-and-take conversation, asking open-ended questions, sharing ideas, or
expressing opinions. These are all skills that not only enhance the development of
friendships but also can improve students' interactions during class activities and
small-group projects. This class meeting should be conducted after completing
the previous class meeting, Are You Listening? in this category.

Learner Outcomes

By the end of this session, students will be able to

- practice attentive listening skills in social situations
- use give-and-take conversation skills
- listen to someone else's opinions

Materials Needed

- How Do You See It? Ten Conversation Starters on page 232
- *Optional:* Kitchen timer with a bell/buzzer
- Grade 4: Chalkboard, dry erase board, or chart paper and chalk or
markers
- Listening from the Heart Tip Sheet (see previous class meeting)

Preparation Needed

- Grade 3: Select one item from the Ten Conversation Starters to read aloud to students. Choose an item you think will generate the most discussion and differences of opinion.
- Grade 4: Select three or four items from the Ten Conversation Starters that you think will spark student interest and copy them onto the board or chart paper for student choice.
- Grade 5: Copy and cut apart enough cards from the Ten Conversation Starters for each pair of students to have one.

Class Meeting Outline

Opening Activity (10 minutes)

1. **We talked about a special kind of listening we called "listening from the heart"** (or active listening). **Listening can be hard work! It means we need to really keep our attention on the person speaking so we can understand what that person wants to tell us.** Review the steps from the Listening from the Heart Tip Sheet from the previous class meeting.

2. Divide students into pairs. (See pages 13–14 for ideas and strategies for grouping students.)
   - Grade 3: Read the discussion topic aloud to all students.
   - Grade 4: Instruct each pair to choose one topic from those written on the board or chart paper to discuss. Read the choices aloud if needed.
   - Grade 5: Give each pair one of the conversation starters to discuss.

3. **In your pairs, each of you will have a turn to be the listener and to be the speaker. Decide who will be the first listener and raise your hand.**
   a. **While the speaker talks, the listener must pay close attention to what his or her partner says, using our Listening from the Heart Tips.**
   b. **When I give the signal, the speaker will be quiet, and the listener will have to tell the speaker what was heard. Tell as much as you can remember. You don't have to repeat word for word.**

c. **I will call time for each part when it is time to switch.** Allow 1 minute for each role, telling pairs when it's time for the speaker to stop. Allow another minute for the listener to restate what he or she heard.

d. **Now you'll switch. The speaker will become the listener. Raise your hand if you're the listener for this round.**

e. Repeat the previous steps, allowing 1 minute for the speaker and another for the listener to restate. Tell students when it's time for the second speaker to stop and the second listener to restate what he or she heard.

Discussion Questions (15 minutes)

1. Process the activity together as a group in a circle.
   a. **What was it like to be the listener? What made it easy or hard for you?**
   b. **What was it like to be the speaker? What did your partners do to show they were paying attention and listening?**
   c. **How did you follow our Listening from the Heart Tips?**
   d. **Was it easier to listen when you agreed with your partner or when you disagreed? Why?**
   e. **If you and your partner disagreed, how did you show you were still listening? How did you make your partner feel you cared about his or her opinion (point of view)?**

2. **Tell something you think was a good or important idea that your partner stated.**

3. **What makes you keep listening when someone is talking? What makes you stop listening?**

4. **It's important to be a good listener. It's also important to be able to carry on a conversation. What things make a good conversation?** (Responses might include taking turns talking, not monopolizing, knowing when to talk or stop talking, or having something interesting to say.)

5. Grades 4–5: **Have you ever been in a situation where someone just talked and talked so you couldn't get a word in? What did that feel like? What did you do?**

Wrap-Up

1. **Being a good listener and being able to have back-and-forth conversations help us be good friends and get along with others. Both take a lot of practice—even for adults!**

2. Encourage additional questions and comments.

Curriculum Connections

Vocabulary: *clarify, conversation, conversationalist, fact, listen, listener, observation, opinion, point of view/perspective, respectful, tactful, truthful*

Language Arts: Use materials such as Marc Brown's "Citizen Frensky" (Arthur Episode #606: http://pbskids.org/arthur or http://pbskids.org/arthur/parentsteachers/index.html) to explore the way words or images can be used to manipulate opinion.

Music/Art: Explore the different ways that artists express their opinions or view of the world.

How Do You See It?
Ten Conversation Starters

Instructions: Grade 3: Choose one topic to read aloud to the class. Grade 4: Write three or four ideas from this list on the board or chart paper for student choice. Grade 5: Copy the cards and cut them apart so that each pair of students has one card.

My favorite thing to do by myself is . . .

The most important qualities in a best friend are . . .

The thing I dislike most about doing chores is . . .

My favorite toy or game is . . .

The best thing to do on a rainy day is . . .

I wish I could . . .

I hope I never have to . . .

The best (or worst) thing about having a pet is . . .

I wish I could spend summer vacation . . .

I think the most interesting person in the world would be someone like . . .

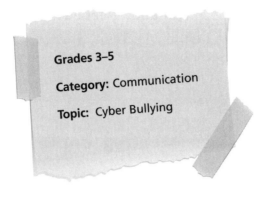

Grades 3–5

Category: Communication

Topic: Cyber Bullying

What Is Cyber Bullying?

Background

When people cyber bully, they use technologies such as the Internet, telephones, and cell phones to bully others. This form of bullying involves new and growing kinds of tools that are fast and have a broad reach. Although it is not the most prevalent type of bullying that students experience, cyber bullying is gaining in popularity, particularly among students in this age group. Many adults may find it challenging to understand these forms of technology and supervise their use. Students need to know what cyber bullying is and how to deal with it both when they experience it and when they witness it.

Learner Outcomes

By the end of this session, students will be able to
- define cyber bullying
- discuss how often, and in what ways, students in their school are involved in cyber bullying
- explain similarities and differences between cyber bullying and more traditional forms of bullying
- discuss ways to deal with cyber bullying

Materials Needed

- Chalkboard or dry erase board and chalk or markers
- What to Do If You Are Cyber Bullied[5] on page 237

Preparation Needed

- Make one copy of the What to Do If You Are Cyber Bullied handout for each student.

Class Meeting Outline

Opening Activity (10 minutes)

1. **How many of you use computers or cell phones? There are lots of good ways these kinds of technology can help us learn and keep in touch with others. What are some good ways to use these technologies? Some students also use these technologies to bully others. When people use computers or phones to bully others, we call that cyber bullying.**

2. Give a couple of examples of cyber bullying:
   - **A student takes a picture of you on his or her cell phone without you knowing it, and sends it to other students in your class with the text message "Biggest Loser." Before long, the picture is passed along to almost all of the students in your grade.**
   - **Someone repeatedly posts mean comments to you through "Club Penguin," like "Nobody likes you! Why don't you go back to your old school?"**

3. **What other examples of cyber bullying can you think of?** (Responses might include sending mean messages through texting, instant messages, photos, email, Web sites, blogs, or chat rooms; pretending to be someone else online; or stealing user names to break into people's accounts. Students might respond by telling something that happened to them.)

4. **What should you do if you are cyber bullied? What can you do if you know someone else has been cyber bullied?**
   a. Pass out copies of the handout and say:
      See if you can unscramble the words on this worksheet to find the answers to these questions. (Answers: 1. Tell an adult; 2. Don't respond; 3. Save the evidence; 4. Kick them off your friends list.)
   b. Ask students to share their answers with the group and correct or fill in correct answers as necessary. **This worksheet**

is yours. **Keep it handy as a reminder of steps you can take to help yourself or someone you know who is cyber bullied.** Consider asking students to take the completed sheets home to discuss with their parents as a homework assignment.

Discussion Questions (15 minutes)

1. Process the activity in a circle as a group.

   a. **If you are cyber bullied or know someone else who is, there are some important steps you can take to get help and stop what's happening.** Refer to the handout. Discuss each of the steps with students. Encourage their thoughts and input:

      - Tell an adult. **What might be some reasons students wouldn't tell adults?** (They are embarrassed, they might be doing something they were told not to do, they might be afraid they won't be allowed to use their phone or the computer.) Reinforce that reporting is the right thing to do, and telling an adult can help you go through the next steps.

      - Don't respond. **Even if it's tempting to send a mean note back—don't! Why? Usually, people who bully want you to get upset. Sending a message back shows them it worked so the bullying might happen more and get worse.**

      - Save the evidence. **What are some different ways to do that? How could you save cyber bullying messages?** (Print out the message or picture that you received or save it to a hard drive or flash drive.) **What if you don't know how to do that?** (Ask an adult or older sibling to help. Turn off the monitor—not the computer.) **Why is this step of saving these messages important?** (Evidence can help in case you need to prove that you were bullied.)

      - Kick them off your friends list. **What are the steps you need to do that?** List ways to take someone off your friend or buddy list for instant messaging or a social networking site. **What can you do to protect yourself so that the cyber bullying doesn't happen again?** (Change

Teacher Tip

Supplement your bullying-prevention program by using Hazelden's cyber bullying curriculum: *Cyber Bullying: A Prevention Curriculum for Grades 3–5.* Sessions in this curriculum are intended for use in class meetings. See www.hazelden.org/cyberbullying or talk to your certified *OBPP* trainer for more information.

your user name and passwords, be careful who you let on your friends list, know your friends, and never share your passwords with others.)

2. Grades 4–5: **Cyber bullying is similar to other types of bullying in many ways. But there are ways that it is different, too.**

   a. **How is cyber bullying similar to other types of bullying?**

   b. **What are differences between cyber bullying and other types of bullying?** (Cyber bullying can be anonymous, it may be easier to bully the other person if you can't see him or her, it can happen even when you're alone or at home.)

   c. **What are ways that cyber bullying can be anonymous?**

   d. **Why can it feel easier to bully someone online than face to face?**

   e. **How does cyber bullying affect students at school even if it doesn't happen at school?**

Wrap-Up

1. **Nobody deserves to be bullied—in *any* way. Cyber bullying can be a very serious form of bullying. If you are cyber bullied or if you know of someone who is, follow these steps!** Encourage students to repeat the steps with you. **Be sure you use your cell phones and computers for the many good ways they help us!**

2. Encourage additional questions and comments.

Curriculum Connections

Vocabulary: *anonymous, cyber bullying, social networking site, technology*

Language Arts: Show webisode 5, "K. B.'s Day" from the Stop Bullying Now! Campaign (www.stop bullyingnow.hrsa.gov). Have students discuss or write about how K. B. might respond to the cyber bullying. Refer to Educator's Corner on this site for questions that can be used for class meeting discussions.

Math/Science: Ask students to predict what types of bullying are most frequent. Compare their predictions to actual data (table 7, page 30; Standard School Report of the Olweus Bullying Questionnaire).

What to Do If You Are Cyber Bullied

Instructions: Unscramble the words in the following sentences for the things you should do if you are cyber bullied.

1. Tlel na dault.

_____   _____   _____.

2. notD' rpsodne.

_____   _____.

3. veaS het deevenic.

_____   _____   _____.

4. cikK mteh fof yuro dfnries silt.

_____   _____   ____   _____   _____   _____.

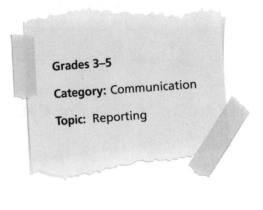

Grades 3–5

Category: Communication

Topic: Reporting

Do Something!

Background

Students need to practice effective ways of letting adults know when they see or hear bullying problems. Because peer pressure is a growing issue at this age, it is helpful to talk about why students may feel uncomfortable reporting concerns to adults, and what can be done to change this "culture of silence" that exists in many schools.

Learner Outcomes

By the end of this session, students will be able to

- discuss reasons why they might feel uncomfortable reporting bullying
- practice techniques for successful reporting of bullying behavior
- brainstorm ideas for changing the "code of silence" to a "code of support"

Materials Needed

- Do Something! Scenarios on page 242
- Grade 3: Blank paper and pencils
- Grades 4–5: Do Something! Worksheet on page 243
- Chalkboard, dry erase board, or chart paper and chalk or markers

Preparation Needed

- Plan how you will group students (five to six per group). (See pages 13–14 for ideas and strategies for grouping students.)

- Grade 3: Write Who? What? When? Where? on the board or chart paper.

- Grades 4–5: Copy the Do Something! Worksheet, at least one for each small group.

- Decide whether all groups will work on the same scenario or on different ones. Grade 3: It may be easier for all students to work on the same situation, with the teacher reading the situation aloud. Grade 5: Students may enjoy the challenge of reading and working on a variety of situations.

- Grades 4–5: Copy and cut enough Do Something! Scenarios to allow one per group (see above about how best to do this for your students).

- Grade 5: *Optional for discussion:* Create three columns on chart paper or the board: Report, Don't Report, Wait/Gather More Facts.

Class Meeting Outline

Opening Activity (15 minutes)

1. **Remember, adults are here at school to help you! Think about times when something happened at school that didn't seem right or that you thought an adult needed to know about. Without naming names, please share some examples.**

2. **What kinds of things should be reported to adults? What do I mean by report?** (Reporting is describing what happened to an adult.)

3. **Today we're going to work in small groups. Each group will have a real-life situation to consider. You will not act out these scenarios. Instead, you will have 10 minutes to discuss what happened.**

4. Grades 4–5: **You will decide as a group what information you know to report, and what information you aren't sure about.**

5. Assign students to their groups. Grades 4–5: Give each group one of the scenarios and a worksheet. Grade 3: Read a scenario to the students, and then give each group paper to write answers to the questions on the board or chart paper.

Discussion Questions (15 minutes)

1. Process the activity with students gathered together in a circle.

   a. **Was it hard or easy for your group to agree on the facts? Why?**

   b. **What surprised you about facts you did not know?**

   c. **Was the situation something you felt an adult should know about? Why or why not?**

   d. **Why do you think students don't report problems to adults? What might get in the way?** Quickly make a list of factors on the board or chart paper. (Responses might include students consider it tattling, a student who bullies might retaliate, students feel that nothing will be done or that information won't be kept confidential, or students feel uncertain about whether something warrants reporting. There is a "code of silence" in the school.)

   e. **What could we do about each of these concerns? How can adults and students work together to make changes?**

2. **Grade 5: Have you heard the saying "code of silence"? What does it mean?**

   a. **What would help students feel better about speaking up?**

   b. **How could students and adults change a "code of silence" into a "code of support"?**

   c. **Do you think students make different choices when they witness or see situations instead of just hearing about what happened? How does that affect your choices?**

   d. **If a situation seems like bullying, but you're just not sure, should you still report what happened? Why or why not?**

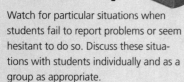

Teacher Tip

Watch for particular situations when students fail to report problems or seem hesitant to do so. Discuss these situations with students individually and as a group as appropriate.

Wrap-Up

1. **Today we talked about the importance of reporting bullying. We also discussed what keeps students from reporting problems to adults. This week, I have a challenge for each of you: when you notice bullying or things that should be reported to adults, get more involved! Let's also keep thinking of ways we can change things. All students should feel more confident and comfortable reporting problems to adults. Remember, adults are here to help.**

2. Encourage additional questions and comments.

Curriculum Connections

Vocabulary: *anonymous, culture or code of silence, emotional, onlookers, opinion, peer pressure, reporting, situation, witness*

Language Arts/Clubs:

- Reinforce the importance of reporting facts and help students differentiate between fact and opinion. Encourage students to apply this skill by writing newspaper articles about school or community events or opinion pieces about topics students feel strongly about.

- Have students read aloud a book that focuses on the importance of reporting bullying situations, such as *Say Something* (Peggy Moss).

Math/Science: Reinforce and practice creative problem-solving with students by having them discuss pros and cons of different choices, and how those choices affect outcomes.

Do Something! Scenarios

Instructions: Copy the cards and cut them apart. Each group will need one card.

Marissa (a popular girl) tells Rachel she'll be her friend if Rachel stops hanging out with Dawn.

Tyrone is really good at sports, but his friend Darren is not. Lately a group of boys has been making fun of Darren, imitating the way he walks and calling him "Darlene."

Kelli and her two best friends hang out at the corner near school every day. Whenever Juan (a boy in their class) walks by, they make fun of his clothes and the way he talks.

It seems that Macy is the center of attention these days—and not in a good way. Every time she is alone, certain boys make comments about her body and the way she looks. Some comments seem stupid, but some make her feel embarrassed and hurt her feelings.

At lunch, Rosa and Max (two older students) take turns tormenting younger students whenever the teacher's back is turned. They trip or bump others, take food off their lunch trays, or block them from sitting down. Whenever students report problems to adults, Rosa and Max deny that they did anything wrong. They never seem to get in trouble.

On the bus, it is a tradition that the back seat is "reserved" for the oldest students to sit. Younger students just KNOW not to sit there. This year, several of the older students have been especially nasty by calling other students on the bus mean names and making fun of them. Next year, you will be one of the oldest students on the bus and some of your friends are already making plans about the ways they'll be mean to the younger students and other kids they don't like.

Do Something! Worksheet

Instructions: Read the situation you received. Decide what information, if any, would be helpful to report, and complete the worksheet.

Where did this situation take place?

What happened first? Include who was involved.

What happened next? Include who was involved.

What happened last? Include who was involved.

What was the result? (Was anyone hurt physically or emotionally? Did any property get taken or damaged? What rules were broken?)

What information DON'T you know?

Who might have seen or heard what happened?

Who would you tell and why?

Grades 3–5

Category: Communication

Topic: Problem-Solving
Difficult Behaviors

Disagree, but Don't Be "Disagreeable"

Background

While many students this age have developed some negotiating and compromising skills, they still need help mastering these techniques. It is helpful for all students to learn how to disagree with others by being tactful and diplomatic, rather than by being offensive. Introduce this session after completing Standing Tall and Speaking Up from category 2: *Identifying Feeling*, and Are You Listening? from this category.

Learner Outcomes

By the end of this session, students will be able to

- practice expressing their opinions or disagreeing with others in tactful ways
- discuss situations where it might be more practical to keep their point of view to themselves

Materials Needed

- Chalkboard, dry erase board, or chart paper and chalk or markers

Preparation Needed

- On the board or chart paper, create two columns: Disagreeable and Polite.

- *Optional:* Open the activity with a short book or selected passage that depicts disagreement or difference of opinion.

Class Meeting Outline

Opening Activity (10 minutes)

1. **Life would be simple if we all had the same ideas and thoughts. Most of us have disagreed with someone at some point. The way you speak and behave when you disagree can make a big difference in how the other person reacts.**

2. **I need a few people to help me demonstrate ways to disagree. You can practice with me. Who can disagree with me without being impolite or mean?**

3. To each volunteer, say: **Winter is definitely the best season of the year.** Encourage volunteers to disagree in a polite way.

4. **What does it mean to be agreeable or polite when we disagree?**

5. **I am going to read some statements. For each one, please disagree in a way that is polite rather than disagreeable.** Read each statement at least two or three times so that each student in your class has an opportunity to respond to one statement.

    - **Rock and roll music is the BEST music there ever was.**
    - **Really short haircuts on girls are so cute.**
    - **Really long hair on boys makes them look cool.**
    - **(Name of sports team) is the best team ever!**
    - **Vegetarians are healthier than people who eat meat.**
    - **How you look and what you wear really matter.**
    - **It's never okay to lie, no matter what.**
    - **Science is MUCH harder than math.**
    - **Girls are better at science than boys.**
    - **Living in a city is better than living in the country.**

Dig Deeper

- Until about age eight or nine, students have difficulty compromising on their own without adult intervention because they lack the cognitive ability to hold two competing ideas in their minds simultaneously.

- Using literature to explore topics from a character's point of view allows students to consider sensitive situations from a more neutral perspective. This makes it easier to evaluate the pros and cons of various decisions, and to propose better choices if the character's decision did not have a positive outcome.

- Whenever possible, avoid literature selections that illustrate magical thinking or poor choices on the part of the characters. If you decide to use these choices anyway, be sure to have students evaluate and propose better solutions.

Discussion Questions (15 minutes)

1. Process the activity.

   a. **What was that like to politely disagree? Did it feel like something you always do anyway, or was it different?**

   b. **What did you notice about the statements that were made in a polite way?** (Answers might include the person uses a calm, even tone of voice, doesn't put down or argue, has a neutral or interested facial expression, acknowledges other person's point of view, keeps an open mind, uses phrases like "in my opinion" or "I think" or "I understand" or "I see this differently," pays attention to receiver's reaction and adapts response.) Write responses on the chart in the Polite column.

   c. **What are ways that people behave when they make statements in disagreeable or impolite ways?** (Answers might include the person uses an angry tone of voice or facial expression, overpowers or belittles the other person, doesn't allow the person to talk after he or she disagrees, shows no regard for other person's point of view, uses phrases like "you're wrong" or "always" or "never" or "everyone else thinks," disregards receiver's reaction.) Write responses on the chart in the Disagreeable column.

   d. **Which way of disagreeing would be more likely to turn into an argument or fight? Why do you think so?**

   e. **What could you do if you think you have hurt someone's feelings?**

2. Grades 4–5: Ask additional questions to help students understand how to disagree in safe ways.

   a. **If you are the person disagreeing, what signals could you look for to tell how the other person is feeling about what you said?** (Possible answers are facial expression looks scared or angry; he or she stops paying attention or argues back.)

   b. **When might it be smart to keep your opinions to yourself?** (Possible answers are to be safe, when you might hurt someone's feelings by telling what you think, when you're not sure what to say.)

   c. **What are examples of when it might be best not to say what you're thinking? What could you say or do instead?**

(Responses might be stay quiet, say what part you do agree with, say "I don't know," or say "I have to think about it.")

d. **In your opinion, can you be polite and still be truthful? What are the drawbacks of always being truthful? of always being polite?**

e. **Do you think people disagree more over facts or opinions?**

Wrap-Up

1. **We all disagree sometimes. You can choose to speak and act in ways that make things worse. Or you can choose to keep peace. We all need to be assertive about saying what we think. But, it's also important to respect other people's points of view and to treat each other kindly.**

2. Encourage additional questions and comments.

Curriculum Connections

Vocabulary: *agree/agreeable, assertive, considerate, difference of opinion, diplomatic, disagree/disagreeable, disagreement, impolite, offend, offensive, polite, rude, tactful*

Language Arts:

- Use age-appropriate literature to discuss ways characters handled disagreements, how they resolved situations, or how they made amends for disagreeable behavior. Examples include *Mrs. Lincoln's Dressmaker: The Unlikely Friendship of Elizabeth Keckley and Mary Todd Lincoln* (Lynda Jones), *Teammates* (Peter Golenbock), *Bridge to Terabithia* (Katherine Paterson), *The Hundred Dresses* (Eleanor Estes), *Wringer* (Jerry Spinnelli), *Tales of a Fourth Grade Nothing* (Judy Blume), *Every Kid's Guide to Handling Disagreements* (Joy Wilt Berry), *The Kids' Guide to Working Out Conflicts: How to Keep Cool, Stay Safe, and Get Along* (Naomi Drew).

- Ask students to write a journal entry about a time when they were on the receiving end of a disagreeable response. Have them describe how they felt and reacted.

Social Studies: As part of your academic curriculum, highlight examples of individuals who have acted as diplomats. Compare them to individuals whose actions escalated conflicts.

Art/Drama: Introduce students to the use of improvisation as a way of trying out positive reactions in difficult situations.

Category 4

Hot Spots

(Five class meetings)

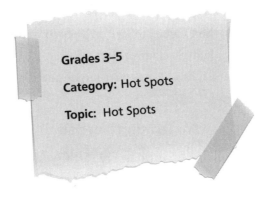

Grades 3–5

Category: Hot Spots

Topic: Hot Spots

Why Do Kids Bully Here?

Background

Students in grades 3–5 are often acutely aware of bullying locations in their schools. However, they may not be able to articulate why their behavior varies in different social situations. Fortunately, students can be guided to examine the reasons for their actions and to think of ways to change their behaviors. Selected data from the Olweus Bullying Questionnaire (OBQ), which should be available from your school's Bullying Prevention Coordinating Committee, can be used as a basis for discussing hot spots where bullying is likely to occur in your building. This session is intended to be conducted after students understand the definition of bullying and is a prerequisite for other class meetings in this category.

Learner Outcomes

By the end of this session, students will be able to
- identify three or four of the most common hot spots for bullying in their school
- discuss why bullying behavior is more common in those locations than in others
- discuss ways to turn hot spots into safe spots

Materials Needed

- Selected data from the Olweus Bullying Questionnaire (OBQ) that was administered to students in your school
- Chalkboard, dry erase board, or chart paper and chalk or markers

Preparation Needed

- Obtain Olweus Bullying Questionnaire (OBQ) data from your school's Bullying Prevention Coordinating Committee. Review and highlight key hot spots from question 18. It is recommended that you also have access to results from questions 4–12 (types of bullying), 14–16 (who was bullied), and 21 and 37–38 (student reactions to bullying) to answer student questions and address issues that may come up during any of the class meetings in this category. If necessary, ask for assistance to interpret this data, as it will be a valuable resource in subsequent sessions as well.
- On the board or chart paper, create a two-column chart. In the left column, list all the areas in your school where students said they experienced bullying. In the right column, write the numbers (Grade 3) or percentages (Grades 4–5:) as they appear in the OBQ chart (results for Boys and Girls). Cover the right column before starting the session so students cannot see the results.

Teacher Tips

- **Hot Spot:** A place inside or outside of school where bullying is likely to happen most often.
- If you do not have data such as the OBQ, list on the board where bullying is likely to occur in most schools, including playground, hallways, classroom, cafeteria, and bus/on way to or from school. Invite students to rank order where they think bullying happens most and discuss why. You may want to follow up with observations in areas students highlighted.

Class Meeting Outline

Opening Activity (10 minutes)

1. **Many places in our school feel safe for most students. But bullying does happen here and we are working to stop and prevent it.**
2. **We asked students here to tell us about their experiences with bullying. Students listed areas of the school where bullying happens more often.**
   a. Read survey question 18 to students if desired.
   b. If students participated in the OBQ, remind them of the date the survey was given.

3. Present the chart with just the left column showing. **Here are some places students said bullying happens in our school. Of these, where do you think bullying is most likely to happen?**

4. Encourage students to state their opinions. Tally votes or ask students to come to consensus on the top three or four locations.

5. **We call these areas "hot spots."** Mark a star beside areas students identified as the most likely places for bullying to occur. Uncover the OBQ data, and have students compare their votes with the OBQ findings.

Discussion Questions (15 minutes)

1. Process the activity with the group in a circle. **How did your answers today compare with the answers students gave on the survey? What looks the same? What looks different?** For differences: **Why do you think we answered differently than the survey results?**

2. Gather students in groups of five or six. (See pages 13–14 for ideas and strategies for grouping students.) Assign each group one of the hot spots on the chart. Give each group 5 minutes to brainstorm an answer to this question: **What do you think makes bullying more likely to happen in this spot?** Encourage students to think of how student attitudes and behavior, supervision, and aspects of the physical space may contribute to bullying in each location.

3. Have groups come back into the circle to share their ideas with the group.

    a. **How does bullying affect your own behavior when you are in (name the most frequent hot spot)?**

    b. **Why do you think students behave differently in hot spots compared to areas where bullying happens less often?**

    c. **What are the areas of the school where you think there is less bullying (or places you might think of as safe spots)?** List student responses.

      • **What makes these areas feel comfortable or safe?**
      • **Compare these "safe spots" to hot spots. What makes hot spots so different from the safe spots?**

    d. **What could our class do to turn our hot spots into more positive places? What can each one of us do to turn our hot spots into safe spots?** List three or four practical ideas from

Teacher Tips

• After conducting the initial class meeting in this category, teachers may want to consider how to present subsequent sessions. For example, you might present all sessions in order, choose only those that are most relevant to your students' experiences, or present sessions in response to specific problems that arise, rather than as a block.

• Revisit the concept of hot spots periodically during the year and continue to seek student ideas for reducing bullying in these locations.

the discussion. **How will we be able to tell whether our ideas worked?** (Examples might include discussion, vote, or adult and student observations.)

Teacher Tip

Adult supervision and intervention is essential to reducing bullying. However, students can learn to take responsibility for how their behavior affects others, and to change behaviors that contribute to bullying. Contributing their own suggestions can improve their commitment to changes.

Wrap-Up

1. Briefly review student observations and ideas.
2. **Adults want to help students feel safe and protected every place at school, including on the bus. We are trying hard to stop bullying behavior in hot spots, but we need your help as well. One way you can help is to let us know when and where there are problems. We need to keep talking about what we can do, and work together. Let's all be active bystanders against bullying. This week, let's see if we can work together to begin changing hot spots to safe spots.**

Curriculum Connections

Vocabulary: *hot spots, percentages, safe spots, solutions, transform, trouble spots*

Language Arts: To help alleviate concerns that younger or new students might have about problems they may face at school, invite older students to write a letter explaining what the school is doing to prevent bullying.

Math: Have students graph the OBQ raw data for questions 14, 15, 18, 21, or 38 and discuss what the graph shows.

Social Studies: Assign students to work in teams to observe student behavior in hot spots. They can use their observations as anecdotal information in class discussions.

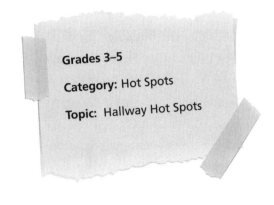

Grades 3–5

Category: Hot Spots

Topic: Hallway Hot Spots

If These Halls Could Talk . . .

Background

Students pass through school hallways numerous times each day. Though these hallways may provide a pleasant opportunity to socialize for some students, hallways are also among the most commonly reported hot spots for bullying. Mixed-age groups can make younger students vulnerable. Hallways that are crowded, noisy, or poorly supervised by adults provide opportunities for more frequent bullying. Adults can dramatically improve transitions through school hallways with a combination of improved supervision, organization, and direct intervention. When students reflect on their own behavior in hallways and practice ways they can help each other, their behavior and investment in reducing bullying improve.

Learner Outcomes

By the end of this session, students will be able to
- identify individual needs for personal space
- give examples of both positive and negative student interactions that occur during hallway transition times
- list possible positive responses to bullying that may occur in hallways or during transition times

Materials Needed

- Chalkboard, dry erase board, or chart paper and chalk or markers
- Kitchen timer with a bell/buzzer

Preparation Needed

- Review your school's Olweus Bullying Questionnaire (OBQ) results for question 18. See Preparation Needed on page 250 for additional data you might need from the OBQ, such as types of bullying, who was bullied, and student reactions to bullying so you are prepared for student questions and discussion.
- On the board or chart paper, create two columns. Label one With Class and label the second On My Own.
- Decide how to group students (five or six students each) for skits. (See pages 13–14 for ideas and strategies for grouping students.)
- Decide when students can perform their skits if they are not able to finish within the class meeting time.

Class Meeting Outline

Opening Activity (15 minutes)

1. **When are you in the hallway? Let's brainstorm together. We'll make two lists: times when you're in a line with our class and I'm with you** (point to the first column on the board or chart) **or times when you're by yourself or with other students** (point to the second column). Brainstorm for a few minutes or until students are out of ideas.

2. **We're going to create some 1-minute skits that tell stories about what happens in the hall—from the point of view of the hall itself. The topic or title of your skit will be "If Our Halls Could Talk . . ." Think about that for a minute. If the walls in our hallway could talk, what would they say about what goes on there? What would they see and hear? How might they view the ways that students behave? What does the hall know that adults might not know?**

3. Divide students into groups of five or six. Each group will pick one situation from either list as inspiration. **Some of your group should pretend to be the talking walls, and some can pretend to be students. The only rules for this activity are that you can't use anyone's name, you can't reveal anyone's personal secrets, and you may not actually act out bullying behavior.**

4. Set the timer for 7 to 10 minutes. **You have until the timer rings to come up with a 1-minute skit. When the timer goes off, everyone will stop talking and sit down with your group in our circle. Ready?**

Discussion Questions (15 minutes)

1. Process the activity. Allow each group time to perform their 1-minute skits in the center of the circle. If there is not time for all groups to perform, tell students when their group will have a chance to do so. You may wish to use the timer to make sure groups stay within the 1-minute time frame.

   a. **Did the skits show things that you've seen or heard happen in our halls?**

   b. **What things seemed funny or didn't seem like problems?**

   c. **What things didn't seem like problems that adults or others needed to watch?**

   d. **What things seemed like problems or concerns where you might like an adult's help?**

   e. **How do you think seeing things from the hallways' point of view might change the way students treat each other in the future in our real hallways?**

2. **What things make it difficult to be in the hallways? What makes our halls a hot spot? Are all the hallways the same?**

3. **How is it different when you are with a group or with a teacher than when you are on your own?**

4. **Do you think students behave differently in the hallways than in our classroom? Why or why not?**

5. **What ideas do you have that could turn our hallways from being a hot spot to being a safe spot? What can adults do? What can you do?**

Wrap-Up

1. **It was very interesting to see how you looked at these situations from another point of view.** If students had time to generate ideas, comment on them. **Let's work together to try some of these ideas to turn the hallway into a safe place.**

2. Encourage additional questions and comments.

Curriculum Connections

Vocabulary: *hot spot, inspiration, observe, organized, perspective, point of view, safe space, secret*

Language Arts: Have students create and publish an advice column that includes pointers about dealing with bullying hot spots.

Science: Assign students to observe "hallway happenings" over a period of time. Have them write about their observations and include at least one possible solution to a problem and the steps needed to put that solution into practice.

Art: Encourage students to develop a cartoon or graphic short story about a hallway problem with a positive solution.

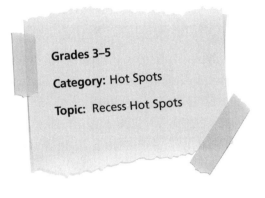

Grades 3–5

Category: Hot Spots

Topic: Recess Hot Spots

Are We Having Fun Yet?

Background

Recess is an essential time for students to socialize with peers and to get much-needed physical activity. Although most children enjoy recess, this time can be the worst time of the day for students who are bullied by their peers. While adults are responsible for making changes to ensure that recess is safe and enjoyable for all students, it is also important to involve students in open discussions about what goes on during recess, about how physical space in play areas is used, and about how students' behavior and interactions affect others.

Learner Outcomes

By the end of this session, students will be able to
- define ways that recess spaces contribute to exclusion or divisions between groups of students
- discuss ideas for offering social support to vulnerable students
- list ideas for changing the playground from a hot spot to a safe spot

Materials Needed

- Are We Having Fun Yet? Recess Scenarios on page 262
- Chalkboard or dry erase board and chalk or markers
- Sheets of paper and pencils for each group
- Copy of current playground/recess rules, if they exist

Preparation Needed

- Review your school's Olweus Bullying Questionnaire (OBQ) results for question 18, where students reported being bullied, to learn how bullying at recess compares to other potential hot spots at your school. Ask your school's Bullying Prevention Coordinating Committee what steps it has taken to address bullying at recess.

- See Preparation Needed on page 250 for additional data you might need from the OBQ, such as types of bullying, who was bullied, and student reactions to bullying so you are prepared for student questions and discussion.

- Select two or three Are We Having Fun Yet? Recess Scenarios to use with your students, or devise your own.

- If possible, invite a playground supervisor or paraprofessional who works with your students at recess to attend this class meeting. Suggest in advance that the supervisor review the scenarios as well and add actual recess situations he or she has dealt with (without using names).

- Decide how you will divide students into groups of three or four for the activity. (See pages 13–14 for ideas and strategies for grouping students.)

- Write the following three prompts on the board: What is the problem? What can be done now? What can happen later?

Class Meeting Outline

Opening Activity (15 minutes)

1. Begin by gathering students' ideas about recess.
   a. **Raise your hand if you enjoy recess. What do you like about it?**
   b. **Now, raise your hand if you think that there are sometimes problems at recess. What kinds of problems?**
   c. **Raise your hand if you've ever seen others teased or bullied at recess.**

2. **Recess is a time to have fun and socialize, but it's also a hot spot where bullying and hurtful teasing happen. Today we're going to talk about different situations that sometimes come up on the playground. Let's see**

if we can make sure that all students are treated fairly and have fun during this important time of the day.

3. Welcome the recess supervisor, if present, and instruct students to do the same. Explain that she or he is there to learn more about difficulties students have on the playground.

4. Assign students to their small groups and give each group a sheet of paper and pencil.

5. **I am going to read a few examples of things that might happen during recess at any school. First I'll read the example. Then, your group will discuss each of these questions.** Point to and read aloud the questions you wrote on the board. **Write your final answer to each question on the paper I gave your group.**

6. Read the first scenario you selected. Give students enough time (about 5 minutes) to discuss the scenario thoroughly before moving to the next one.

Dig Deeper

Adults may miss negative acts that occur during recess because students appear to be having fun. Games such as chasing, keep-away, and Simon Says can quickly escalate to become forums for group bullying and a means to torment socially vulnerable students.

Discussion Questions (15 minutes)

1. Process the activity together in a circle.

   a. Reread each scenario. Have groups share what they decided for each of the three questions. To save time, ask each group to share one idea for each question, and not to repeat if their ideas are the same as some already given.

Dig Deeper

Boy-girl friendships and gender competition are prevalent at this age. To avoid possible problems, do not promote boy-versus-girl competitions in sports and other activities.

   b. Ask students to comment about their group discussion experience. **Was it hard to agree on points? What are some examples of opinions where you disagreed? Did boys and girls feel the same way?**

   c. **What things did you think about in making a decision (popularity, peer pressure, following the rules, acting cool)?**

2. Have students compare the scenarios to their observations of recess at their school.

   a. **Are there some areas of the playground that seem off-limits to certain groups of students? I don't mean that an adult says you can't use the space, but whether certain groups of students claim it or make it hard to play there.**

b. **In your opinion, are all students involved in activities at recess? Why or why not? When students aren't involved, what are they doing?**

c. **Do you think most students get involved with just one activity or group? Or do they move around between different activities or groups during recess?**

d. **Do you see students who aren't involved in any activity and seem to be left out? What can you do to include these students in recess activities?**

3. **What can you do if you see bullying happening when you are at recess?** Discuss how students might apply their solutions to problems in the scenarios to actual problems during recess at their school.

4. Grades 4–5:

a. **Do you think some students have more privileges at recess than others? Explain. Do you think that's fair? Why or why not?**

b. **Aside from our school rules about bullying, are there any other rules you know of that are just for recess? What are they? Are these rules made by adults or students?**

c. **Do students listen when adults tell them to do things at recess? Why or why not? What are some examples?** Caution students not to use names.

5. Collect the papers from each group at the end of the discussion for reference or follow-up.

Wrap-Up

1. **Adults here at school want recess to be a fun time of day for all students to enjoy. Recess is a time for exercise or games, relaxation, and being with friends. It should not be a time when anyone feels left out or bullied.**

2. Recap student observations and suggestions for improvement.

3. Summarize how you will work with students to follow up on putting some of their plans into action.

4. Thank the playground supervisor for participating.

Teacher Tip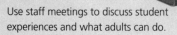
Use staff meetings to discuss student experiences and what adults can do.

Curriculum Connections

Vocabulary: *anticipate, anxious, entitlement, isolate, percentages, privileges, turf*

Math/Art: Have students design maps or layouts for their ideal recess space.

Social Studies: After exploring recess issues, have students consider and propose ideas for change. If some ideas require administrative action, suggest that students present a plan of action to decision-makers. Be sure to discuss this with decision-makers in advance.

Community Service/Cross-Grade Activity: Create opportunities for "playground buddies" to form so younger students have an older peer they can go to if they need assistance or support. As with other buddy activities, providing structure for pairs to get to know each other is essential to developing a successful match.

Are We Having Fun Yet? Recess Scenarios

Instructions: Select two or three scenarios to read aloud to your students.

1. Allie can't find anyone who will play with her.
2. Tony isn't very good at throwing or hitting a softball. The teacher says some students have to let Tony play with them, but they moan and roll their eyes whenever it's Tony's turn at bat.
3. A group of students invites Rashad to play, but then uses his cap to play keep-away.
4. You are playing with a group of students and suddenly one student says, "Hey, you can't do that, it's against our rules!" You never heard this rule before and it doesn't seem fair.
5. Renee is playing ball with her friend, Nimay. Other students keep calling them names and grabbing their ball.
6. You are playing a circle game with a ball. Every time Kayla gets it, she throws it really hard and tries to hit a student who is younger than her.
7. James is not very good at sports. When teams are picked for kickball, he is always picked last. Everyone complains when they end up with him on their team.
8. You and your friends are playing with a jump rope and a group of other students start kicking the rope to make you miss.

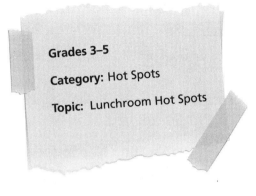

Grades 3–5

Category: Hot Spots

Topic: Lunchroom Hot Spots

Lunch, Anyone?

Background

Lunch is a positive part of many students' days, offering a time to enjoy food, to be with friends, and to take a break from school routines. Like other common hot spots, bullying is more likely to occur in the lunchroom, leaving some students feeling embarrassed, anxious, or left out. Long tables, multi-age groupings, and large groups of students can pose particular challenges for adults and students alike and contribute to bullying when supervision is insufficient. Although bullying can occur anywhere students gather for meals, this session focuses on lunchrooms. Teachers are encouraged to make adaptations as appropriate to their circumstances. As with other hot spots, shifts in both adult and student behaviors are required to achieve lasting changes.

Learner Outcomes

By the end of this session, students will be able to
- discuss common lunchtime dilemmas and bullying
- rehearse positive ways to deal with bullying that occurs in lunchroom scenarios
- review lunchroom/cafeteria rules and determine what needs to be added to these rules

Materials Needed

- Lunch, Anyone? Dilemmas on page 267
- Drawing paper and colored pencils for pairs of students
- Tape or stapler
- Chalkboard, dry erase board, or chart paper and chalk or markers

Preparation Needed

- Review your school Olweus Bullying Questionnaire (OBQ) data for question 18, regarding bullying hot spot locations. Ask a member of your school's Bullying Prevention Coordinating Committee to assist you in interpreting the data so that you can (1) note differences between the incidence of lunchtime bullying for girls and boys; (2) make some inferences from the data about your class (for example, if 60 percent of students on the OBQ reported lunchtime bullying problems, assume the same percentage for your classroom and calculate how many of your students might be affected); and (3) have a sense of how common lunchtime bullying is in your school (how did it rank compared to other hot spot areas?). You will use these facts in the opening activity.

- See Preparation Needed on page 250 for additional data you might need from the OBQ, such as types of bullying, who was bullied, and student reactions to bullying so you are prepared for student questions and discussion.

- Copy and cut enough Lunch, Anyone? Dilemmas for each pair of students.

- Decide how to divide students up into pairs or trios. (See pages 13–14 for ideas and strategies for grouping students.)

- You may wish to invite your lunchroom supervisors or monitors to join your class to participate in this discussion. Give them an opportunity to talk about their expectations and to hear students' concerns. Doing so will help to reinforce the idea that building a positive school climate includes adults and students sharing the same goals.

Class Meeting Outline

Opening Activity (15–20 minutes)

1. **Lunchtime gives everyone a break from our work times. We all need to take regular breaks to eat and to relax!**

2. **How would you describe our lunchtime?** (Where do you sit? Do you usually sit with the same people? Do you have enough time to eat? What do you like most or least about lunchtime?)

3. **Some students don't enjoy lunchtime as much as others. Let me share some facts that might surprise you.** Refer to facts you collected from your OBQ data:

   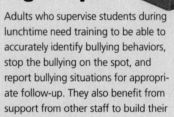

   Dig Deeper

   Adults who supervise students during lunchtime need training to be able to accurately identify bullying behaviors, stop the bullying on the spot, and report bullying situations for appropriate follow-up. They also benefit from support from other staff to build their credibility with students.

   - **Bullying at lunch was the (rank) most common place students reported bullying happened here at our school.**
   - **When we did our bullying survey, about (how many or what percent of) students in our school said that lunchtime was a hot spot for them.**
   - **If we just thought about our classroom, that would mean about (number) boys and (number) girls in our class alone have difficulties with bullying at lunch! Does that seem like a lot to you?**

4. Divide the class into their assigned pairs or trios. **I will give each pair a slip of paper with a dilemma (problem) that students might run into at lunchtime.**

   a. **With your partner(s), decide what someone could do to help or respond in that situation, and then draw a picture of your solution. Remember to try to include bystanders in your solution.**

   b. **Write a brief caption describing your solution on your dilemma strip. Tape or staple it to your drawing when you are done.**

5. Distribute scenarios, paper, and colored pencils to each pair or trio. Allow about 10 minutes for students to work.

Discussion Questions (10–15 minutes)

1. Process the activity with all students gathered as a group in the circle.

   a. Give each pair an opportunity to present its dilemma and solution.

b. Guide the discussion: As each pair presents, ask the class to discuss ways the solution is useful, realistic, and safe.

c. Ask the pairs where they would like to display their captioned drawings.

2. **What do you think are the most common kinds of problems students your age have at lunchtime?** List these on the board or chart paper.

3. Refer back to the OBQ data. **In our school more (provide information about which gender had more issues: boys or girls) reported having difficulties with bullying problems at lunch. Why do you think so? What kinds of things go on at lunchtime that make it harder for (boys or girls)? What can we do about that?**

4. **Even though adults supervise lunchtime, it seems that some students still find ways to bully and exclude others.**

   a. **Why do you think that is?**

   b. **What could adults do differently?**

   c. **What can students do differently to help each other or to stop behaving in mean or hurtful ways?**

Wrap-Up

1. **You came up with lots of clever ideas! Lunch should be fun and relaxed for everyone at our school. Let's all work together to try to make it that way.**

2. Collect drawings and display them in the room.

Curriculum Connections

Vocabulary: *dilemmas, percentages*

Social Studies/Language Arts: Assign students to interview food preparers or lunchtime paraprofessionals to find out more about their jobs. Have them write a feature article for the school newspaper or for morning announcements to highlight these often underappreciated school workers.

Health: Without singling out students, discuss food allergies or intolerances (nuts, dairy, gluten) or special health concerns that affect students' mealtimes (Crohn's disease, cystic fibrosis, diabetes). Build understanding about the impact these diseases have on individuals and ways students might help.

Community Service: Contact a local food pantry or community service organization that provides meals to seniors, homeless individuals, or needy families. Determine how your students may be able to help.

Lunch, Anyone? Dilemmas

Instructions: Copy the cards and cut them apart. Distribute one card to each small group to discuss and draw a solution for a dilemma. Instruct students to use the card to write a caption about their solution.

Cutting in line

Saving seats or not letting someone sit with the group

Making fun of someone's lunch or food choices

Taking someone's lunch money

Bumping or knocking someone's food to the floor

Making rude comments or spreading rumors about someone

Breaking a lunchroom rule on purpose when an adult is not looking

---

Touching or ruining someone's lunch

Moving away when someone sits down

Taking or trading lunch items

Whispering about someone sitting across the table

Ignoring or pretending not to notice someone

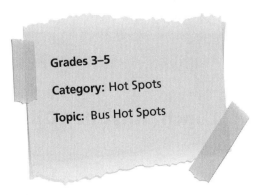

Grades 3–5

Category: Hot Spots

Topic: Bus Hot Spots

What a Way to Start or End the Day

Background

The trip to and from school sets a tone for every student's day. Buses may not be the single greatest hot spot for bullying behavior in most schools, but they do pose challenges for students and the adults who drive them. Not only are buses difficult to supervise but also some students may feel that school rules don't apply to bus behavior. Additionally, buses typically involve students of mixed ages, where older students may bully those who are younger or who, like students with special needs, are perceived as more vulnerable. Regardless of how students travel, adults need to be aware of ways students' passages might expose them to bullying so that problems can be addressed promptly and effectively.

Learner Outcomes

By the end of this session, students will be able to
- identify how bullying happens on the way to or from school
- identify positive ways to respond to difficult behaviors encountered in getting to or from school
- identify "safe" individuals they can turn to as needed on the way to and from school
- identify the school's system for reporting bullying problems when they do occur on the way to or from school

Materials Needed

- Grades 3–4: Chairs
- Grades 4–5: Paper and pencils
- Chalkboard, dry erase board, or chart paper and chalk or markers

Preparation Needed

- Review your school Olweus Bullying Questionnaire (OBQ) data for question 18, particularly answers to "on the way to and from school," "on the school bus," and "at the bus stop."
- See Preparation Needed on page 250 for additional data you might need from the OBQ, such as types of bullying, who was bullied, and student reactions to bullying so you are prepared for student questions and discussion.
- Grades 4–5: Write the following words on the board or chart paper: Introduction, Problem, Solution, and Result.

Class Meeting Outline

Opening Activity (15–20 minutes)

1. **Let's take a quick poll: How do you get to school each morning? Raise your hand if you**
   - take a school bus
   - come alone by car
   - car-pool with others
   - walk
   - ride a bike, scooter, or skateboard
   - take public transportation
   - travel to school another way
2. **What happens before we get here can make a big difference in how we feel as we start our day! Unfortunately, we know that some students are bullied as they travel back and forth to school.**

3. Grades 3–4: Line chairs to look like a bus in the center of your circle area.

   a. As a class, brainstorm problems students may have on the bus. List students' suggestions on the board or chart paper.

   b. Divide the class into two groups. Invite each group to sit in the chairs and act out one solution to each problem, thus giving students alternate solutions for a particular dilemma.

   c. Follow with discussion questions between each skit.

4. Grades 4–5: Assign students to work individually or in groups. Distribute paper and pencils. **Create your own short stories about bullying problems that can happen on the way to and from school. Try to think of bullying problems that might happen to students who walk to and from school or take public transportation, as well as problems for students who ride the school bus.**

   a. **Include four parts to your story** (refer to words on the board or chart paper) **and write one or two sentences for each section:**

      • **Introduction: Who are the characters?**
      • **Problem: What is the problem?**
      • **Solution: Tell how the characters and others worked together to resolve the problem.**
      • **Result: How did the solution work? How did it turn out?**

   b. Allow students 15 minutes to work on their stories.

Discussion Questions (10 minutes)

1. Process the activity with all students in a circle.

   a. Grades 3–4: Discuss the skits.

      • **How did those solutions work?**
      • **How do you think students could use those solutions to resolve problems?**
      • **What help might you need from other students? from adults?**
      • **Why don't the same solutions work every time? What can you do about that?**
      • **Are some choices better than others? Why?**

   b. Grades 4–5: Invite students to read their stories.

      • **What were some creative ways the main and supporting characters handled their problems?**

Dig Deeper

• How students begin and end their day affects how they will be able to attend to learning. When each student has at least one caring adult who can check in with them each day, it can make a big difference.

• Adults can improve student confidence and safety on the way to and from school by helping students develop support systems with peers on their route.

- What were pros and cons to each of the solutions?
- What were the most realistic solutions?
- What could you do if you tried a solution and it didn't work?
- Why is it important to have more than one solution ready to go?

2. **Each of us needs someone to turn to for help sometimes.**

    a. **If you ever need help on the way to or from school, what kind of help would you need? How could someone help you?** List answers on the board or chart paper.

    b. **What backup or "safe people" could you go to if a teacher is not nearby?**

    c. **What plans could you make to keep yourself safe from bullying on the way to and from school?** Write plans on the board or chart paper and ask each student to choose one to put into practice. (Possible plans include carry a cell phone, walk with a friend, carry "phone money" in your shoe, identify places with your parents' approval where you could go if you get into difficulties, call 9-1-1.)

Wrap-Up

1. **Whenever we face problems, there isn't just one solution that works every time. We need to have many solutions we can use to solve problems. Please be thinking of more ideas, and try those out the next time you see negative behavior on the way to and from school. You just might help make someone's school day much better!**

2. Encourage additional questions and comments.

Teacher Tips

When helping students consider or generate solutions to bullying problems, consider the following points:

- Because of the power difference in bullying situations, conflict resolution techniques (which focus more on give-and-take or negotiated solutions) are generally not appropriate to use in resolving bullying problems.

- Students often need a "toolbox" of skills to draw from to find an option that works. They may have to try out a variety of choices before they are successful, so the more options they have considered and tried in advance, the more likely they have something they can rely on in the heat of the moment.

- Keep in mind that it is never the bullied student's responsibility to stop the bullying. Bystanders find they have power in numbers when responding to bullying.

- Bus drivers should be trained to recognize bullying behavior, know how to intervene, and support the child who is being bullied. If there is a lot of discussion about bullying on your school's bus routes, this information should be passed on to your school's Bullying Prevention Coordinating Committee.

Curriculum Connections

Vocabulary: *advantages/pros, backup, disadvantages/cons, introduction, problem, resolve, result, skit, solution, spare*

Language Arts: Use materials and webisodes from Take a Stand, Lend a Hand to discuss difficulties on the way to and from school at http://stopbullyingnow.hrsa.gov/PDFs/SBN_Comic_V1_F.pdf and http://www.stopbullyingnow.hrsa.gov/kids/webisodes/webisode-04.aspx. Accompanying teacher guide materials are available online.

Math/Geography: Suggest that students map their travel routes to school. Have them mark alternative routes or the locations of their "safe person" if they need help on the way.

Health: Ask each student to identify one or more people they could go to for help on the way to and from school. Encourage them to get phone numbers for each of these people.

Category 5

Peer Relationships

(Ten class meetings)

Grades 3–5

Category: Peer Relationships

Topic: Friendship

Friendship Relay

Background

It is important for every child to have at least one friend at school. Students without friends at school are more likely to experience bullying and to feel excluded. They also are at higher risk for being bullied and having lower academic achievement. While most students have basic social skills, they still need to improve those skills for building and maintaining friendships. Students in third through fifth grade need adult assistance to help them form friendships and learn effective ways of responding to social problems, including bullying.

Learner Outcomes

By the end of this session, students will be able to

- practice friendship-related skills such as greetings, starting a conversation, and asking for help
- discuss attributes of a good friend
- be aware of ways they may fail to act like a good friend

Materials Needed

- Friendship Relay Cards on page 277
- Chalkboard, dry erase board, or chart paper and chalk or markers

Preparation Needed

- Copy, cut, and select enough Friendship Relay Cards for at least half the number of students in your class.
- Decide how to divide the class into two teams so there are students with varying social skills on each. (See pages 13–14 for ideas and strategies for grouping students.)

Class Meeting Outline

Opening Activity (15 minutes)

1. **If someone asked what *the most import*ant part of being at school was, what would you say?**
2. **One important part of being at school is learning how to make friends and be a friend to others. We all need friends to be happy. But being a friend takes practice and hard work.**
3. **We're going to play a game to practice things we need to do to make and keep friends. We'll work in two teams. Everyone will have a turn and your teammates can help you when it's your turn.**
4. Divide students into two teams and have each team form a straight line. Give the following directions for play:
   a. **I will choose a card from this pile. It will tell you to do something that is related to making or keeping friends.**
   b. **When you are at the head of the line, you will do what's on the card. Use your teammates to help you come up with the best response you can think of as quickly as you can.**
   c. **Once you've had your turn, go to the end of the line.**
   d. **Each person who I think performs the task correctly will get a point for his or her team. Let's see which team can earn the most points. Let's play!**
5. Keep a tally of points on the board or chart paper. Play until everyone on each team has had a turn. Alternate which team gets to respond to the relay card first.

Discussion Questions (10–15 minutes)

1. Process the activity with all students in a circle. Announce which team got the most points and have everyone give both teams a hand.

a. What were examples of words or behaviors that were most friendly or welcoming?

b. Which of these were hardest for your team? Which were easiest?

2. What makes some situations harder for students your age to handle? (They might be shy, have to think fast, not sure what to say, be embarrassed or afraid.)

3. How can you tell if someone is being friendly to you? How can you tell when someone isn't being friendly to you?

4. What can you do to be a good friend? What makes a good friend?

5. Once you have made a friend, what are things you can do to keep that friend?

6. What determines whether or not people become friends with each other? What things can get in the way of making friends?

7. Why do students sometimes stop being friends with each other?

Wrap-Up

1. Friends are an important part of life for everyone. None of us are close friends with everyone—and sometimes our friends change over time. Making and keeping friends is hard work for many of us. But the more we practice, the better we all get.

2. Encourage additional questions and comments.

Curriculum Connections

Vocabulary: *acknowledge, appreciate, chat, compliment, conversation, friend, greet, sincere*

Language Arts:

- Ask students to write personal reflections on the topic What makes you a good friend? or What can you do to be a better friend?

- Provide books with friendship themes in your classroom for free reading or for reading aloud to the class. Selections might include *Mr. Lincoln's Way* or *Thank You, Mr. Falker* (Patricia Polacco), *The Hundred Dresses* (Eleanor Estes), *Mrs. Lincoln's Dressmaker: The Unlikely Friendship of Elizabeth Keckley and Mary Todd Lincoln* (Lynda Jones), *Molly's Pilgrim* (Barbara Cohen), *The Butter Battle Book* (Dr. Seuss), *Babe: The Gallant Pig* (Dick King-Smith), *Charlotte's Web* (E. B. White), *Wringer* (Jerry Spinelli), *Bridge to Terabithia* (Katherine Paterson), *Because of Winn-Dixie* (Kate DiCamillo), *Fudge* and *Superfudge* (Judy Blume), *The Twits* or *The BFG* (Roald Dahl).

Art: Create a class poster entitled "What Makes a Good Friend?" Use ideas from the class meeting for the poster.

Friendship Relay Cards

Instructions: Copy the cards and cut them apart. Select which cards your class will use for the Friendship Relay. Prepare enough cards for at least half the number of students in your class. For example, if you have twenty students, prepare ten cards.

Introduce yourself to a student you have seen, but not met	Greet and welcome a guest to our classroom
Give someone a compliment	Congratulate a friend for something he or she did
Invite someone to join you for lunch	Invite someone to play at your home
Offer to help someone	Encourage someone who is having a hard time doing something difficult
Say something that would start a conversation	Politely end a conversation or excuse yourself to go do something else
Thank someone for helping you	Say something that shows you appreciate another person just the way they are
Offer to share something with someone	Politely ask for directions
Sincerely apologize for something you did accidentally	Sincerely apologize to a friend for something you did and offer a way to make it up to them
Politely ask if you can join an activity or game	Politely interrupt a conversation

Grades 3–5

Category: Peer Relationships

Topic: Friendship and Popularity

Friends for Real?

Background

Friendship alliances among students this age can divide students according to gender, social class, ethnicity, and abilities. As peers become more central in their lives and popularity becomes more important, students begin to distinguish casual friendships from real friendships. As students form social hierarchies, they may resort to bullying and relationship manipulation to gain social status. As a result, longstanding friendships may abruptly end as new alliances form—sometimes leaving devastated students in their wake. Students need support learning to respect and value differences, and form friendships based on sincere rather than superficial qualities.

Learner Outcomes

By the end of this session, students will be able to
- discuss why friends are important
- discuss what "being popular" means
- explore ways that focusing on popularity has a negative effect on relationships and may limit true friendships

Materials Needed

- Colored pencils or markers
- One sheet of paper for each student

Preparation Needed

None

Class Meeting Outline

Opening Activity (15 minutes)

1. **Some of us have had the same good friends since kindergarten. And making new friends is important, too. We all need friends in our lives, but sometimes it's hard to know how to choose new friends.**

2. Pass out a sheet of paper to each student. **We're going to do something called a self-reflection—these are your own private thoughts and feelings. It's private, so don't put your name on this sheet or share it with any other student.**

3. **Draw a circle at the top of your paper. Write Me in that circle. Then, underneath that circle, jot the name or initials of every student in this class, and draw a circle around each. When you are finished, look up here. I am going to ask you some questions and tell you what to do next.**

4. Read the following instructions aloud, one line at a time, giving students time between each to complete an item before moving on.

   a. **First, draw a line from your Me circle to the circles of all the classmates you feel you know pretty well.**

   b. **Put a star next to the circles of people you don't know very well.**

   c. **Write an F next to the circles of anyone you consider a real friend.**

   d. **Draw a heart next to the circles of people you think are kind and considerate to everyone.**

   e. **Write an A next to the circles of people you feel you could rely on to give you good advice about a problem.**

   f. Grade 5: **Write a T next to the circles of people you can trust.**

   g. Grade 5: **Write a P next to the circles of anyone you think is popular.**

Teacher Tips

- Be aware of students in your class who might be isolated, excluded, or considered to be outcasts.

- If you have students with particular social difficulties, consider co-leading this session with a school social worker or other such support person.

    h. **Finally, think of any questions you have about friendships or making friends. Write those on the back of the page.**

Discussion Questions (15 minutes)

1. Process the activity. **As we talk, I want to remind you not to use any names of other students.**

    a. **How many feel you know lots of your classmates very well?**

    b. **How many of you had stars on your papers?** (For students they didn't know well.) **What things might keep students from getting to know each other better? How do you think you could get to know other students in this class better?**

2. Grade 3: **How many of you have ever been asked by your parent to be friends with another child who you don't really know, like the son or daughter of your mother's best friend? What was that like? How did it turn out? What happened?**

3. **In your opinion, what does it mean to be "friends for real" (or "close friends" or "BFFs"—"best friends forever")? How do real friends talk and act with each other? How is a real friend different from relationships you have with other students your own age?**

4. Grade 5: **What makes a person popular or not? Does popularity among students change? What is it based on?**

5. Discuss students' questions about friendship from their worksheets, as time permits.

Wrap-Up

1. **We all need friends. Some of us have many, some only a few. We need to be on the lookout to include and welcome students who seem lonely or left out, or who don't have friends yet. I don't expect you to be friends with everyone in our class, but I do expect you to treat every person here with kindness and respect. Think about ways you can be the best friend possible.**

2. Ask students to fold their worksheets in half so that no one can see their answers. Collect the worksheets to ensure that they don't "float" around.

Curriculum Connections

Vocabulary: *confidential/private, personal values, popular, self-reflection*

Language Arts: Ask students to write a letter to a younger student about what they've learned about being a friend or what friendship means to them.

Art: Show students how to make friendship bracelets. Encourage students to make two—one to keep and one to give to someone they don't know very well yet.

Media Literacy: Show students examples of advertisements targeted to people in their age group or a bit older. Ask them to identify how advertisers attempt to appeal to the target audience's desire to be more popular, seem older, be richer, or be more attractive to the opposite sex.

Grades 3–5

Category: Peer Relationships

Topic: Peer Pressure

Be True to Yourself

Background

Students are subjected to many forms of peer pressure and need help from adults to learn how to go against the crowd and make good choices about their behavior. Adults can help them by providing options and a supportive environment that reinforces the idea that being kind and helping others is "cool." This class meeting helps students learn to make good choices and reinforces using positive peer pressure to do what is right. Prior to conducting this session, complete Standing Tall and Speaking Up in category 2: *Identifying Feelings*.

Learner Outcomes

By the end of this session, students will be able to

- describe what peer pressure is
- discuss ways that peer pressure can play a role in bullying
- practice options for responding to peer pressure
- discuss ways peer pressure can help students make good choices

Materials Needed

- Peer Pressure Vignettes on page 286
- *OBPP* Bullying Circle diagram (Teacher Guide CD-ROM, document 18)

Preparation Needed

- Copy, cut apart, and select the Peer Pressure Vignettes so each group of four students has one.
- Make one copy of the Bullying Circle for each student.
- Decide how you will divide students into groups of four. (See pages 13–14 for ideas and strategies for grouping students.)

Class Meeting Outline

Opening Activity (15 minutes)

1. **What is peer pressure? Peer pressure can be a good thing and it can also be a bad thing.** (Example of positive peer pressure: a friend or group of friends convinces you to try a new sport, and you end up liking this activity that you wouldn't have tried on your own. Example of negative peer pressure: someone dares you to do something or makes you feel like you won't be included if you don't go along with something he or she says.) **Peer pressure can be really difficult to resist.**

2. Quickly go through a few of the following questions without asking students to elaborate for now. **Think to yourself—have you ever**
   - **worried about what others would think if you did or didn't go along with something?**
   - **worried you'd get in trouble if you did what was asked?**
   - **worried someone would end up getting hurt if you did what was asked?**
   - **done something you really didn't want to do and felt bad about it?**
   - **felt bad or guilty about the choice you made?**
   - **felt good about the choice you made?**
   - **felt good about the choice a group made?**

3. Divide students into groups. Give each group a vignette to discuss. Encourage groups to think about the following questions: **What can you do in this situation? Can you get your friends or others to change their minds or back you up on this?** Have group members decide on an assertive response and then role-play the situation. Roles might be student(s) applying the pressure, student being pressured, and bystanders (parents, friends, other students).

4. If students need a review of assertive behavior, demonstrate with one of the vignettes before breaking into groups.

Discussion Questions (15 minutes)

1. Process the activity. Have each group explain its vignette. Give each student a copy of the Bullying Circle handout.

   a. **What would make it hard to go against the group in this situation?**

   b. **How did you decide what you'd do?**

   c. **Do you think there was more than one right decision or solution?**

   d. **Is it especially hard to make a decision when you feel someone won't like you if you don't do what that person wants? Why?**

   e. **How can peer pressure lead to bullying?**

   f. **How can peer pressure be a positive thing?**

2. **How is negative peer pressure related to bullying? Remember the Bullying Circle and all the roles students can play when they are involved in a bullying situation? Look at the roles on your handout and tell me which ones are giving in to negative peer pressure.**

3. **How do you think positive peer pressure can be used in our school to reduce bullying? Which roles on your handout are most important when we think of using positive peer pressure to reduce bullying in our school?**

4. **Grade 3:** **Is it hard to be different from others in a group? Why do we sometimes feel like we have to be like others? If someone popular is bullying another student, why do you think some kids join in? Why is it hard to step up and help the child being bullied?**

5. **Grade 4:** **Describe a situation when someone might feel pressured to do something he or she didn't want to do in order to be liked. If someone popular is bullying another student, why do you think some kids join in? Why is it hard to step up and help the child being bullied?**

6. **Grade 5:**

   • **What are ways you can step in and help if you see someone who is being pressured to do something he or she doesn't want to do? How can you use positive peer pressure to help more kids be friends to children who are being bullied?**

- Do you think students your age ever pretend to like something (or hide something they like) because they are worried about what other students will think? Are there ways students can stand up for what they believe in and still keep their friends?

Wrap-Up

1. Facing peer pressure to make poor choices is difficult for all of us. One solution won't work every time, so you need to try different things and encourage your friends to make good choices, too. Real friends don't pressure you to do things that hurt you or others. It takes courage to go against a group. Standing together with friends to be kind to others is a positive way to use peer pressure. It feels great to be a part of a group that does good things for others. Let's try to use positive peer pressure to reduce bullying at our school. If you ever need help, please let me know!

2. Encourage additional questions and comments.

Curriculum Connections

Vocabulary: *conscience, peer pressure, popular*

Language Arts/History: Ask students to write a letter to themselves, saying what is important to them now, what they believe, and what they like to do. At the end of the year, return the letters to the students so they can compare ways they have changed and grown.

Social Studies/Science: Have the class create a dated time capsule of things that are popular now. Make a date to reopen it (or open time capsules from other groups of students from previous years) and see if the same items are still popular.

Art/Health: Have students create "T-shirts" from construction paper. On one side, they can list things of which they are proud, and on the other, write one way they can be a better friend. Decide with students whether to display the T-shirts or keep them for personal reflection.

Peer Pressure Vignettes

Instructions: Copy the cards and cut them apart. You will need one card for each group of four students.

You and a friend are going to a movie and you are excited because you haven't spent much time together lately. But when your friend comes to pick you up, she has another person with her. You and this person don't really get along. You are disappointed but feel like you have to hang out with both of them.	There is a tray of cookies in the lunchroom. Each cookie costs 50 cents, but someone who sits at your lunch table just took one without paying. When you say something, the person starts calling you a "goody-goody."
You are shopping for new school clothes. You pick out something that you know everyone is wearing, but you don't really like. You know if you don't wear something like this, you will be teased.	A person you like who is popular wants you to join in playing a mean prank on someone who is a friend of yours. The person says, "You can be friends with us if you do it."
You and some classmates are trying out a new stunt with skateboards or bikes. You see a sign that says "No bikes or skateboards allowed." When you hesitate, the others start yelling, "You baby! We dare you!"	Your friends are tired of a student in your class who has been mean to other students. One friend suggests spreading a rumor about that student to "teach him/her a lesson." When you say you don't want to take part, your friend says, "Oh you're just afraid you'll get caught. C'mon! We're all going to do it. No one will know."
One of your friends wants to do something he/she isn't supposed to and asks you to tell a lie as a cover—saying, "If you really were my friend you'd do it."	You are at the mall with your friends. One of the girls puts a T-shirt in her purse without paying for it and tells you that if you are going to be a part of the "in-crowd," you need to always look good. She says that shoplifting is a good way to get really cool stuff and that you are dumb if you don't take things, too.

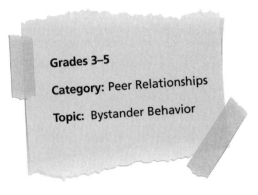

Grades 3–5

Category: Peer Relationships

Topic: Bystander Behavior

Stepping Up and Stepping In

Background

The majority of students in any bullying situation are bystanders who can help in some way. Not all bystanders react the same way. Some may watch bullying with pleasure or even join in, others may try to ignore what is going on, and still others may want to help but feel powerless to take action. Some bystanders ("defenders") may try to help those who are bullied in the moment or afterwards. Students in grades 3–5 are concerned about how they are viewed by peers so it is essential that bullying-prevention efforts create an environment where being a prosocial bystander, or defender, is valued and rewarded. In this class meeting, students will practice making good choices as bystanders. Conduct class meetings from the *OBPP* Teacher Guide that define bullying behavior and establish school rules before conducting this session. This session should also follow Be True to Yourself in this category.

Learner Outcomes

By the end of this session, students will be able to
- identify different roles bystanders play in bullying situations
- identify different options bystanders have to act before, during, or after a bullying incident
- discuss positive and negative ways that peer pressure can affect how and whether bystanders take action

Materials Needed

- Stepping Up and Stepping In Stories on page 291
- Stepping Up and Stepping In Worksheet on page 292
- Bullying Circle diagram (Teacher Guide CD-ROM, document 18)

Preparation Needed

- Copy Stepping Up and Stepping In Stories and Worksheet. Make enough for each group of four students.
- Become familiar with the Bullying Circle diagram and have it ready for class discussion.
- Decide how you will divide the class into groups of four. (See pages 13–14 for ideas and strategies for grouping students.)

Class Meeting Outline

Opening Activity (15 minutes)

1. **Have you ever heard of the expression "stepping up to the plate"? What does it mean? It's a baseball expression. It means it's your turn to help. It's your job to support the team. You're getting ready to do something important or take responsibility. We've talked about ways bystanders can get involved and help when they know about or see bullying that's happening. Today, we'll talk about many good ways we can step up to the plate and step in when we see bullying occur.**

2. **Let's quickly review different roles bystanders play in bullying situations.** Refer to the *OBPP* Bullying Circle diagram. Note: if your students know the diagram well or you have recently reviewed it with them, skip this step.

3. **It is always important to tell an adult about bullying. But there are options that bystanders can take in addition to telling an adult.**
   a. **We're going to work in groups of four.** (Teachers may want to model the use of the worksheet with the class before breaking into work groups.)
   b. **Each group will have both a story and a worksheet.**

   c. **One group member will read the story aloud. Then, the group will talk about what could happen next. What could the bystanders do now?**

   d. **Brainstorm at least two choices the bystanders could make (besides asking for help from an adult) to help stop the bullying. Write those ideas on your worksheet.**

   e. **For each choice, think about the advantages and disadvantages and write those on the worksheet, too.** Explain what advantages and disadvantages are, if necessary.

Discussion Questions (15 minutes)

1. Process the activity. Have the groups return to the circle. Ask each group to read its story and tell how it completed the worksheet.
   a. **What can bystanders do to stop the bullying right when it is happening?**
   b. **What things could bystanders do afterward?**
   c. **Do you think there are more advantages to your choices than disadvantages? Why or why not?**
   d. **What kinds of things might keep students from reporting problems to adults, or from stepping up in a situation like the one you worked on?**

2. Grades 4–5:
   a. **What opportunities did the student(s) who bullied have to prevent what happened? to make it up to the bullied student afterward?** Relate this question to a specific story you used. Give a few examples.
   b. **What are some reactions or feelings students can have when they witness bullying?**
   c. **What things might make it more comfortable for students to respond to bullying? What things might make it uncomfortable for students to step in?**
   d. **How do you think bystanders feel if they watch but don't get involved?**
   e. **What could you do if a choice you made seemed to make the bullying worse?**
   f. **What if you were being bullied and nobody stood up for you?**

Wrap-Up

1. **At some point, all of us have been or will be bystanders to bullying situations. It's hard to know what to do and how to act quickly to help someone. That's one of the reasons it's good for us to practice. But it's also important for you to know that our school wants students to help only if it's safe. Adults are here to help you. Bullying is a big problem that affects all of us. This isn't something only you should try to fix alone. It's up to ALL of us to step up to the plate!**

2. Encourage additional questions and comments.

Curriculum Connections

Vocabulary: *advantages/disadvantages, automatic, bystander/up-stander, choices, escalate/de-escalate, make amends, options, pros/cons, reactions*

Language Arts: Ask students to write about a personal experience as a defender in a bullying situation.

Social Studies: Assign students to look at current events for examples of public figures who bully others, and for examples of ways that bystanders have taken action to right wrongs.

Stepping Up and Stepping In Stories

Instructions: Copy the cards and cut them apart. You can choose to give a different story to each group, or use the same story for every group. Read the story or stories aloud before students begin discussing solutions.

Kiesha

Kiesha is sitting on the bus. Her good friend Sara is walking down the aisle to sit next to her. Just then, Alana pushes in front of Sara and sits down next to Kiesha instead. Sara is very upset and starts to cry.

Marcus and Ben

Marcus and Ben are waiting to go into school. Robert, an older boy, grabs Marcus's backpack. Robert and his friends start playing keep-away with the backpack. A group of students watch and laugh at Marcus.

Alex

Alex is walking down the hall. He sees Janine bullying the new boy whose locker is right next to Alex's. Jason is standing nearby and says something to Janine, but she tells him, "Shut up!"

Bart

Bart thinks Daniela is a pest and tries to find ways to keep away from her, but she won't leave him alone. Some boys say, "Barty has a girlfriend . . . Are you in looovvve, Bart?" Bart yells, "Daniela is an idiot!" Another boy says, "Yeah, no 'girls' play ball with us, Bart." Daniela sees what happens. Mike is in the group, just standing around.

Jess and Anna

Jess is smart, good in sports, and friends with Anna. Kids call Anna "weirdo" and "stupid" and make fun of her clothes. Some other girls Jess likes say she can be friends with them as long as she stops hanging out with Anna. Jess mentions what happened to another friend on her soccer team.

Rocky

Rocky doesn't get along very well with other students. He always interrupts and when he plays ball, he accidentally does things that mess up the game. A group of boys and girls start calling him names and he starts to yell and cry. The other students laugh. Mary is just watching, but looks uncomfortable.

Matt and Andrew

Matt and Andrew have been friends since kindergarten. Lately, they haven't spent much time together and are interested in different things. Matt hears other boys talking about a text message they sent about Andrew. Matt knows it isn't true and is just a rumor. A new friend asks him about it.

Stepping Up and Stepping In Worksheet

Instructions: Read your story aloud as a group. Then fill in the chart below.

Situation Title: _____

Names of Bystander or Bystanders: _____

1. What choices might the bystander or bystanders have to stop the bully-ing either before, during, or after the situation? List three options in the left-hand column of the chart. The first option has been done for you.
2. Write down the advantages and disadvantages of each choice in the chart.

How could the bystander/s try to stop the bullying?	Advantages	Disadvantages
Option 1: Always tell an adult		
Option 2:		
Option 3:		

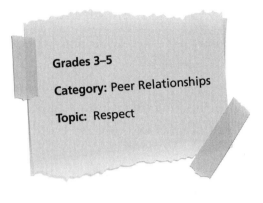

Grades 3–5

Category: Peer Relationships

Topic: Respect

Show a Little Respect

Background

Showing respect for others, even if they seem different from us, is a key to living together harmoniously. Respect plays an important role in bullying prevention by contributing to the development of healthy relationships and communication. By grades 3–5, students grasp the need for fair play, following rules, boundaries, and caring about the feelings of others, all of which can contribute to the development of respect. Schools and classrooms where respect is evident among students and between adults and students are likely to have a lower incidence of bullying.

Learner Outcomes

By the end of this session, students will be able to
- define respect as being thoughtful and considerate
- discuss the link between showing respect and having friends
- demonstrate respectful behavior by role-playing common situations

Materials Needed

- Show a Little Respect Game Cards on page 297
- Object to use as a spinner (wooden rod or game spinner)
- Tape
- Chalkboard, dry erase board, or chart paper and chalk or markers

Preparation Needed

- Review the vocabulary words in Curriculum Connections prior to conducting the class meeting.
- Copy, cut, and select Show a Little Respect Game Cards.
- Place the spinner in the center of your meeting circle and arrange the Show a Little Respect cards face down and evenly spaced around it (like the face of a clock).
- Write the word "respect" on the board or chart paper.

Class Meeting Outline

Opening Activity (15 minutes)

1. **We're going to play a game today called Show a Little Respect.**
2. **Before we start, let's review what respect means. How many of you have heard the phrase "Respect your elders"? What does "respect" mean in that case?** (Answers include obey, honor, don't talk back, don't question what grown-ups say.) **The kind of respect we are going to use in our game has to do with our vocabulary words: *considerate, courteous, tactful, thoughtful,* and *polite.*** Define the vocabulary words, if necessary.
3. **I'd like a few of you to quickly demonstrate what these words mean. Pretend I am a person (adult or child) who is visiting the school. Introduce yourself to me and welcome me to the school.** Ask two or three students to show several ways of being considerate, courteous, tactful, thoughtful, and polite.
4. **Here's how the game works:**
   a. **There are (number) cards laid out in the middle of our circle—sort of like the numbers on a clock. Each card has a tricky situation written on it.**
   b. **You will each take turns spinning this spinner.** Demonstrate. **When the spinner stops and points, turn over the card it's pointing to.**
   c. **Silently read the situation, and quickly decide what you might do and say.**

Dig Deeper

- Adults must clearly convey the message that respect for others does not mean that a bullied person is expected to passively accept the bullying.
- Self-respect is an important concept as well. In relation to bullying prevention, it might include notions like defending others, doing the right thing even if it's unpopular, or using assertive behavior to stand up for yourself or others.

    d. **Then, act out what is on the card for the rest of us, using your most respectful words and body language.**

5. Play the game. Each time someone has a turn, instruct him or her to place the card upside down in the same spot. If one card is selected more than twice, you may remove that card from the mix, so students have an opportunity to practice other scenarios.

Discussion Questions (10–15 minutes)

1. Process the activity.
   a. **Which of these tricky situations were hardest? easiest? Why?**
   b. **What kinds of words or phrases were the most respectful? the least respectful? Why?**
   c. **What were ways that people showed respect nonverbally, or through their body language or tone of voice?**
2. **What are benefits to us for showing respect to others?**
3. **Have you ever had to tell someone the truth in a gentle way (or maybe just part of the truth) to be respectful and to avoid hurting that person's feelings?** (Refer to the examples on the cards, like responding to a friend who asks about a haircut you don't like, or telling someone you don't want to be close friends anymore.) **What did that feel like? What's a good way to handle these situations? What made it hard for you?**
4. **Why is it important for all of us to show respect to each other here at school?**
5. **What role does respect play in preventing bullying?** (Bullying is a form of disrespecting others, showing respect can help avoid bullying, respectful language can help bystanders confront bullying without making the problem worse.)

Wrap-Up

1. **None of us is friends with everyone we meet. But everyone deserves to be treated with respect, whether or not they are a friend. We can show that respect through the words we use and through our actions. Whether you agree or disagree with someone, please keep practicing being thoughtful, considerate, tactful, and polite.**
2. Compliment students on their respectful behavior.

Curriculum Connections

Vocabulary: *considerate, courteous, nonverbal, polite, respect, respectful, tactful, thoughtful*

Language Arts: Many writing assignments can be based on the topic of respect. Have students use the letters of the word as inspiration for a poem, write an essay about the importance of respect, or write a journal entry about a time they showed respect to someone who wasn't a friend.

Math: Select a hot spot in the school where bullying tends to happen. Encourage students to keep a tally of respectful/nonrespectful choices they witness there over a period of two to five days, and then graph the behavior. Post the graph in the hot spot for all to see. If students find a high amount of disrespectful behavior, brainstorm ways to make positive changes.

Physical Education: Emphasize fair play through competitive and non-competitive games. Encourage students to show respect by developing inclusive rules that support students who have disabilities or other limitations to participate in all play.

Show a Little Respect Game Cards

Instructions: Copy the cards and cut them apart. If possible, tape or glue them to pieces of construction paper or index cards.

Say no to an invitation to come to someone's house	Ask for help from someone you don't know well
Disagree with someone's opinion	Tell someone that his or her shirt is on inside out
Reply when a friend asks if you like his or her haircut (and you really don't like it)	Tell a friend you don't like something he or she did
Deny a rumor about someone you know	Tell a friend why other students have been laughing at him or her
Tell someone he or she is not following the rules or playing fair	Tell someone who has been bullying a classmate to leave the person alone
Interrupt a conversation	Someone sends you a text message in which he or she calls another student a mean name
Someone cuts in front of you in line after you've been waiting a long time	Tell a group who wants you to stop a game and move that you were there first and aren't finished playing yet
Tell someone who just told you some gossip or a rumor that you don't want to be involved	Tell an old friend you want to make some new friends, too

Grades 3–5

Category: Peer Relationships

Topic: Trust

Trust Talk

Background

All successful relationships require a mutual sense of trust. Not surprisingly, trust is important in bullying prevention as well. First, students need to trust their emotions about situations to keep safe and to know when to seek assistance from adults. Second, they need to trust that both adults and peers will protect them by providing social, emotional, and physical support when they need it. Finally, they need to feel secure that they can share confidences, show weaknesses, and laugh at their own mistakes without worrying that they will be judged or criticized.

Learner Outcomes

By the end of this session, students will be able to

- discuss the role trust plays in relationships with peers
- explain that it takes work and practice to trust each other
- explore concrete examples of how and when to show trust in common situations

Materials Needed

- Trust Talk Situations on page 301
- Three cards or sheets of paper, 5 x 8 inches or larger

Preparation Needed

- Use the cards to create three signs: Trust, Not Sure, and Do Not Trust.
- Locate a place with room to create a long, imaginary line. Place the cards labeled Trust and Do Not Trust on opposite ends of the line. Place the Not Sure card in the center.
- Preselect three or four Trust Talk Situations for the class activity.

Class Meeting Outline

Opening Activity (15 minutes)

1. **What does it mean to trust someone?**
2. **How many of you have ever had to trust someone else to help you with something that was new or hard for you? What are some examples?**
3. **What made it hard or easy for you to depend on that person? How did you know you could trust that person?**
4. Tell students about the imaginary line. Point out the signs you placed at either end and in the middle.
5. **I am going to read you some situations. When I do, think about how you feel: Does the situation make you feel like you can trust? like you can't trust? or aren't you sure? Then, you'll go stand on the spot along our line that best describes your feeling.**
6. Begin the activity. Note that situations 4, 8, and 9 ask if others can trust the student.

Discussion Questions (15 minutes)

1. Process the activity in a circle.
   a. **Did everyone feel the same way for every situation?**
   b. **What kinds of situations made it harder to feel trust or depend on someone?**
   c. **How do you know when you can trust someone? Describe how it feels to be able to trust.**
   d. **How does it feel when you don't trust someone?**
   e. **What gets in the way of trust?**
   f. **When you were in the middle or not sure, what made you feel confused or uncertain?**

2. **Why is it important to be able to trust your friends? classmates? Give examples of others we may need to trust.**

3. **How is trust important when it comes to bullying situations?**

4. If you did situations 4, 8, or 9, ask:

    a. **What does it mean to be trustworthy?**

    b. **How do you let your friends know that they can trust you? What kinds of things do you do?** (Responses might include talk to them, be honest, listen to what they say, believe them, or respect them.)

Wrap-Up

1. **We feel trust when we know we can count on someone. We need to trust every day that we will be safe and welcome. Trust helps us keep friends because we know we are there for each other. Talking and working together can help us learn to trust each other. Look for qualities of trustworthy people in your family, your friends, and adults at school, and in yourself.**

2. Encourage additional questions and comments.

Curriculum Connections

Vocabulary: *confident, depend on, qualities, rely, safe/secure, trust/trustworthy*

Language Arts: Encourage students to write poems or journal entries with trust and trustworthiness as themes.

Social Studies: Explore examples in current events where trust was violated (for example, countries violating cease-fire agreements, public figures violating election promises, businesses polluting the environment).

Music: Teach students the song *Lean on Me* by Bill Withers, and have them perform it for another class. Lyrics for this song can be found online.

Physical Education: Use strength-training and other challenges to help build each student's sense of trust in their own bodies.

....

Trust Talk Situations

....

Instructions: Select three or four situations to read aloud to students.

1. A new friend says (he/she) will call you tonight to make a plan for you to come over after school one day this week. Do you trust that your new friend will call tonight?

2. You have a secret that you don't want anyone but your close friend to know. You decide to tell, but you ask your friend to promise not to tell anyone else. Do you trust your friend to keep the secret?

3. A (girl/boy) who lives in your neighborhood loves the new game you got for your birthday. (She/He) wants to take it home to show (her/his) dad and says (she'll/he'll) bring it back tomorrow. Do you trust your neighbor to bring it back tomorrow?

*4. Someone at school says you can come to (his/her) party, but only if you stop playing with a friend in your class. Can your friend trust you to stand by (him/her)?

5. Students play the same ball game at every recess, and they never let you play. Today, they say you can play. Do you trust them to include you and not play a trick on you?

6. Another student at school is always making fun of your glasses. You tell the person to stop. Your friends are upset about it, too. Can you trust your friends to tell the person to stop, too?

7. An adult you've seen before stops you outside of school and asks you for directions. You know where (he/she) wants to go. The adult asks if you'll go along in the car to show the way. Do you trust this person and go with (him/her)?

*8. A friend tells you a secret about (himself/herself) and asks you not to tell anyone else. Can (he/she) trust you?

*9. Your parents tell you to meet them at a certain place outside the school so they can pick you up on their way home. Can they trust you to be there on time?

*Questions 4, 8, and 9 are a bit different, as they ask whether others can trust YOU. If used, ask students to stand on the spot along the line that describes how much others can trust their behavior.

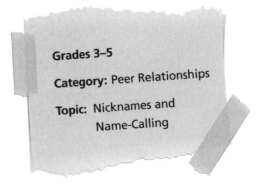

Grades 3–5

Category: Peer Relationships

Topic: Nicknames and
        Name-Calling

What's in a Name?

Background

Our names are an integral part of our personal identity. While nicknames can be positive, students sometimes use nicknames and name-calling as a way of taunting peers. At this age, name-calling frequently focuses on issues of appearance, culture, popularity, and gender put-downs, often including inappropriate or offensive language. Teachers can use name-calling incidents as opportunities to address the forms of bias that these nicknames reflect.

Learner Outcomes

By the end of this session, students will be able to

- describe cultural customs related to choosing names for children, the meaning of names, and use of nicknames
- describe the continuum of positive or wanted nicknames, negative or unwanted nicknames, and name-calling
- demonstrate ways to respond to name-calling from the perspective of bystanders and recipients of name-calling

Materials Needed

- Paper or index card for each student
- Pen or pencil for each student

- Three to five sources for finding meanings and origins of names: baby name books, dictionary with a "names" section, or Internet sites that list popular names for different nationalities
- Three sheets of chart paper and markers
- *OBPP* Our School's Anti-Bullying Rules poster (Teacher Guide CD-ROM, document 8)

Preparation Needed

- On the first sheet of chart paper, print Wanted Nicknames; on the second, print Unwanted Nicknames, and on the third, print Unsure. Note: these sheets will be used to list factors that make a nickname feel good or bad.
- Hang the Four Anti-Bullying Rules poster where all students can see it.
- Decide how you will divide students into three to five groups. The number of groups will depend on the number of sources available for finding meanings and origins of names. (See pages 13–14 for ideas and strategies for grouping students.)

Class Meeting Outline

Opening Activity (15 minutes)

1. **Our names and nicknames are used to identify who we are. Sometimes we like them, and sometimes we don't.**
2. **Do any of you know what your given name means or where it comes from?**
3. **We're going to start our class meeting today by working in small groups to find out what our names mean.** Divide students into three to five groups. Give each student an index card and pencil. Then give each group a resource for learning about their names.
4. **Write your real or given name (not your nickname) on your index card. Use the resource I gave your group to find out where your name came from, and what it means. Write this information on the index card also.**

Teacher Tips

- If students who have been adopted know both their birth and adoptive names, encourage them to look up both.
- If students are unable to find their names, encourage them to find a name that is very close to their name.

Please share your resource with other groups if you need to. Allow 10 minutes for this portion of the activity.

5. **Was everyone able to find his or her name? If not, that's okay. Lots of people have great names that these books don't include. Were you able to find a name that was very close to your name?**

Discussion Questions (15 minutes)

1. Process the activity: Use students' responses to take advantages of opportunities to build sensitivity and respect for each other, and to discuss sensitive topics related to name-calling, put-downs related to gender, and cultural or other biases.

    a. **Were you surprised by what you did or didn't find out about your name? Why?**

    b. **How did this information affect the way you feel about your name?**

2. **What is a nickname? What family nicknames do you have, if you are comfortable saying?**

3. **Have you ever heard the old saying "Sticks and stones . . ."?** Ask students to finish it—there are different variations. **Do you think that's true? Why or why not?**

4. Using the chart paper sheets, ask: **What makes some nicknames wanted or okay and others unwanted and not okay? On what does it depend?** Write student responses on each sheet. Summarize the key points by starring or circling them. Remember not to use the sheets for listing particular nicknames.

5. **Who decides if a nickname crosses the line?** (Make sure students know that this is the person who is being called the name. Even if someone uses a name that he or she didn't think was hurtful, another student may feel offended by the use of the name. When this happens, the use of the offending name should stop.)

6. **What are ways you can deal with name-calling if it happens to you or someone you know?** Refer to the *OBPP* Anti-Bullying Rules. **Are there any other things you could try?** Generate pros and cons of different sorts of responses, such as stating the facts, stating the bullying rule that was violated, or using humor.

Dig Deeper

- Many families have cultural traditions about choosing names for children. Some are based on what they mean or represent in a family. Some names are considered lucky or blessed. Sometimes a certain person is required to choose the name.

- Immigrant families from some cultures feel it is very important to keep a child's given name. Other families feel strongly about adopting more traditional American names so that their children will be more accepted at school or in the broader community. Educators can help children accept unusual names of others by talking about the name and explaining the name's significance.

7. **If someone calls someone else a name, is it ever okay to call that person a name back? Why or why not?**

Wrap-Up

1. **Our names are an important way that we identify ourselves. That's one of the reasons it can feel so painful when people use our names against us. The same is true of nicknames. When we agree on a nickname, it's a way we can connect with friends. But when nicknames are used as put-downs, this is bullying behavior and will not be tolerated in our school. Let's always be sure to only use wanted names for others, and if you're not sure, ask!**

2. **Your homework tonight is to ask someone at home how your name was chosen and who chose it. Write that on the back of your card. If you weren't able to find the meaning of your name in class today, ask a family member to tell you what special meaning it has for him or her. Bring your cards back because we will use them for some other activities.**

Curriculum Connections

Vocabulary: *alias, connotation, culture, flattering/unflattering, gender put-down, given name, heritage, name-calling, nickname, pen name, pet name, positive/negative, stereotype*

Language Arts: Create a word-scramble puzzle or word-find puzzle with the names of all class members, and invite students to work on these.

Social Studies: Create a nickname-scramble puzzle using nicknames of famous men and women in history or current events. Place nicknames in one column and scrambled real names in the other. Students will match names with nicknames.

Art: Invite students to create symbols that represent some aspect of their name.

Grades 3–5

Category: Peer Relationships

Topic: Creating Healthy
Boundaries

Make Space for Me

Background

Personal space and setting boundaries are linked to bullying prevention in several important ways. First, personal space affords us a sense of privacy, which should be respected by others. Second, personal space helps us define our relationships with others—who to allow into our inner circle to share confidences, humor, or interests. Third, personal space relates to setting healthy boundaries in relationships, including how we are willing to be treated by others, standing up for what we believe in spite of what others think, and responding assertively to protect ourselves and those in our circle. Students should have practice reading nonverbal cues and body language prior to this session. (See Watch Closely! in category 3: *Communication*.)

Learner Outcomes

By the end of this session, students will be able to
- discuss ways of creating healthy personal boundaries
- acknowledge that individuals have different needs for personal space and discuss ways to respect those different needs
- differentiate between creating healthy boundaries and creating barriers to respect

Materials Needed

- Make Space for Me Scenarios on page 310
- Three bowls or containers
- Chalkboard, dry erase board, or chart paper and chalk or markers

Preparation Needed

- Select six to ten scenarios from the Make Space for Me Scenarios. Copy and cut enough scenarios so that each group has the same set. Each set should have one scenario for every group member.
- Place each set in a bowl or container.
- List on the board or chart paper: Healthy boundary? Disrespectful?
- Assign students to one of three groups. (See pages 13–14 for ideas and strategies for grouping students.)

Class Meeting Outline

Opening Activity (15 minutes)

1. **Who remembers what a personal boundary is? What are reasons people need these boundaries?**
2. **Sometimes we interfere with or don't pay attention to someone else's personal boundaries, either by accident or on purpose. When that happens, we need to let that person know we are sorry and try to do something that shows we respect his or her boundaries.**
3. Split the class into three groups. Give each group a container with scenarios in it.
4. **Each person in your group will take turns picking a slip from the container and reading it aloud to the group. The group will talk about each. Use these questions on the board to guide your discussion.**
5. Give groups 10 minutes to work.

Discussion Questions (10–15 minutes)

1. Process the activity.
   a. **What did your group discover?** Invite groups to share ideas and insights to the questions they discussed.

    b. How do people use words and tone of voice to set healthy personal boundaries?

    c. How does eye contact or body language play a role in setting boundaries?

    d. In some of these situations, students' words or actions were disrespectful instead of creating healthy boundaries. Give some examples and explain why you think so.

    e. Some words or actions went way too far and may have really harmed friendships. Give some examples and explain why you think so.

    f. What situations weren't so clear?

    g. Do students ever use personal boundaries as an excuse to leave others out? How?

2. Are there good ways to let others know that you need alone-time or privacy?

3. If someone crosses into your personal space, what can you do if you tell that person to stop but he or she won't?

4. What can you say to a friend who has treated you in a way that feels bad?

5. Why is it important to be alone sometimes? How do we know when we need that personal space? How do we know when others need personal space?

6. Have you ever done something that got in the way of someone else's personal space? How did you know? What did you do afterwards?

7. Grade 5: Are there differences between how you show respect for other people's privacy or personal boundaries at home or school? between close friends and others? What are the differences?

Wrap-Up

1. We all need our own personal space to feel safe and comfortable. But sometimes we do things that get in the way of someone else's personal space, or someone may do the same to us. When this happens, we need to find ways to fix the problem. You ALL have the right to set your own healthy boundaries at school and everywhere.

2. Encourage additional questions and comments.

Curriculum Connections

Vocabulary: *boundaries, confidence, healthy/unhealthy, personal space, privacy, secrets, trust*

Science: Have students read about how animals behave in groups in their natural habitats, and in confinement (like in zoos). How do they establish turf? What happens if they lack the companionship of a pack? How does their behavior change if they are overcrowded?

Social Studies: Provide opportunities for students to explore ways cultures respect boundaries when people live in small spaces without rooms. Examples to study include people in hiding during the Holocaust or escaping on the Underground Railroad; Eskimo igloos, ships, or single-room frontier cabins; or ancient civilizations such as at Pompeii, at Machu Picchu, or Anasazi tribes of Native Americans.

Make Space for Me Scenarios

Instructions: Copy the cards and cut them apart. Each group will need a card for each person. Each group should have the same set of cards.

Someone next to you at lunch sits so close that you keep having to move over.

You are tired and a friend keeps asking you to play. You tell him, "I'm really tired. I just want to be alone, okay?"

You had asked to play a game at indoor recess, but someone pushes in front of you and says, "I reserved this spot already, sorry" and now you can't play.

Someone on the bus says, "Hey! You're in my space. Move it!"

You are supposed to be working on a group science project. Every time one student tries to get involved, someone else says, "Hey, back off. I got this covered."

You have a ton of homework to do and your little sister keeps asking you to play with her. Finally you yell, "Get out of my face!"

Your close friend told someone a secret about you that she promised not to tell. You tell her, "We need to talk. I'm really upset about what you did."

You are mad at a friend who hurt your feelings. You say, "You made me really mad. Please leave me alone."

At recess, a classmate asked for the kickball you were using. You told him you weren't done with it. Finally, he grabbed it and ran off.

An older student pushes you every day in the hallway when you pass by. You are tired of it, and it scares you. You finally say, firmly, "KEEP YOUR DISTANCE!"

You heard a rumor about a girl in another class. You can't wait to tell all your friends. You email them all about it and say, "Keep this secret!"

A friend of yours always wants to play with you—and only you—at recess. You tell her, "I want to play with other kids, too."

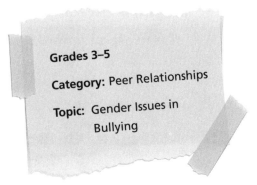

"Real" Boys and "Real" Girls: What Does It Mean?

Background

Societies establish all kinds of rules for behavior, including those about gender roles. People who don't conform to these expectations may be ridiculed, excluded, or subjected to harassment and assault. Boys are often expected to show bravado and aggression rather than sensitivity, and they are often seen as independent when being assertive or challenging authority. In contrast, girls are often advised to be quiet and to take more passive roles. When girls act assertively or challenge authority, they are more likely to be viewed in negative terms like "bossy." Such stereotypes limit both boys' and girls' development, affecting their ability to form relationships with peers.

Learner Outcomes

By the end of this session, students will be able to
- identify their own views and biases about what is considered "normal" behavior for girls and for boys
- identify words and beliefs related to gender that are hurtful to others and unacceptable at school
- use critical thinking to explore ways gender stereotypes are formed

Materials Needed

- Chalkboard, dry erase board, or chart paper and chalk or markers

Preparation Needed

- On two separate sheets of chart paper (or two columns on the board), write "Real" Girls and "Real" Boys.

Class Meeting Outline

Opening Activity (10 minutes)

Dig Deeper

- *Gender roles* are based on a society's rules about what is considered "normal" in terms of masculinity or femininity. These rules (or stereotypes) may vary according to culture or ethnicity. Students who don't feel they fit in according to their gender role do more poorly in school and have a much higher rate of suicide.

- All students need to be taught the harmful effects that certain words and attitudes have on others, whether based on perceptions about race, ethnicity, abilities, or gender. Gender put-downs deserve the same immediate interventions as a racial or ethnic slur.

1. **Do you think it is acceptable for boys to play with dolls if they choose to do so? Why or why not?**
2. **Do you think it is acceptable for girls to play with toy tractors, trucks, and other construction vehicles if they choose to do so? Why or why not?**
3. **In our world, there are many rules that we follow without really knowing why. Some of these rules are written down but most are not. Some of these rules are about what it means to act like a boy or act like a girl.**
4. Point out the columns on the board or chart paper.
5. **Think about words people might use to describe what it means to act like a "real" girl or "real" boy, whether you agree with them or not.**
6. **Let's list your ideas on each of these charts.** As needed, remind students about categories such as appearance or ways of dressing, interests and skills, ways of talking or communicating, codes of conduct related to aggressive or passive behavior, leadership skills, friendships, or ways of expressing emotions.

Discussion Questions (10–15 minutes)

1. Process the activity. Focus on one list at a time and ask:
   a. **Do any of these words we've listed surprise you? Would you agree with everything we listed?** If needed, explain that people often disagree on these issues, and that we may not come to an agreement. We all have the right to our personal views.
   b. **Which of these words make you feel good about being a boy? a girl?**

   c. **Which of these words do you think make it hard to be able to show our true selves?** Circle those that students mention.

2. Guide students in analyzing the lists.

   a. **How does it make you feel when you see these lists?**

   b. **What do you think happens when boys and girls behave in ways that are different from these expectations we listed? Do you think that is fair?**

   c. **Where do you think we learn these stereotypes?** If necessary, define the word "stereotype."

   d. **Why do you think we sometimes agree or go along with stereotypes like these? What are some good things about this? What are some not so good things about this?**

Wrap-Up

1. **We have discussed a lot of stereotypes about the way boys and girls are expected to behave. These are attitudes we live with every day—but it doesn't mean we shouldn't question or challenge them. You should never feel limited in what you can do no matter what your gender is. Let's keep this in mind in the way we treat each other.**

2. Encourage additional questions and comments.

Curriculum Connections

Vocabulary: *attitudes, bias, challenge, expectations, gender, limit, masculine/feminine, roles, stereotype, tradition*

Language Arts: Add books to the class library that allow students to explore and challenge gender-role stereotypes. Examples include *Anna Banana and Me* (Lenore Blegvad), *The Art Lesson* (Tomie dePaola), *Boy, Can He Dance!* (Eileen Spinelli), *William's Doll* (Charlotte Zolotow), *Mama and Me and the Model T* (Faye Gibbons), *Pinky and Rex and the Bully* (James Howe), *The Hundred Dresses* (Eleanor Estes), *The Bully of Barkham Street* (Mary Stolz). Encourage students to identify and critique gender stereotypes in age-appropriate literature.

Math/Media Literacy: For homework, assign students to watch their favorite TV program (including commercials) for 30 minutes. Have them count the number of times they see men or boys and women or girls portrayed in "traditional" roles. Or have students look through toy catalogs and count the number of boys and girls shown playing with toys that are stereotypically for boys and for girls.

Social Studies: Encourage students to read about people whose work and experiences defied or challenged gender-role stereotypes: historical figures such as Amelia Earhart (aviator) and Indira Ghandi (political leader); female race car drivers, astronauts, and surgeons; male ballet dancers, designers, and nurses.

Grades 3–5

Category: Peer Relationships

Topic: Gender Issues in
Bullying

Hey, Did You Notice That?

Background

Stereotypes about the roles of boys and girls are prevalent in our society, and these stereotypes can sometimes lead to bullying. Students in elementary grades need help from adults to sort out the ways these stereotypical attitudes and behaviors are harmful to boys and girls alike. Depending on your students' reading and writing levels, this class meeting may take more than one session, or it could be extended into an academic area. This class meeting should follow "Real" Boys and "Real" Girls: What Does It Mean? in category 5: *Peer Relationships*.

Learner Outcomes

By the end of this session, students will be able to

- discuss the relationship between gender-role stereotyping and bullying
- use critical thinking skills to explore ways that their own views about boys and girls are shaped by the world around them

Materials Needed

- Borrow six to eight picture books from your school library or colleagues. Choose from the following selections that deal with bullying but also reflect varying degrees of gender bias or gender-role stereotyping: *The Berenstain Bears and the Double Dare* (Stan and

Jan Berenstain), *Enemy Pie* (Derek Munson), *King of the Playground* (Phyllis Reynolds Naylor), *The Recess Queen* (Alexis O'Neill), *Princess Prunella and the Purple Peanut* (Margaret Atwood), *The Paper Bag Princess* (Robert Munsch), *Petronella* (Jay Williams), *The Three Little Wolves and the Big Bad Pig* (Eugene Trivizas).

- Hey, Did You Notice That? Book Reviewers' Worksheet on page 317
- Chalkboard, dry erase board, or chart paper and chalk or markers
- Pencils for each group

Preparation Needed

- Copy one worksheet for each group of students, or write questions on the board for reference.
- Decide how you will assign students to groups of three or four. (See pages 13–14 for ideas and strategies for grouping students.)

Class Meeting Outline

Opening Activity (20 minutes)

1. **Messages about the roles that girls and boys should play are all around us and can make us think we should behave in certain ways. Books for children have a lot of these messages, too!**

2. **Who can tell me what a book critic is? Today, we're all going to be book critics.**

3. Split the class up into their assigned groups. **Each group will get a book to review. There are questions on this worksheet that your group will think about while you read the book.** Give each group a book and a worksheet to record their observations.

4. **Think about our discussions about gender stereotypes. See what you notice about the words and illustrations. For this activity, it's okay to skim your book.**

5. **You will have about 8 minutes to review your book and another 10 minutes to discuss and answer the questions on your worksheet.**

Teacher Tip

This class meeting and "Real" Boys and "Real" Girls: What Does It Mean? are intended to help teachers address specific types of gender-based bullying common at this age. Teachers are encouraged to take a broader view about the role gender may have in shaping school and classroom climate and its effect on academic achievement.

6. Tell students when it is time to make the transition from reading to the discussion.

Discussion Questions (10–15 minutes)

1. Gather students in a circle and process the activity. Have each group show its book.

    a. **What did your book have to say about boys or girls?**

    b. **Did you discover any myths about bullying?**

    c. **Would you recommend this book to other students? to teachers?**

    d. **Do you have any suggestions for the author and illustrator? If they were to rewrite or reillustrate this book, what might you want them to say or show differently?**

2. **How do gender messages in books affect children?**

Wrap-Up

1. **It may be impossible to avoid stereotypes about how boys or girls are supposed to act in our society. But, we can learn to recognize, question, and speak up about stereotypes when we see them. We can also make a pledge to follow our dreams, even if those dreams don't seem to fit into what others think we should do. Remember, there are no limits to what boys or girls can do if they set their minds to it. When you set your goals and stick to them, you set a good example for brothers and sisters and other students in the school.**

2. Encourage additional questions and comments.

Curriculum Connections

Vocabulary: *feminine, gender role, masculine, misconception, myth, stereotype*

Language Arts/Art: Use fairy tale "fracturing" to explore gender-role perspectives and biases. Ask students to rewrite well-known fairy tales, reversing the gender of the main characters. Suggest that they illustrate their fractured tales as well.

Social Studies: Ask students to develop hypotheses about why women and minorities are not as present or visible in history, politics, the art world, or sports. Use books like *Gutsy Girls: Young Women Who Dare* (Tina Schwager and Michele Schuerger) to present ideas about the challenges girls have had pursuing interests and hobbies that are traditionally considered masculine.

Hey, Did You Notice That?
Book Reviewers' Worksheet

Instructions: Look through your book as a group. Then answer the following questions.

Title of Book: _____

Author: _____

Reviewers' Names: _____

What examples of stereotypes about gender did you find in the words and pictures?

1.

2.

3.

Did you find any myths about bullying? Describe any that you found:

Would you recommend this book? ❏ Yes   ❏ No   ❏ Maybe
Why or why not?

Category **6**

Respecting Differences and Promoting Acceptance

(Three class meetings)

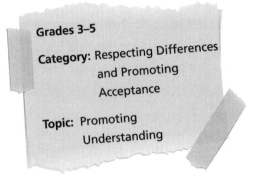

Grades 3–5

Category: Respecting Differences and Promoting Acceptance

Topic: Promoting Understanding

Cultural Expedition

Background

Students' desires to fit in make them susceptible to biases about "normal" behavior, including stereotypes about gender. Since students generally befriend peers they perceive as being like them, accepting others they view as different can pose challenges. Encouraging students to interact with classmates from diverse backgrounds can help promote learning about each other, but doing so in isolation is insufficient to promote acceptance. Adults must show they genuinely embrace differences and teach students to challenge stereotypes, prejudice, and perceptions leading to exclusion, bullying, and discrimination. This session encourages student observation about how perceived differences can lead to bullying. The class meeting is divided into three short parts, including an observation. With coordination, it can be completed during a single school day.

Learner Outcomes

By the end of this session, students will be able to
- define diversity
- describe how accepting diversity can lead to understanding or forming relationships with others who are different
- discuss ways students choose friends
- observe their own and peer behavior to identify ways peers socialize with each other
- discuss how intolerance of differences might lead to bias and bullying

Materials Needed

- Chalkboard, dry erase board, or chart paper and chalk or markers
- Cultural Expedition Observation Report on page 324
- Pencils for each student for observation segment

Preparation Needed

- Copy enough Cultural Expedition Observation Report forms for each pair of students.
- Coordinate as needed with other adults regarding times and places to conduct the observation portion of this class meeting.
    - a. Observations may be done during transitions in the hall, at lunch, at recess, at the bus stop, or on the bus—whatever suits your schedule and seems appropriate for your class. Obtain hall passes for students as needed.
    - b. Grade 3: Assign specific observation locations. Grades 4–5: Allow students to choose the observation locations.
    - c. While students should always be appropriately supervised, they may be observing in locations where adult supervision does not routinely occur. For this reason, it is recommended that students report back to you as they complete their observations.
- Decide how to allocate time for each portion of this class meeting and whether parts might be integrated into specific curriculum content areas during the day.
- Decide how you will assign pairs for the observations. (See pages 13–14 for ideas and strategies for grouping students.)

Class Meeting Outline

Opening Activity (10–20 minutes total)

Part 1: Describe and assign the expedition (5–10 minutes)

1. **We're going on an expedition. Does anyone know what an expedition is? It is a kind of journey or trip for exploring or researching an interesting topic.**

2. **You are going to be explorers and you will be watching to find out more about the culture of students at our school. The word "culture" can mean different things. What are meanings you know about?** (Refer to the explanation in Teacher Tips.)

3. **For our cultural expedition, you will work in pairs. Each pair will observe in a particular area. Wherever you are, you will watch how groups of students behave with each other. We are not looking for bullying or misbehavior, but how students talk or play with each other. For example:**
   - **Who do they choose to be with? Who do they avoid?**
   - **Are students who play or talk together the same as or different from each other? in what ways?**
   - **Are they the same as or different from students they avoid? How?**

4. Assign observation pairs and discuss the logistics of how they will observe. Assign locations as appropriate for your group. **Check in with me before you start your observation (and confirm details). Then let me know when you have finished.**

5. Pass out copies of the Cultural Expedition Observation Report. Briefly review the Tips for Careful Observation at the top of the form and explain what students will write on the form:

   a. **When doing careful observation, you try not to be noticed—you try to "keep a low profile." What does that mean? What are some ways you can do that?**

   b. **Careful observers record facts about what they see. They do not use names in their reports or in conversations with others. How could you describe details of what you see without using names?** (Examples include some older girls, two boys from the same grade, a group of girls who play on the same soccer team, students from chorus, or a group of students with special needs.)

Teacher Tips

- When observations are conducted in pairs and at a variety of places or times, students will be able to work less obviously.

- **Culture:** For the purposes of this activity, culture refers to values and beliefs students at your school have and how those affect the ways they interact—specifically, who they choose to associate with, and how they make those choices.

Part 2: Conduct the cultural expedition observation (5–10 minutes)

1. Have students check in with you before beginning their observations. Tell them to observe for about 5 to 10 minutes, depending on their locations. Assigned observations during passing time in the hall may

be limited to 5 minutes, but an observation at lunch might last 10 minutes or longer.

2. Have students notify you when the observation is completed, or as soon after as is reasonable.

3. Allow students to keep their observation reports to bring to the discussion.

Discussion Questions (15 minutes)

1. Process the activity in a circle as a whole group. List each observation location on separate sheets of chart paper or columns on the board. Write responses in the appropriate chart or column.

   a. **What was hard about being an observer? What did you like about it?**

   b. **How did students group together? Did you notice patterns by gender? by classroom or grade? by an activity they're in or sport? by popularity? by race or ethnicity? other?**

   c. **Raise your hand if the group you observed included or welcomed a variety of students. Raise your hand if the group you observed didn't include others. Why do you think that happened?**

   d. **Raise your hand if other students seemed to ignore the group you watched or simply left them alone. Raise your hand if others seemed to avoid them on purpose.**

   e. **Based on your observations, do you think students choose to be with people who are more like them or doesn't it seem to matter? Why do you think so?**

   f. **Did you and your partner observe students who were more like you? Why do you think so?**

2. **Diversity means variety. Some of your observations tell us about how well we accept people who are different from us—how much we accept diversity.**

   a. **Do you think it's harder to be friends with someone who is very different from yourself? Why or why not?**

   b. **Why do you think some people feel comfortable with people who are different or more diverse from themselves and some don't?**

   c. **What things can we learn by getting to know diverse groups of people?**

3. **What did you learn from our cultural expedition that might help you get along better with other students?**

4. Collect the observation sheets or have students keep them for follow-up or extension activities in another content area.

Wrap-Up

1. **We all like to be with people we feel understand us or who share our interests. In our school, it's never okay to be disrespectful toward, make fun of, or exclude students for any reason. It's especially important to learn to get along with lots of different people.**

2. Note ways students showed they valued differences and appreciate diversity. **We can learn a lot by getting to know people who are different from us. You all did a wonderful job as explorers!**

Teacher Tips

- Students' friendships at this age may reflect biases about gender, race, and ethnicity, and perceived differences. You will want to discuss these sensitive topics in more depth during class meeting discussions or as part of Curriculum Connections.

- **Diversity:** This can most easily be explained to students as "variety"—specifically, a variety of people from different backgrounds, races, or points of view. (For more information on diversity and topics related to this class meeting, refer to pages 9–12.)

Curriculum Connections

Vocabulary: *associate (v), avoid, culture, diversity, exclude, expedition, explorer, gender, observe/ observation*

Science: Use the *National Geographic* magazine and Web site to encourage students to learn about actual cultural expeditions and what they revealed about diverse groups of people.

Social Studies: Have students explore their family's cultural heritage. Use their work as a basis for highlighting customs or interesting facts about different cultures.

Cultural Expedition Observation Report

Tips for Careful Observation

1. Watch quietly and keep a low profile
2. Write the facts (NO names!)

Explorers: _____

Place: _____

Date: _____ Time Started: _____ Time Ended: _____

Instructions: Find a group of students to watch. Answer the following questions. How many students are part of the group?

_____ (at the start of the Expedition) _____ (at the end)

What are they doing? ❏ sitting   ❏ standing   ❏ talking   ❏ eating

❏ playing   ❏ walking   ❏ other: (what?) _____

Does the group include other students who want to join them?
❏ Yes   ❏ No   ❏ It depends

Please explain how they were included or excluded.

Do other students avoid or ignore them?
❏ Yes   ❏ No   ❏ It depends

Please describe their behavior.

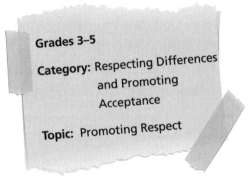

Grades 3–5

Category: Respecting Differences and Promoting Acceptance

Topic: Promoting Respect

Don't Judge a Book by Its Cover

Background

Although diversity adds richness to our world, some people perceive diversity as threatening. It is natural to compare ourselves to each other, but when comparisons lead to biases and stereotypes, our ability to have positive relationships with others becomes limited. Biases about characteristics such as the color of our skin, our family heritage or origin, our cultural identity, our gender, or our abilities are hurtful and may impinge on our civil rights. Stereotypes can lead to bullying and can extend beyond bullying to prejudice, harassment, hazing, discrimination, hate crimes, and other forms of violence. Conduct this class meeting after conducting Cultural Expedition.

Learner Outcomes

By the end of this session, students will be able to
- discuss reasons people judge others based on outward appearances
- discuss ways that intolerance of differences can lead to disrespect and bullying
- discuss ways to change their own biases

Materials Needed

- Book that is unfamiliar to students, old or new, any grade level
- Don't Judge a Book by Its Cover Conversation Starters on page 329

Preparation Needed

- Select two or three items from Don't Judge a Book by Its Cover Conversation Starters. Adapt as appropriate.

- Grade 5: Select two or three additional conversation starters that represent situations that have crossed the line between bullying and more serious forms of aggression, such as prejudice, sexual harassment, hazing, and discrimination based on someone's race, culture or ethnicity, socioeconomic status, religion, disabilities, gender, or perceived sexual orientation.

Class Meeting Outline

Opening Activity (10 minutes)

1. **How many of you have ever heard the expression "Don't judge a book by its cover"? What does that expression mean?**

2. Show the book you selected. **What can you tell about this book just by looking at it? What can't you tell about it?**

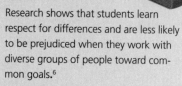

Dig Deeper

Research shows that students learn respect for differences and are less likely to be prejudiced when they work with diverse groups of people toward common goals.[6]

3. **How do we sometimes "judge a book by its cover" with people?**

4. **How do you think this judging relates to our discussions about accepting differences and bullying?**

5. Read selected Don't Judge a Book by Its Cover Conversation Starters one at a time to students. Follow each conversation starter by asking discussion questions from the list below.

Discussion Questions (10–15 minutes)

1. Process the activity. Choose questions appropriate for your students' grade level and experiences and build on their responses.

   a. **Why do some people judge others based on how they look?**

   b. **Where do attitudes and beliefs like this come from?**

   c. **Is it bullying to make fun of others because they are different, even before we know them? Why or why not?**

   d. **How might beliefs like this lead to bullying?**

e. **Have you ever been in a situation where someone was made fun of for being different? What did you do? How did you feel?**

f. **How could you get to know this person better?**

g. **What could you do or say to help change what is happening in the situation?**

Dig Deeper

Students this age often have opportunities to work with others who are different from them (through school projects, group activities and play, sports, youth clubs, scouting, community service, or faith-based group activities), but they require adult guidance and support to succeed.

h. **What are some ways we can change our own biases?** (Responses might include get to know people better, try new things, learn more about people around the world, ask more questions, be more observant.)

2. **Can you recall a time when**

   • **someone made you feel good about you just the way you are? The person appreciated that you are not exactly like everyone else? How did he or she do this?**

   • **you encouraged someone else or gave someone positive feedback about a way that person is different from you? What did you do?**

3. Grade 5: **Some bullying behavior crosses the line. It goes beyond bullying.** Refer to conversation starters you selected that might be termed discrimination, harassment, or hazing and use those terms as appropriate.

Wrap-Up

1. **It's hard to know how to act when we are faced with situations like those we talked about today. It takes a lot of courage, even when we think we know what we should do. Some of the behavior we talked about could even be considered bullying. It's wrong to judge people by how they look or because of things they can't change about themselves. Let's keep working together to find ways to really get to know each other.**

2. Encourage additional questions and comments.

Curriculum Connections

Vocabulary: *attitudes, beliefs, bias, diversity, discrimination, fact, gender, human rights, impressions, judge, opinion, prejudice, respect*

Language Arts: Suggest that students read age-appropriate literature that deals with topics of diversity and respecting differences: *Wringer* (Jerry Spinelli), *The Hundred Dresses* (Eleanor Estes), *Crow Boy* (Taro Yashima), *Ugly Duckling* (Hans Christian Andersen), *Rainbow Fish* (Marcus Pfister), *The Noonday Friends* (Mary Stolz), *Dominic* (William Steig), and *Magnus Powermouse* (Dick King-Smith).

Social Studies: Use the Bullying Circle Role Cards (Teacher Guide CD-ROM, document 18) to role-play situations from this class meeting.

Art/Social Studies: Have students create collages about diversity, using ideas from current events.

Don't Judge a Book by Its Cover
Conversation Starters

Instructions: Read two or three examples to your students and discuss each situation in depth.

1. Some students in your school dress a certain way because their religion requires it. You have heard other students call them names because of their clothing.

2. A girl at school wears clothes that are old or out-of-style and don't always fit well. Some students comment that her clothes must come from (insert name of a well-known local thrift store).

3. A boy in your grade cries every time he doesn't get his way.

4. A student in the special education class who talks very loud and interrupts people all the time wants to be your friend.

5. Students say they don't like another student they say is "fat."

6. A girl in your class has a lot of allergies. Other students play tricks on her to get her to eat or touch things that might make her have an allergic reaction.

7. One of the boys on the bus was teasing another boy about being interested in fashion. He tells other students that he's seen the boy play with dolls.

8. A friend tells you not to go to some other students' home because that person (goes to a different church, isn't "American," has a different color skin than yours, lives in a "bad" neighborhood).

9. A girl and boy in your grade have been best friends since preschool. Students say things about their being in love and call the boy names for playing with and spending time with a girl.

10. A student in your class doesn't have friends because she brags a lot and sometimes tells lies to impress others.

11. Some boys in your class are really good at art but not at sports. People say they act like girls. The girls in your class who are good in sports but not at art don't get teased about that.

Grades 3–5

Category: Respecting Differences and Promoting Acceptance

Topic: Biases, Stereotypes, and Privilege

The Trouble with Privilege . . .

Background

Some groups are afforded a greater degree of privilege than others, simply because of who they are. For those in the majority, the ways in which they are privileged are often invisible to them. Elementary-aged children generally have a strong sense of fairness, and when they are confronted by the ways that unearned privilege creates injustice, they can be motivated to try to help and to "right wrongs." Privilege and injustice are complex concepts, and the process of exploring them may be somewhat difficult for younger students in this age range, and it may raise strong feelings among students and adults alike. Adults need to provide sensitive guidance to help students handle and respond to injustice appropriately.

Learner Outcomes

By the end of this session, students will be able to
- discuss how privilege can be earned or unearned
- identify ways that unearned privilege can be invisible to some and harmful to others
- call attention to prejudice and discrimination when they occur

Materials Needed

- Chalkboard, dry erase board, or chart paper and chalk or markers

- Eight to ten small objects (such as pennies or paper clips) for each student
- Three containers (shoe boxes, baskets, or paper bags)
- The Trouble with Privilege . . . Teacher Reference List on page 335

Preparation Needed

- Label one container Earned, the second, Unearned, and the third, Not Sure. Place the containers on the floor in the center of the meeting circle so that all students can reach them without having to get up.
- Place several piles of small objects around the circle, so they will be within easy reach of students when they sit in the circle.
- Add your own ideas to The Trouble with Privilege . . . Teacher Reference List based on privileges you know students can earn at your school.

Class Meeting Outline

Opening Activity (15 minutes)

1. Have students sit in a circle on the floor, so each has easy access to the three containers and the small objects.
2. **Who can tell us in their own words what a privilege is?** If students have trouble defining the word, help them paraphrase what it means (a benefit, a special favor, a reward for doing something, an honor, a freedom, or an advantage). Write all responses on the chart paper or board.
3. **Sometimes we get privileges for things we do. Those privileges are earned.** Ask students for a few examples of earned privileges. (Examples might include getting an allowance for helping around the house, getting to do something special for good grades, getting extra free time for working well together as a class.)
4. **Sometimes privileges aren't earned. What are examples of privileges you know of that people get just because of who they are?** (These privileges are often based on things students have no control over, such as how they look, where they live, who their family is, whether they are smart or have a special talent, or whether their families have money

or live in a nice house.) Be sensitive to the background of students in your group as you continue to explore these issues.

5. **Unearned privileges can be confusing and unfair.**

   a. **Sometimes people who have the privileges think they are better than those who have few. They may judge them without knowing anything about them. They may be unkind to them or even bully them.**

   b. **Sometimes people who don't have the same kinds of privileges may feel they are not being treated fairly. Some may act angry or unkind, too.**

   c. **Sometimes, people who enjoy unearned privileges don't even realize they have them. Or, they don't realize that their unearned privileges can make others feel bad about themselves.**

6. **I'm going to read you examples of different kinds of privileges people have. After I read each one, take one of these** (indicate small objects) **and put it into one of these containers. Decide whether you think the privilege I say is earned** (point to first container) **or unearned** (point to second container). **If you're not sure, put it here** (point to third container). **Ready?**

7. **Here is the first one: If you make your bed every day for a week, you are allowed to watch your favorite TV show on Friday night. Do you think this is an earned or unearned privilege, or you're not sure? Cast your vote now.** Students don't have to take turns and should be able to reach the containers by stretching.

8. Continue reading eight to ten items from The Trouble with Privilege . . . Teacher Reference List. Be sure to include some items that are earned and some that are unearned.

Discussion Questions (15 minutes)

1. Process the activity.

   a. **What were examples of things you felt were earned? Why did you feel these were earned? Do you all agree?**

   b. **What were examples of things you felt were unearned? Why do you think this?**

   c. **Let's talk about some examples you weren't sure about.**

2. **What are some examples of privileges you think people get just because of who they are?** Be aware, there are no "right" or "wrong" answers! This question helps to identify feelings and perceptions about bias

and privilege. Handle student responses sensitively, reminding them these are difficult issues to talk about and encouraging them to disagree in respectful ways.

3. **When people get unearned privileges, why does that seem unfair? What can we do about that?**

4. **How would it feel if I decided that, for the rest of the day, all the students whose first names start with the letter** (choose one that is in the majority) **would get to do anything they wanted? The rest of you would have to study and do regular schoolwork. How do you think it would feel if that happened every day?**

5. **What does it mean to be in the majority? What does it mean to be in the minority? Have any of you ever experienced a situation where someone was bullied because that person was in the minority? What happened?**

Wrap-Up

1. **Unearned privileges can create situations where some people feel they are better than others. This can lead to bullying and unfairness and treating people poorly. It's hard to talk about these things, but it's an important part of understanding and accepting each other and getting along. We all need to work together to find ways to help others who have been treated unfairly.**

2. Invite students to state one thing they learned or one idea to help others.

Dig Deeper

The following recommendations for taking action against prejudice and discrimination were adapted from guidelines developed by the Anti-Defamation League (www.adl.org):

- Whenever students are exposed to bigoted language, adults at home and school can calmly respond by stating, "Please don't talk that way around my children." Students need to know this language is not acceptable and to see how adults take action.

- Students who are victims of prejudice need adults to support them and to acknowledge the seriousness of the behavior without minimizing their experiences.

- Adults should give students ideas for how they can respond to hateful name-calling and bigotry in ways that are not likely to escalate the situation. If students feel unsafe, or when hateful words are used, they should walk away and get help from an adult right away. If they feel safe enough to respond, they can say, "That's not right to talk/act that way." Or "Please don't use words like that." Or "Our school taught us not to use words like that." Or "_____ is a hate word." In keeping with the *OBPP* model, bystanders should be encouraged to step in the latter situations to offer support as defenders.

Curriculum Connections

Vocabulary: *bias, bigotry, earned/unearned, injustice, intolerance, minority/majority, prejudice, privilege, unfair*

Language Arts: Use age-appropriate literature to discuss concepts raised in this class meeting. Examples include *The Table Where Rich People Sit* (Byrd Baylor), *The Rag Coat* (Lauren Mills), *The Lotus Seed* (Sherry Garland), *Sarah, Plain and Tall* (Patricia MacLachlan), *Love That Dog* (Sharon Creech), *Felita* (Nicholasa Mohr), *Araboolies of Liberty Street* (Sam Swope), *Wringer* (Jerry Spinelli), *Charlotte's Web* (E. B. White), and *Lily's Crossing* (Patricia Reilly Giff).

Math: Have students tally the number of items in each container as you conduct the activity.

Cross-Curricular/Community: Encourage students to participate in social action projects to instill a sense of responsibility. Ideas include collecting contributions of books, food, or clothing for displaced families; raising money or collecting goods for a local animal shelter; visiting shut-in or elderly neighbors; learning about ways to make playgrounds more accessible for students with disabilities.

The Trouble with Privilege . . .
Teacher Reference List

Instructions: Choose eight to ten items from the following list to read to the class. There is space to add your own as well.

1. You get to watch a favorite TV show if you make your bed every day.
2. You get to call a friend after you finish your homework.
3. If you are popular, people choose you first for teams.
4. Older students get the best seats on the bus.
5. You get an allowance.
6. You get to pick out a gift if you get a really good grade on your report card.
7. People want to be your friend because you wear nice clothes.
8. You have your own room at home.
9. You are allowed to paint your room any color you want.
10. You have enough food to eat every day.
11. You're good at music, so you get to be first in line when you go to music class.
12. Your sports team won a trophy for winning the most games this year.
13. Students who are first in line get the best choice of seats in the cafeteria.
14. A student who raises her hand the most gets called on most often even though she usually has the wrong answer.
15. Boys get more turns to play on the computer than girls.
16. Every vacation, some students travel to special places like Disneyland.
17. You get paid to help clean the yard.
18. You get to be on the team because your parent is the coach.

Category 7

Serving the Community/Reaching Outward

(Two class meetings)

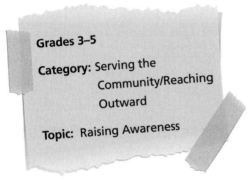

Grades 3–5

Category: Serving the
           Community/Reaching
           Outward

Topic: Raising Awareness

Be Aware!

Background

Students in grades 3–5 have strong opinions about what is right and wrong. This is a great age to build on students' desires to share what they know about helping others. Communicating the effect bullying has on others builds empathy and reinforces bullying-prevention concepts. It is recommended that this class meeting be conducted after students have had ample opportunities to learn the basic principles and practice the techniques taught as part of the *Olweus Bullying Prevention Program*. The two class meetings in this category are intended as a pair and should be conducted consecutively.

Learner Outcomes

By the end of this session, students will be able to

- identify what they have learned about bullying and the effect it has on others
- reflect on how what they have learned might help other students

Materials Needed

- Index card or paper for each student
- Pencil for each student
- *OBPP* Our School's Anti-Bullying Rules poster (Teacher Guide CD-ROM, document 8)

Preparation Needed

- Make sure the *OBPP* Our School's Anti-Bullying Rules poster is hung in a place where all can see it.

Class Meeting Outline

Opening Activity (15 minutes)

1. **Over the past months, we have talked a lot about bullying: what it is, why it happens, and how it affects students in our whole school. We have these school rules about bullying to remind us how to help** (refer to *OBPP* poster). **We've also practiced things we can each say and do to stop bullying from happening.**

2. **Close your eyes for a minute. Think quietly about what you have learned about bullying so far this year. How have you changed the way you think or act to make our school safer and more peaceful?**

3. While students are thinking, place an index card or piece of paper and a pencil on each of their desks.

4. **Open your eyes. You'll see a card in front of you. Write your name at the top of your card. Then write an example of something you've learned about bullying or how you've changed the way you act about bullying.**

Discussion Questions (15 minutes)

1. Process the activity. If students have been working at their desks for the opening activity, move to a circle for the discussion.

   a. Invite students to share their reflections about what they have learned and ways they have made positive changes related to bullying prevention.

   b. Comment on the learning and growth expressed by students; add your own observations. **These are great examples of personal accomplishments you each have made!**

   c. **Think about how things were before we started our bullying prevention program. In your opinion, what has made the biggest difference in how students look at bullying now?**

   d. Grade 3: Collect student cards to refer back to for the next class meeting.

   e. Grades 4–5: Wait to collect student cards until the end of step 2, below.

2. Grades 4–5:

    a. **Have you heard the expression "Actions speak louder than words"? What does that mean? Look at what you wrote on your cards. What do your own actions say about what you've learned or how you've changed?**

    b. **Think about your own experiences with bullying. What advice would you give other students about how to stop or prevent it? For example, what would you tell a friend in another school? students who are new here? younger students?**

    c. **What is one wish that you have for making our school a better place for everyone?** (This can be about anything.)

    d. **In your opinion, how can that make school better?**

    e. **On the back of your card, write your one wish.** Remind students to make sure their names are on their cards. Collect cards to use in the next class meeting in this category.

Wrap-Up

1. **You have made important changes in the way you look at bullying. You have become more aware of bullying problems and how they affect your classmates and our whole school. And you are taking responsibility to make changes that affect all of us. That's very important work that you can feel very proud of!**

2. Encourage additional questions and comments.

Curriculum Connections

Vocabulary: *accomplishments, actions, attitudes/beliefs, aware/awareness, influence, reflect, responsibility*

Social Studies: Refer to student ideas about ways they have taken personal responsibility to make positive changes, and relate those ideas to excerpts from famous speeches that encourage individuals to take responsibility for public change. (Some examples include Barack Obama's "Yes We Can" speech, John F. Kennedy's "Ask Not" speech, Martin Luther King's "I Have a Dream" speech, and Abraham Lincoln's Gettysburg Address.)

Music/Art:

- Have students translate what they've learned into a drawing, storyboard, rap, song, or skit.

- Collect index cards from students in classes across the school so that students' reflections can be shared. (Remove students' names before doing so.) Invite students to create a wall mural on which the index cards will be glued.

Grades 3–5

Category: Serving the Community/Reaching Outward

Topic: Reaching Out

Messages for Change

Background

Third-, fourth-, and fifth-grade students can be called on to become leaders in their schools and share positive examples of how to prevent bullying. They can also be encouraged to share their knowledge with their broader school communities, including after-school programs, youth activities, scouting groups, and sports or recreation programs. This class meeting is a continuation of the previous class meeting in this category. Both sessions should come after students have had enough experience to reflect on ways their behaviors and attitudes about bullying have changed over time. In this class meeting, students will develop a community outreach project. They will need more than one session to complete their projects.

Learner Outcomes

By the end of this session, students will be able to
- discuss ways that heightened awareness about bullying has led to positive changes in their own attitudes and behaviors
- communicate messages for positive changes in bullying behaviors to the broader school community

Materials Needed

- Student responses (index cards) from Be Aware! (previous class meeting in this category)
- Chalkboard, dry erase board, or chart paper and chalk or markers

Preparation Needed

- Coordinate efforts with colleagues who are using this same class meeting. Classes may be given a choice of either activities or locations to focus their projects (see ideas below in Opening Activity).
- Students will need more than one class meeting to complete their projects. Decide whether to carry the project into another class meeting, into free periods, as homework, or as part of an academic curriculum connection.

Class Meeting Outline

Opening Activity (20 minutes)

1. Return students' index cards from the previous class meeting and briefly recap what they learned.
2. **Younger students look up to you. When you decide to make good choices, they are more likely to do the same. We are going to create a class project using what you've learned about bullying. We'll share ways you have made positive changes in your own behavior with others in our school.**
3. **Let's talk about ways we can share your ideas with others.** Select a project and location based on whether your class will be collaborating with other classes. Either allow students to brainstorm their own options and then vote to choose an idea, or preselect a few for which students can vote.
   a. Ideas for projects might include
      - write a letter to a friend about what you've learned
      - create a bulletin board

Teacher Tips

- Incorporate as many different student ideas regarding project choices and locations as possible.

- If you have the opportunity, work collaboratively with other classes or do this as a longer-term project.

- compile and categorize ideas from the index cards into lists to post in different locations of the school
- select and share key ideas during schoolwide morning announcements
- publish selected or compiled ideas in the school newspaper
- videotape student "testimonials"
- create a presentation or skit to perform for other students

    b. Ideas for locations to present projects might include
- in school with younger students
- at another school in your community
- in an after-school program or youth recreation program
- to a scouting troop or other youth organization

4. Allow the remainder of the class meeting for students to work on the project. Reserve the final 5 minutes of the session for discussion and wrap-up.

Discussion Questions (5 minutes)

1. Process the activity.
   a. Decide how and when to complete the project.
   b. Discuss how to celebrate the completion of the project, including whom to invite.
2. Grade 3: Tell how you will distribute or post students' work.
3. Grades 4–5: Decide together on the best ways to publicize, distribute, or circulate information at the location(s) students chose to share their messages.

Wrap-Up

1. **You can each set good examples for doing the right thing when it comes to how to handle bullying. Sharing your positive ideas with other young people can really help make a difference. Even small changes lead to bigger changes. That makes a positive difference in our whole school and in our community. Let's keep up this good work that you have started!**
2. Hold your celebration to mark the completion or debut of the project.

Curriculum Connections

Vocabulary: *disseminate, distribute, market research*

Language Arts: Work with students to

- practice the correct format for writing a letter (for a letter-writing project)
- practice using public speaking skills (for a morning announcements project), including giving and receiving constructive feedback
- write invitations announcing the project completion or unveiling
- write a public service announcement (PSA) announcing the debut of the project

Math/Science: Help students conduct "market research" about the best ways to distribute information in different locations.

Art: Work with lower grade level "reading buddies" to create anti-bullying posters to hang throughout the school. Older students can help younger students learn important lessons about not bullying others.

Category 8

....

Using Current Events

(One class meeting)

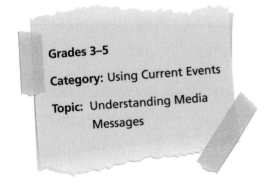

Grades 3–5

Category: Using Current Events

Topic: Understanding Media
Messages

In the News Scavenger Hunt

Background

Students in the upper elementary grades are increasingly concerned about how they fit in with peers and how they are viewed by others. Media messages play a role in shaping their attitudes about a wide range of issues such as what products to buy, how appearance affects popularity, expectations about gender roles, and using violence to solve problems. Both print and visual media are useful as classroom teaching tools to initiate discussions about human relationships, peer pressure, social responsibility, and violence—all of which are relevant bullying-prevention themes.

Learner Outcomes

By the end of this session, students will be able to

- discuss ways the media can affect their views of people, events, and cultural issues
- give an example of how media images and content can affect how students get along
- identify ways that media messages are used to trigger emotions and influence attitudes, as well as to convey information

Materials Needed

- In the News Scavenger Hunt List on page 349
- Samples of age-appropriate news media for each student. Print examples include *Time for Kids, National Geographic Kids, New Moon, Weekly Reader, Sports Illustrated for Kids,* and *Popular Mechanics.* Online examples include *Scholastic News Online* and www.PBS.org.
- Kitchen timer or bell
- Scissors or adhesive notes or "flags"

Preparation Needed

- Obtain copies of age-appropriate news media for viewing.
- Obtain copies of news media that can be cut up.
- Make a copy of In the News Scavenger Hunt List for each team.

Class Meeting Outline

Opening Activity (15 minutes)

1. Divide the class into teams. (See pages 13–14 for ideas and strategies for grouping students.)

2. **We are going on a scavenger hunt for things in newspapers and magazines! Each team will take three or four newspapers or magazines from this pile.** Give each team scissors or adhesive notes to cut out or mark samples that they find.

3. Give each team the In the News Scavenger Hunt List. **Here is a list of things your team will need to find for the scavenger hunt. Use it as you look through your newspapers or magazines. You might not find everything, but try to find as many as you can.** Briefly review the terms *headline, current event, editorial, human interest story,* and *caption* and show examples.

4. **Each time you find something on the list, put a check mark next to it in the box. Then cut or tear it out (or mark it with an adhesive note). You will have about 15 minutes. When you hear the bell, stop.** To help students find more items, you might suggest that teams divide up the list among members. Each member of the team might also have a copy of the list.

Discussion Questions (15 minutes)

1. Process the activity with students gathered as a class in a circle.

   a. **Was it harder to find some items on your list than others? Which ones? Why?**

   b. **What did you discover about how facts and opinions were shown? Is there a difference between telling facts and advertising (getting someone to buy something)? How could you tell the difference?**

   c. **Give an example of how a picture was used to make you feel a certain way.**

   d. **How did words or pictures influence your opinions about certain people or events?**

   e. **How many found examples of beliefs students your age have about what it means to be "popular"? How about "normal"?**

2. Grades 4–5:

   a. **How many of you found stories about acts of violence? stories about peacemakers? Why do you think there are often more stories about acts of violence in the news?**

   b. **What were examples of the ways courage was shown?**

   c. **What groups of people were missing (or "invisible") in your magazines and newspapers? How does that influence how we feel about them? how they might see themselves?**

   d. **How does what students read or hear influence whether they are willing to stand up for what they believe in?**

3. Grades 4–5: Have students look at the examples of age-appropriate news media that you brought in. Talk about different news formats the examples use.

   a. **Look at the front page or the cover. What story is most important or most interesting to you? Do you all agree or do you have different points of view? Do you think that is what the editor intended?**

   b. **Give an example of how something in the news, on TV, or on the Internet affects how students in our school get along.**

Teacher Tips

Use the following definitions to help students understand ways information is highlighted in news media:

Headline, cover, feature, top, or lead story: Items that appear on the cover or front page of print media, or that come first in a TV newscast. Editors decide which stories go first, based on what they feel is either most important or most interesting to their audience.

Current events: Things happening right now locally or in different parts of the world.

Editorial: An opinion about something that happened in the news or the way it was reported.

Human interest stories: News items that focus on people and their problems, achievements, or concerns in a way that makes us feel interested in or care about them. These target our feelings to help us understand a complicated story or events like wars or natural disasters.

Caption: A title or short explanation attached to a picture or illustration.

Wrap-Up

1. **When we pay close attention to TV and what we read, we learn something about other people and about ourselves, too. Learning about the different ways each of us sees things can help us get along and be better citizens in the world.**

2. Encourage students to keep on paying attention to current news events.

Curriculum Connections

Vocabulary: *audience, caption, current event, editor, editorial, format, headline, human interest story, intended, local, national/international, opinion, top/lead/feature/cover story*

Language Arts:

- Read *Harriet the Spy* (Louise Fitzhugh) with students as a starting point for discussing points of view and fact versus opinion.

- Instruct students how to write a lead or feature story about a class, school, or local current event.

Social Studies: Provide newspaper or magazine pictures, or ask students to select some they find interesting. Assign individuals or small groups to create different headlines or captions that convey different meanings or interpretations of the selected pictures.

Art: Have students create a collage about a topic identified in the scavenger hunt and how it makes them feel.

In the News Scavenger Hunt List

Instructions: Using newspapers and magazines, find examples of as many of the items on this list as you can. When you find an item, put a check mark next to it on the list. Mark or cut out the examples you find.

An article about a current world event.	☐
A picture that makes you have a strong feeling about a person, place, or event.	☐
A human interest story.	☐
A cartoon about a subject important to students your age.	☐
An article about being kind to animals or helping the environment.	☐
A picture or article that suggests that certain clothing will make you more popular.	☐
An advertisement that would make students your age feel they were cool if they had the item shown.	☐
A human interest story about older people, people who are disabled, people from certain racial or ethnic groups, people with certain body builds, or people who are poor.	☐
A picture, advertisement, or article that reinforces ways that "normal" boys or girls are "supposed" to act or play.	☐
An article about aggression or violence.	☐
An article about a peaceful act of courage.	☐
A caption that is funny.	☐
A caption that gives a message that seems different from what the picture shows.	☐
A headline or picture that reinforces a negative stereotype or point of view about people.	☐
A headline or a picture and caption you think most students your age would agree is true.	☐
A picture or headline about what a "normal" or "attractive" person should look like.	☐
A headline or story that seems based on rumors or opinions, not facts.	☐

....

Notes

....

1. Definitions from *Cyber Bullying: A Prevention Curriculum for Grades 3–5* by Susan Limber, Patricia Agatston, and Robin Kowalski. Center City, MN: Hazelden, 2009.

2. Anselmi, D. L., and A. L. Law. *Questions of Gender: Perspectives and Paradoxes.* New York: McGraw Hill, 1998.

3. Stern-LaRosa, Caryl, and Ellen H. Bettmann. *The Anti-Defamation League's Hate Hurts: How Children Learn and Unlearn Prejudice.* New York: Scholastic Inc., 2000.

4. Olweus Bullying Prevention Group. *OBBP Trainer's Manual: Who-What-When-Where-How-Why Training Activity;* Tab 11, Document 6. Used with permission.

5. Adapted from *Cyber Bullying: A Prevention Curriculum for Grades 3–5* by Susan Limber, Patricia Agatston, and Robin Kowalski. Center City, MN: Hazelden, 2009.

6. www.adl.org (Anti-Defamation League)

Recommended Resources

Kindergarten–Grade 2

Books

Aliki. *Feelings*. New York: HarperCollins, 1986.

Amnesty International (contributor). *We Are All Born Free: The Universal Declaration of Human Rights in Pictures*. London, UK: Frances Lincoln Children's Books, 2008.

Andersen, Hans Christian. *The Ugly Duckling*. New York: HarperCollins, 1999.

Bedford, David. *It's My Turn!* London, UK: Little Tiger Press, 2001.

Berger, Carin. *The Little Yellow Leaf*. New York: HarperCollins, 2008.

Blegvad, Lenore. *Anna Banana and Me*. New York: Simon & Schuster, 1987.

Bottner, Barbara. *Bootsie Barker Bites*. New York: Putnam Juvenile, 1997.

Bourgeois, Paulette. *Franklin's New Friend*. Tonawanda, NY: Kids Can Press, 1997.

———. *Franklin's Nickname*. New York: Scholastic, 2004.

———. *Franklin's Secret Club*. Tonawanda, NY: Kids Can Press, 1998.

Braman, Arlette N. *Kids Around the World Play! The Best Fun and Games from Many Lands*. Hoboken, NJ: John Wiley & Sons, 2002.

Brinckloe, Julie. *Fireflies*. New York: Simon & Schuster, 1986.

Brown, Laurie Krasny, and Marc Brown. *How to Be a Friend: A Guide to Making Friends and Keeping Them*. New York: Little, Brown, 2001.

Brown, Marc. *Arthur's April Fool*. New York: Little, Brown, 1985.

———. *Muffy's Secret Admirer*. New York: Little, Brown, 1999.

Brumbeau, Jeff. *Miss Hunnicutt's Hat*. Freemont, CA: Orchard Publications, 2003.

Bunting, Eve. *Fly Away Home*. New York: Houghton Mifflin, 1993.

Carle, Eric. *Do You Want to Be My Friend?* New York: Harper Festival, 1995.

———. *The Very Lonely Firefly*. New York: Penguin Young Readers Group, 1995.

Carlson, Nancy. *Arnie and the Skateboard Gang*. New York: Puffin Books, 1997.

———. *How to Lose All Your Friends*. New York: Puffin Books. 1997.

Casteneda, Omar. *Abuela's Weave*. New York: Lee & Low Books, 1995.

Cheltenham Elementary School Kindergartners. *We Are All Alike . . . We Are All Different*. New York: Scholastic, 2002.

Choi, Yangsook. *The Name Jar*. New York: Random House, 2003.

Cohen, Miriam. *Best Friends*. New York: Simon & Schuster, 2007.

Cole, Babette. *Prince Cinders*. New York: Putnam Juvenile, 1997.

Coleman, Evelyn. *White Socks Only*. Morton Grove, IL: Albert Whitman & Company, 1999.

Coles, Robert. *The Story of Ruby Bridges*. New York: Scholastic, 2004.

Cook, Deanna F. *The Kids' Multicultural Cookbook*. Nashville: Williamson Books, 2008.

Cottin, Menena. *The Black Book of Colors*. Toronto, ON: Groundwood Books, 2008.

Couric, Katie. *The Brand New Kid*. New York: Doubleday, 2000.

Curtis, Jamie Lee. *Today I Feel Silly: And Other Moods That Make My Day*. New York: HarperCollins, 1998.

Danneberg, Julie. *First Day Jitters*. Watertown, MA: Charlesbridge Publishing, 2000.

dePaola, Tommie. *Andy, That's My Name*. New York: Scholastic, 2000.

———. *The Art Lesson*. New York: Putnam Juvenile, 1997.

———. *Oliver Button Is a Sissy*. New York: Houghton Mifflin, 1979.

DeRolf, Shane. *The Crayon Box That Talked*. New York: Random House, 1997.

Dubé, Pierrette. *Sticks and Stones!* Richmond Hill, ON: Firefly Books, 1998.

Duke, Kate. *The Tale of Pip and Squeak*. New York: Dutton Juvenile, 2007.

Fox, Mem. *Whoever You Are*. Fort Worth, TX: Harcourt Education, Inc., 2006.

Gainer, Cindy. *I'm Like You, You're Like Me: A Child's Book about Understanding and Celebrating Each Other*. Minneapolis: Free Spirit Publishing, 1998.

Golenbock, Peter. *Teammates*. New York: Houghton Mifflin, 1992.

Hallinan, P. K. *My First Day of School*. Nashville: Ideals Publications, Inc., 1987.

Hamanaka, Sheila. *All the Colors of the Earth*. New York: HarperCollins, 1999.

Hammerseng, Kathryn M. *Telling Isn't Tattling*. Seattle: Parenting Press, Inc., 1995.

Henkes, Kevin. *Chester's Way*. New York: HarperCollins, 1997.

———. *Chrysanthemum*. New York: Mulberry Books, 1996.

———. *A Weekend with Wendell*. New York: HarperCollins, 1995.

Hills, Tad. *Knock, Knock! Who's There? My First Book of Knock-Knock Jokes*. New York: Simon & Schuster, 2000.

Hoffman, Mary. *Amazing Grace*. New York: Dial Books for Young Readers, 1991.

Jones, Rebecca C. *Matthew and Tilly*. New York: Puffin, 1995.

Kachenmeister, Cherryl. *On Monday When It Rained*. Boston: Sandpiper, 2001.

Kellogg, Steven. *Best Friends*. New York: Dial Books for Young Readers, 1986.

Lehman, Dana. *I DOUBLE Dare You!* Allenton, MI: Lehman Publishing, 2008.

Lester, Helen. *Hooway for Wodney Wat*. New York: Houghton Mifflin Books for Children, 1999.

Lionni, Leo. *A Color of His Own*. New York: Random House, 2006.

———. *Frederick*. New York: Random House, 1973.

———. *It's Mine!* New York: Random House, 1996.

———. *Swimmy*. New York: Random House, 1973.

Lobel, Arnold. *Frog and Toad Are Friends*. New York: HarperCollins, 1979.

Lovell, Patty. *Stand Tall, Molly Lou Melon*. New York: Putnam Juvenile, 2001.

Ludwig, Trudy. *Just Kidding*. Berkeley: Ten Speed Press, 2006.

———. *My Secret Bully*. Berkeley: Ten Speed Press, 2005.

———. *Trouble Talk.* Berkeley: Ten Speed Press, 2008.

Luvmour, Josette, and Sambhava Luvmour. *Everyone Wins! Cooperative Games and Activities.* Gabriola Island, BC: New Society Publishers, 2007.

Maestro, Marco. *What Do You Hear When Cows Sing? And Other Silly Riddles.* New York: HarperCollins, 1996.

Marshall, James. *George and Martha.* New York: Houghton Mifflin, 1972.

———. *George and Martha One Fine Day.* New York: Houghton Mifflin, 1978.

Mauterer, Erin. *Laugh Out Loud: Jokes and Riddles from Highlights for Children.* Honesdale, PA: Boyds Mills Press, 2005.

McCain, Becky Ray. *Nobody Knew What to Do: A Story about Bullying.* Morton Grove, IL: Albert Whitman & Company, 2001.

McCloud, Carol. *Have You Filled a Bucket Today?* Northville, MI: Nelson Publishing, 2006.

Meiners, Cheri J. *Share and Take Turns.* Minneapolis: Free Spirit Publishing, 2003.

Moss, Peggy. *Say Something.* Gardiner, ME: Tilbury House Publishers, 2008.

Nolan, Allia Zobel. *What I Like about Me.* Pleasantville, NY: Reader's Digest Children's Books, 2005.

Orlick, Terry. *Cooperative Games and Sports: Joyful Activities for Everyone.* Champaign, IL: Human Kenetics Publishers, 2006.

Park, Barbara. *Junie B. Jones and the Stupid Smelly Bus.* New York: Random House, 1992.

Polacco, Patricia. *Thank You, Mr. Falker.* New York: Penguin Young Readers Group, 2001.

Pryor, Kimberly Jane. *Cooperation.* New York: Macmillan Young Library, 2008.

Recorvits, Helen, and Gabi Swiatkowska. *My Name Is Yoon.* New York: Farrar, Straus, and Giroux, 2003.

Reibstein, Mark. *Wabi Sabi.* New York: Little, Brown, 2008.

Rose, Maddy. *The Adventures of Pinkie: A Nickname.* New York: Random House, 2007.

Rosenberry, Vera. *Vera's First Day of School.* New York: Macmillan, 2003.

Scieszka, Jon. *Squids Will Be Squids.* New York: Puffin Books, 2003.

———. *The True Story of the Three Little Pigs!* New York: Puffin Books, 1996.

Seskin, Steve, and Allen Shamblin. *Don't Laugh at Me.* Berkeley: Ten Speed Press, 2002.

Seuss, Dr. *The Butter Battle Book.* New York: Random House, 1984.

———. *The Cat in the Hat.* New York: Random House, 1957.

———. *Thidwick the Big-Hearted Moose.* New York: Random House, 1948.

Steig, William. *Amos and Boris.* New York: Farrar, Straus, and Giroux, 1992.

Stihler, Cherie B. *The Giant Cabbage: An Alaska Folktale.* Seattle: Sasquatch Books, 2003.

Stolz, Mary. *Emmet's Pig.* New York: HarperCollins, 2003.

Surat, Michele. *Angel Child, Dragon Child.* New York: Scholastic, 1989.

Swope, Sam. *The Araboolies of Liberty Street.* New York: Farrar, Straus and Giroux, 2001.

Terzian, Alexandra M. *The Kids' Multicultural Art Book: Art and Craft Experiences from Around the World.* Nashville: Williamson Books, 1993.

Thomas, Iolette. *Mermaid Janine.* New York: Scholastic, 1993.

Tyler, Michael. *The Skin You Live In.* Chicago: Chicago Children's Museum, 2005.

Waber, Bernard. *Ira Sleeps Over.* New York: Houghton Mifflin, 1975.

Whitcomb, Mary. *Odd Velvet.* San Francisco: Chronicle Books, 1998.

White, E. B. *Charlotte's Web.* New York: HarperCollins, 2001.

Willems, Mo. *Don't Let the Pigeon Drive the Bus!* New York: Hyperion Press, 2003.

———. *I Love My New Toy!* New York: Hyperion Books for Children, 2008.

———. *Knuffle Bunny: A Cautionary Tale.* New York: Hyperion Books for Children, 2004.

———. *My Friend Is Sad.* New York: Hyperion Books for Children, 2007.

Wing, Natasha. *The Night Before First Grade.* New York: Penguin Young Readers Group, 2005.

———. *The Night Before Kindergarten.* New York: Penguin Young Readers Group, 2001.

Woodson, Jacqueline. *The Other Side.* New York: Putnam Juvenile, 2001.

Yashima, Taro. *Crow Boy.* New York: Puffin Books, 1976.

Yolen, Jane. *Sleeping Ugly.* New York: Putnam Juvenile, 1997.

Zolotow, Charlotte. *William's Doll.* New York: HarperCollins, 1985.

Magazines

National Geographic Kids
Ranger Rick
Time for Kids
Weekly Reader

Web Sites

Bluestein, Jane, "What's Wrong with 'I-Messages'?" www.janebluestein.com/articles/whatswrong.html (accessed May 1, 2009).

Cyber bullying and cyber-safe information: www.wiredsafety.org, www.isafe.org, www.wiredkids.org, www.netsmartz.org, and www.cyberbullyhelp.com

NetSmartz Workshop: www.netsmartz.org

Scholastic Fractured Fairy Tales and Fables: www.teacher.scholastic.com/writewit/mff/fractured_fairy.htm

Scholastic News Online: www2.scholastic.com/browse/scholasticNews.jsp

Grades 3–5

Books

Allen, Debbie. *Dancing in the Wings.* New York: Puffin Books, 2003.

Andersen, Hans Christian. *The Ugly Duckling.* New York: HarperCollins, 1999.

Atwood, Margaret. *Princess Prunella and the Purple Peanut.* New York: Workman Publishing Company, 1995.

Baylor, Byrd. *The Table Where Rich People Sit.* New York: Simon & Schuster, 1998.

Berenstain, Stan, and Jan Berenstain. *The Berenstain Bears and the Double Dare.* New York: Random House, 1988.

Berry, Joy Wilt. *Every Kid's Guide to Handling Disagreements.* New York: Scholastic Library Publishing, 1991.

Blegvad, Lenore. *Anna Banana and Me.* New York: Simon & Schuster, 1987.

Blume, Judy. *Iggie's House.* New York: Simon & Schuster, 2002.

———. *Superfudge.* New York: Puffin Books, 2007.

———. *Tales of a Fourth Grade Nothing.* New York: Puffin Books, 2007.

Bosch, Carl W. *Bully on the Bus.* Seattle: Parenting Press, 1988.

Bridges, Ruby. *Through My Eyes.* New York: Scholastic, 1999.

Cohen, Barbara. *Molly's Pilgrim.* New York: HarperCollins, 1998.

Copeland, Brian. *Not a Genuine Black Man.* New York: Hyperion, 2006.

Creech, Sharon. *Love That Dog.* New York: HarperTrohpy, 2003.

Dahl, Roald. *The BFG.* New York: Puffin Books, 2007.

———. *The Twits.* New York: Puffin Books, 2007.

dePaola, Tommie. *The Art Lesson.* New York: Putnam Juvenile, 1997.

de Saint-Exupéry, Antione. *The Little Prince.* Translated by Richard Howard. New York: Houghton Mifflin, 2000.

DiCamillo, Kate. *Because of Winn-Dixie.* Cambridge, MA: Candlewick Press, 2000.

Drew, Naomi. *The Kids' Guide to Working Out Conflicts: How to Keep Cool, Stay Safe, and Get Along.* Minneapolis: Free Spirit Publishing, 2004.

Estes, Eleanor. *The Hundred Dresses.* New York: Houghton Mifflin, 2004.

Fitzhugh, Louise. *Harriet the Spy.* New York: Random House, 2001.

Garland, Sherry. *The Lotus Seed.* Fort Worth, TX: Harcourt Education, Inc., 1997.

Gibbons, Faye. *Mama and Me and the Model T.* New York: HarperCollins, 1999.

Giff, Patricia Reilly. *Lily's Crossing.* New York: Random House, 1999.

Going, K. L. *The Liberation of Gabriel King.* New York: Puffin Books, 2007.

Golenbock, Peter. *Teammates.* New York: Houghton Mifflin, 1992.

Hoose, Phillip, and Hannah Hoose. *Hey, Little Ant.* Berkeley: Ten Speed Press, 1998.

Howe, James. *Pinky and Rex and the Bully.* New York: Simon & Schuster, 1996.

Jones, Lynda. *Mrs. Lincoln's Dressmaker: The Unlikely Friendship of Elizabeth Keckley and Mary Todd Lincoln.* Washington, DC: National Geographic Children's Books, 2009.

King-Smith, Dick. *Babe: The Gallant Pig.* New York: Random House, 2005.

———. *Magnus Powermouse.* New York: HarperCollins, 1984.

Lowry, Lois. *Number the Stars.* New York: Random House, 1998.

Ludwig, Trudy. *Just Kidding.* Berkeley: Ten Speed Press, 2006.

———. *Sorry!* Berkeley: Ten Speed Press, 2006.

MacLachlan, Patricia. *Sarah, Plain and Tall.* New York: Scholastic, 2005.

McCain, Becky Ray. *Nobody Knew What to Do: A Story about Bullying.* Morton Grove, IL: Albert Whitman & Company, 2001.

Meiners, Cheri J., and Meredith Johnson. *Reach Out and Give.* Minneapolis: Free Spirit Publishing, 2006.

Mills, Lauren. *The Rag Coat.* New York: Little, Brown, 1991.

Mohr, Nicholasa. *Felita.* New York: Puffin Books, 1999.

Moss, Peggy. *Say Something.* Gardiner, ME: Tilbury House Publishers, 2008.

Munsch, Robert. *The Paper Bag Princess.* Toronto, ON: Annick Press, 1992.

Munson, Derek. *Enemy Pie.* San Francisco: Chronicle Books, 2000.

Naylor, Phyllis Reynolds. *King of the Playground.* New York: Simon & Schuster, 1994.

O'Neill, Alexis. *The Recess Queen.* New York: Scholastic Press, 2002.

Paterson, Katherine. *Bridge to Terabithia.* New York: HarperTeen, 2004.

Peet, Bill. *Farewell to Shady Glade.* New York: Houghton Mifflin, 1981.

Pfister, Marcus. *The Rainbow Fish.* New York: Scholastic, 2000.

Polacco, Patricia. *Mr. Lincoln's Way.* New York: Penguin Young Readers Group, 2001.

————. *Thank You, Mr. Falker.* New York: Penguin Young Readers Group, 2001.

Schwager, Tina, and Michele Schuerger. *Gutsy Girls: Young Women Who Dare.* Minneapolis: Free Spirit Publishing, 1999.

Seuss, Dr. *The Butter Battle Book.* New York: Random House, 1984.

————. *Horton Hears a Who!* New York: Random House, 1954.

————. *The Sneetches and Other Stories.* New York: Random House, 1961.

Spinelli, Eileen. *Boy, Can He Dance!* New York: Simon & Schuster, 1997.

Spinelli, Jerry. *Wringer.* New York: HarperTeen, 2004.

Steig, William. *Dominic.* New York: Macmillan, 2007.

Stolz, Mary. *The Bully of Barkham Street.* Des Moines, IA: Perfection Learning, Corp., 1985.

————. *The Noonday Friends.* New York: HarperCollins, 1971.

Swope, Sam. *The Araboolies of Liberty Street.* New York: Farrar, Straus and Giroux, 2001.

Trivizas, Eugene. *The Three Little Wolves and the Big Bad Pig.* New York: Simon & Schuster, 1997.

White, E. B. *Charlotte's Web.* New York: HarperCollins, 2001.

Williams, Jay. *Petronella.* North Kingstown, RI: Moon Mountain Publishing, 2000.

Yashima, Taro. *Crow Boy.* New York: Puffin Books, 1976.

Zolotow, Charlotte. *William's Doll.* New York: HarperCollins, 1985.

Magazines

National Geographic Kids
New Moon
Popular Mechanics
Sports Illustrated for Kids
Time for Kids
Weekly Reader

Web Sites

Anti-Defamation League: www.adl.org

Arthur (PBS Kids): http://pbskids.org/arthur

Arthur for Parents and Teachers: http://pbskids.org/arthur/parentsteachers/index.html

Do Something: www.dosomething.org

Hazelden's Cyber Bullying curricula: www.hazelden.org/cyberbullying

Heifer International: www.heifer.org

National Geographic: www.nationalgeographic.com

Network for Good: www.networkforgood.org

Public Broadcasting Service: www.pbs.org

Scholastic News Online: www2.scholastic.com/browse/scholasticNews.jsp

Stop Bullying Now: www.stopbullyingnow.hrsa.gov